# ENGAGING
# DISCOURSE

A **21**ST Century
Composition
Reader **&** Curriculum

**Bradley Summerhill**
Truckee Meadows Community College

**Kendall Hunt**
publishing company

Cover image © Shutterstock.com

www.kendallhunt.com
*Send all inquiries to:*
4050 Westmark Drive
Dubuque, IA 52004-1840

Copyright © 2020 by Kendall Hunt Publishing Company

ISBN 978-1-5249-6906-6

Published in the United States of America

# OUR CLASSROOM IS AMERICA

We are diverse. We come from different parts of town, maybe even from different parts of the country. We do not share the same ideology. We do not share the same religion, or ethnicity, or socio-economic background. We do share this classroom space. If we value our choice to attend this classroom, then it would seem we are obligated to listen to one another and to foster a community of mutual respect. We do not need to agree, but we do need to share ideas and to learn to communicate with a clear and open mind, in clear and meaningful language. We need to do what our leaders, increasingly, seem incapable of doing. We need to speak and to write with thoughtfulness, even mindfulness, and with honesty. We need to accept that it's OK if we do not all agree all of the time. We don't need to feel fearful, or angry, when we don't agree with others, even when the authority figure at the front of the classroom is the person with whom we disagree. We need to accept that not everyone shares the same personal values, or they don't share those values equally or to a similar degree.

Some of us have already checked out. Some of us never learned how to check in. Some of us are full of passionate engagement with world affairs. Some of us have barely ventured beyond our own neighborhoods.

We gather here to engage in public discourse. We gather here to learn how to do so.

Think of "public discourse" as the lost art of meaningful conversation. Our "conversation" takes place in writing, in language that is composed in accordance with the guidelines of standard written English.

We gather here to learn how to:

- evaluate source material,
- analyze an author's language,
- develop and sustain a reasonable point of view,
- persuade others to respect, value, and share our own point of view,
- and compose a piece of writing that empowers its author through the composition's capacity to evaluate and to control language.

Blue = Important
Purple = Evidence
Pink = Writing Importances

Green = Main
yellow

# BRIEF CONTENTS

# CONTENTS

## Unit Four: An Introduction to Research in the 21st Century   131

## Unit Five: Social Psychology   159

# WELCOME TO ENGAGING DISCOURSE

## Author's Note

Unlike most textbooks, this one has a personality—namely, me. Over the years, I have developed my own perspective, of course, but I feel no need to force the world to inhabit my viewpoint. In fact, when this course functions according to plan, students are forced to develop their own independent perspectives. Yet we live in a time and in a cultural moment where we, at least we so-called adults, are suspicious of each other's social and political motives. So let me make it clear: I have no agenda.

That's not true, actually. I do have one item on my agenda. I would like us to avoid binary modes of thinking: either/or, yes/no, us/them. Complexity is embedded in the textbook's title. *Engaging Discourse* can be understood as an adjective modifying a noun, as in, *We appreciate this engaging discourse. Engaging Discourse* can also be understood as a verb acting upon a direct object, as in, *We are engaging discourse.* Maybe that's not as clever or complex as I would like it to be, but it's the best I've got at the moment. Nevertheless, *Engaging Discourse* reflects my belief that college students must, for a wide variety of sound reasons, learn how to engage in complex and respectful modes of discourse.

Any claims that I make in my unit or article introductions I try to substantiate with good evidence, usually cited on the "Further Inquiry & Research" page at the end of each unit. I am not, however, attempting to persuade anyone of anything. I wish only for students to develop their own views based on sound principles of critical reasoning and mutual respect for others. I am more likely to ask open-ended questions than to attempt to sway anyone toward a particular viewpoint. The fancy term for this effort is "dialectic." I prefer the more homey term "dialogue." Maybe we ought to say "conversation." More than a few cultural critics have bemoaned conversation as a lost art in our society.

For the sake of complete transparency, let me add that my own views have developed over the years as a result of my conscious stance as a "radical moderate." I have never been comfortable with the noise of *either/or* and *us/them*. Americans seem to love to saddle one another with labels. I find it a tiresome, unproductive practice. Learning, cognitive development, and the sound practice of composition are the goals here. Having worked with college students for two decades now, I am more hopeful than ever that the current generation can and will improve the tenor of our nation's civic discourse.

Bradley Summerhill
*Reno, Nevada*

# The Definition of "Discourse"

1. verbal <u>interchange</u> of ideas; *especially* : <u>conversation</u>
2. a : formal and orderly and usually extended expression of thought on a subject
   b : connected speech or writing
   c : a <u>linguistic</u> unit (such as a conversation or a story) larger than a sentence
3. a mode of organizing knowledge, ideas, or experience that is rooted in language and its concrete contexts (such as history or institutions)
   - critical *discourse*
4. *archaic* : the capacity of orderly thought or procedure : <u>rationality</u>
5. *obsolete* : social familiarity

First Known Use: 15th century
Examples of "discourse" in a Sentence:

He likes to engage in lively *discourse* with his visitors.
She delivered an entertaining *discourse* on the current state of the film industry.

—Merriam-Webster Dictionary, *www.merriam-webster.com*

## Discourse as Dinner Conversation

American literary theorist Kenneth Burke (1897–1993) famously describes "discourse" as an ongoing conversation. He creates the following metaphor to describe the process of literary discourse and academic scholarship: Imagine that you arrive at a dinner party. A lively conversation has been going on for some time. You must listen for a moment even to figure out what the conversation is all about. Before you jump in, you want to make sure that you have heard from several voices in order to determine not only the subject matter but also the tone and the manner of the conversation—in other words, in order to determine how these people are communicating. Once you feel familiar enough with the subject matter, and once you are confident in how you will approach the subject, you offer your own insights and contributions.

It's a useful metaphor. In composition, we often paraphrase the main points of one or two authoritative sources in order to familiarize ourselves (and our audience, the imaginary readers of our text) with the subject matter, and in order to establish a proper tone and context into which we can then set forth our own insights, our own contributions.

We use the term "public discourse" in this text because the conversation is not really taking place at a private dinner party. These conversations take place in all kinds of public venues. For example, public discourse takes place in many forms via social media. Public discourse takes place on news broadcasts, in podcasts, on talk shows, and in college classrooms. Open public discourse enjoys a rich history that predates the founding of the United States and reaches back to the ancient Greek and Roman civilizations.

We want to learn how to write college essays. Yes, that's our immediate goal. At the same time, we strive to maintain a rich legacy of meaningful public conversation in order to carry these traditions into the 21st century and beyond.

# READ THIS NOW! *A Preface for Students and Instructors*

There is a constant that distinguishes many university students from the college students whom I teach. The distinction is evident at the start of a recent semester when I ask a late afternoon class of 28 students, "How many of you work a job at least 20 hours per week?" Every hand in the room goes up. I know that, sad as it may seem, not all 28 students will make it to semester's end. This lack of retention has little to do with academic preparedness, however. Typically, their employments are not the sort of student-friendly jobs you might find on a university campus. These are mainly "real world" service sector positions.

Then I get a little worked up. I say, "Your boss doesn't care about you. You are a warm body to fill a shift. As soon as you get a college degree, you move on and your manager has to find another warm body. So they don't want you to succeed."

You think that's bad? Wait till you hear what comes next: "And many of you are first generation college students, the first in your family to attend college. Don't expect support from your family." Harsh, right? So I make a joke about what if your boss is your family, then you're in real trouble. Students who are engaged in family businesses crack a smile. I go on to explain that though they are filled with love and good intentions, some families new to the college experience don't understand the kind of support it takes to prioritize higher education.

Work and family obligations keep about 25 percent of our department's students from passing English 101, our first semester composition course. People don't understand this statistic. They think it's a matter of academic preparedness, but it's not. Students need help with composition, but that's true of all students. It's grinding work hours—often 40 hours or more per week, and family obligations—that spell academic discord.

The generation called the Millennials (birthdates circa 1985 to 2000s) has been criticized in academia, in media, and in popular culture for "having no grit," for being entitled whiners, for lacking a work ethic and a learning ethic. OK. Maybe so. Maybe that's true of 21st century Americans. I have a hard time seeing it, though, especially when all those hands go up in the room. I see students struggling with a new world and a tough economy. Yes, even when unemployment rates hit historic lows, it's still a tough economy for college and high school students who aspire beyond the service sector. I see a 21st century that welcomes part-time service sector employment and a world where an elite four year university degree costs a quarter million dollars. And the saddest notion is that few Millennials seem to possess the wherewithal or the knowledge to stand up against the unfair criticism. Various and sundry measures reveal that Millennials are ignorant. Yet that hardly distinguishes them from the youth of prior ages. What's unprecedented is the global spread and flow of information. Information of all sorts, factual and otherwise, spreads across our world at light speed, while knowledge (that is, understanding how to make use of the information) seems to become more scarce. Studies and experts bear out these observations. A few clicks of the keyboard can confirm it.

Yet all young human beings are ignorant. We are not born with knowledge. We must learn. In our current age where literature has retreated to the realm of fantasy and mythology (*Harry Potter, Hunger Games, A Song of Fire and Ice i.e. Game of Thrones,* etc., etc.) we continue to believe in a human creature who is and remains exactly who he or she is at birth—chosen boy, girl of destiny, call it what you will. (The latest Disney Company iterations of *Star Wars* have turned "The Force" into a magical birthright rather than a discipline that requires training under wise masters.) Science tells us that we *become*. Myth tells us that we *are*.

Our environment ("nurture," training, practice, learning) allows us to maximize the innate qualities with which we are born ("nature").

Each of the six units that follow in this textbook meditates upon a dialectic of "nature" and "nurture." The immediate issues do not touch on these ideas directly; however, you can find an element of the dialectic behind each chapter. Besides, it's useful (and essential to our cognitive-oriented learning outcomes) to familiarize ourselves with a cognitive process of thesis + antithesis = synthesis. That is, an idea that converses with the counter to that idea results in concepts that acknowledge and blend both prior concepts. (Look up "dialectic" in your Merriam-Webster phone app or online via *Dictionary.com*. Use your new world tools to acquire knowledge, not just information.)

As science reveals more and more regarding our genetics, scientists simultaneously discover more and more the importance of one's surrounding in terms of development, behavior, and even social and political attitudes. Recent experimental philosophers go so far as to question the reality and existence of personal choice or what we call "free will." Whether we engage in an ancient dialogue on the role of fate versus free will, or whether we engage in a modern dialogue on the role of nature versus nurture, we are engaged in a longstanding human struggle to discover who we are and who we can become.

Once a person is engaged in such an epic conversation and develops a viewpoint which he or she wishes to express, the most difficult aspects of literary composition suddenly become much easier and less daunting. Our step-by-step approach offers an opportunity for success to every college student. At the same time, the course cultivates the student's work ethic, a vital ingredient to meet the high literacy standards required for achievement in the 21st century.

Guided discussions and small writing assignments lead to formal essay assignments. There are multiple essay options for each unit. Each unit also provides an opportunity for further inquiry and research. Each assignment has a suggested evaluation rubric to assess and measure certain critical fundamental skills, such as the ability to identify an author's thesis, the ability to introduce a published article to an outside audience, the ability to quote from the article using signal phrases and other means of proper integration, the ability to follow MLA (Modern Language Association) or another acceptable format, and the ability to compose in standard written English. Instructors are free, of course, to modify the evaluation rubrics as they see fit. Instructors can also add (or subtract) readings from provided lists and develop their own analytical and research writing assignments. Each rubric includes a segment of holistic assessment where the instructor uses his or her expertise and good judgment to offer up an overall or "holistic" assessment of the student's written product. We used to call this holistic assessment a "grade." Am I allowed to use a smiley face emoticon in an academic textbook?

I'll go old school: :-)

## Millennials or Gen Z?

This textbook is addressed to Millennials and to Generation Z, to people born between about 1985 and 2015. You are the inheritors and the creators of a new century. You have access to more information and to more data than any prior human generation. Your lives have been shaped by forces that were unimaginable to prior human generations. And you will certainly have experiences unlike any prior human generation.

Drawing distinct parameters around an entire generation is an exercise in faulty generalizations. Yet cultural commentators have labeled and shaped our general understandings of prior American generations: the Greatest Generation (early 1900s–1946) who grew up in the Great Depression and fought World War II, the Baby Boomers (1946–1964) who stirred drastic cultural change. My own generation is called Generation X (late 1960s–early 1980s). I'm not sure what we're known for other than punk rock and never being satisfied.

Marketers and demographers describe the generation born between about 1985 and 2000 as the Millennial generation, or simply "Millennials." Sometimes this group is called Generation Y, because "y" comes after "x," I suppose. So, naturally, the generation following the Millennials must call itself Generation Z. I'm not sure this label has caught on completely, but it probably will. And then the sons and daughters of the Millennials and Gen Z must clearly be labeled "Generation A." I can already imagine the start of a dystopic sci-fi series.

The dates and the definitions that I give above aren't set in stone. Other authorities may reject the dates I use to distinguish generations or may bristle because I have absorbed the Silent Generation (circa 1925–1942) under the auspices of the Greatest Generation. I'm pretty sure, though, that these folks would rather be called "Greatest" than "Silent."

The study and definitions of generations is not an exact science. We can certainly determine some valid parameters, but there is a bit of art involved in this particular discourse. For my part, I don't want to get too hung up on names.

Some members of "Generation Z" may bristle at being grouped with the "Millennials." The Millennials, they say, have a distant memory of a time prior to social media, whereas we don't. OK. Fair enough.

The overriding factor that distinguishes both the Millennials and Generation Z, however, is exactly the same: the internet. The so-called Internet Era cannot be given an exact birthdate, although many scholars point to the early 1990s when the "world wide web" became a viable public medium connecting servers and computers through common communication protocols. The explosive growth of the internet thereafter justifies a new epoch's place in the history books, whatever scholars decide to call it. The development of the internet changed not only information systems but the economy itself, along with the very nature of human communication.

You can decide for yourself whether you belong to the Millennials or to Generation Z. I'll leave it to others to make the fine, or not so fine, distinctions between these groups. If, in this textbook, I use the term "Millennials," understand that I mean "Millennials and Generation Z," but I'm just too lazy to write it out.

# ABOUT THE AUTHOR

Bradley Summerhill is a tenured English professor at Truckee Meadows Community College in Reno, Nevada. He graduated with Highest Distinction from the University of Virginia and obtained a Master of Fine Arts degree from the University of Arkansas. He has worked as a journalist and paperboy (Google it). He is the author of a novel, *Gambler's Quartet*, and a songwriter for the most excellent garage band Adapter. He is father to one daughter and dreams of leading a full reggae orchestra on sold-out world tours.

© Judy Prutzman

Bradley Summerhill stands at the graveside of Jim Morrison, the Lizard King (Google it).

# UNIT ONE

# Education

## Suggested Timeline: Two to three weeks

Our first unit requires you to read two short essays and one longer essay about learning and education and to reflect upon your own education. In her 2011 book *Now You See It,* education reform advocate Cathy Davidson observes, "The formal education most of us experienced—and which we now often think of when we picture a classroom—is based on giving premium value to expertise, specialization, and hierarchy. It prepared us for success in the twentieth century, when those things mattered above all. Yet what form of education is required in the information age, when what matters has grown very different?" Reflect on your own education. Have you experienced an outdated 20th century mode of hierarchical learning? To what extent have you experienced an education well suited to the realities of the 21st century? Davidson opines, "Rather than thinking of ways we can be preparing our students for their future, we seem determined to prepare them for the past." She sees the form of education that you have likely experienced as based on an industrial model where students were being prepared for work in an industrial world. Numerous scholars and critics claim that we have entered a new phase of human existence and a new post-industrial economy. How should education transform in order to prepare students for this post-industrial world where the internet has altered so many fundamental aspects of our lives?

## Readings

Naturally, you don't have to agree that education needs transformation at all. The following readings may inspire you to analyze and reflect upon the world of education that you have experienced and are experiencing:

1. Isaac Asimov, "What Is Intelligence, Anyway?" (circa 1979)
2. Russell Baker, "School vs. Education" (1975)
3. Mike Rose, "I Just Wanna Be Average" (1989)

## Responsibilities

In order to help you think about these essays, review and respond to the pre- and post-reading questions that appear in the textbook. If need be, take it upon yourself to form a study group so that you can engage in group discussions. Making eye contact with a classmate is always a plus, in my view, but if that's not possible, why not text, email, or chat? Further, you will complete the **Reader Response #1** and **Reader Response #2** assignments in order to prepare you for **Essay One**.

## Objectives

✓ Students will annotate texts, engage in group discussions, and produce critical, creative connections in discussion and in formal compositions between the texts themselves and between the texts and the student's life experience.

✓ Students will demonstrate the ability to produce clear, accurate, and correct academic discourse that reflects an acceptable level of critical thinking while employing the conventions of standard written English.

## Resources

Reader Response Guidelines
Why MLA?
The Principle of Rising Rigor
Introducing Texts or Sources for the Benefit of the "Outside" Audience
Quotation Integration
Suggested Outline for Essay One, Option 1a
Further Inquiry & Research
Additional Source Materials by Topic

Readings

College students suffer the same fallacy as does popular culture when it comes to the thing we call "intelligence." They think that intelligence is something that you are born with, a fixed entity. Moreover, they believe that intelligent students succeed, while other students struggle. Evidence and experience, on the other hand, suggest that intelligence is something that develops, a matter of effort, a matter of *nurture* as much as *nature*.

## Questions to Consider

*Answer these questions as you read and annotate the text:*

- How does Asimov's brief essay support or contradict the assertions made in the introductory paragraph above?
- Look up some information on Isaac Asimov. (Be sure to record what sources and methods you use to find this information.) Why or how is Asimov qualified to speak of the quality that we call "intelligence" or "genius"?
- What is Asimov's basic argument in this composition?
- What methods does Asimov use to persuade his audience of the validity of his viewpoint? Do you find these methods effective? Why or why not?
- When was this essay written? Why might it matter when the essay was written?
- Asimov writes, "A small subsection [of society] has managed to foist itself on the rest as an arbiter of such matters." What does he mean? Begin by looking up the meaning of "arbiter" on *dictionary.com* or in another resource. If by "such matters" he means the measuring of aptitude and intelligence via testing, do you have any relevant experience in this regard?

## Isaac Asimov, What Is Intelligence, Anyway?

What is intelligence, anyway? When I was in the army, I received the kind of aptitude test that all soldiers took and, against a normal of 100, scored 160. No one at the base had ever seen a figure like that, and for two hours they made a big fuss over me. (It didn't mean anything. The next day I was still a buck private with KP—kitchen police—as my highest duty.)

All my life I've been registering scores like that, so that I have the complacent feeling that I'm highly intelligent, and I expect other people to think so too. Actually, though, don't such scores simply mean that I am very good at answering the type of academic questions that are considered worthy of answers by people who make up the intelligence tests—people with intellectual bents similar to mine?

For instance, I had an auto-repair man once, who, on these intelligence tests, could not possibly have scored more than 80, by my estimate. I always took it for granted that I was far more intelligent than he was. Yet, when anything went wrong with my car I hastened to him with it, watched him anxiously as he explored its vitals, and listened to his pronouncements as though they were divine oracles—and he always fixed my car.

Well, then, suppose my auto-repair man devised questions for an intelligence test. Or suppose a carpenter did, or a farmer, or, indeed, almost anyone but an academician. By every one of those tests, I'd prove myself a moron, and I'd be a moron, too. In a world where I could not use my academic training and my verbal talents but had to do something intricate or hard, working with my hands, I would do poorly. My intelligence, then, is not absolute but is a function of the society I live in and of the fact that a small subsection of that society has managed to foist itself on the rest as an arbiter of such matters.

Consider my auto-repair man, again. He had a habit of telling me jokes whenever he saw me. One time he raised his head from under the automobile hood to say: "Doc, a deaf-and-mute guy went into a hardware store to ask for some nails. He put two fingers together on the counter and made hammering motions with the other hand. The clerk brought him a hammer. He shook his head and pointed to the two fingers he was hammering. The clerk brought him nails. He picked out the sizes he wanted, and left. Well, doc, the next guy who came in was a blind man. He wanted scissors. How do you suppose he asked for them?"

Indulgently, I lifted by right hand and made scissoring motions with my first two fingers. Whereupon my auto-repair man laughed raucously and said, "Why, you dumb jerk, he used his voice and asked for them." Then he said smugly, "I've been trying that on all my customers today." "Did you catch many?" I asked. "Quite a few," he said, "but I knew for sure I'd catch you." "Why is that?" I asked. "Because you're so goddamned educated, doc, I knew you couldn't be very smart."

And I have an uneasy feeling he had something there.

## Questions for Comprehension

*Answer these questions as a comprehension reading quiz and/or for further clarification on the text:*

1. True or False. In this essay, Asimov argues that he is, in fact, a stupid person.

2. True or False. Asimov argues that aptitude tests are relative indicators of ability; therefore, he is doubtful of the capacity of these tests to reveal an individual's true abilities.

3. As briefly and coherently as possible, explain what the author means when he claims that his intelligence "is not absolute but is a function of the society I live in."

When you are reading and analyzing a work (also called a "text"), it is usually important for you to understand the historical and publication context of the written material. In this case, the author's text was published more than forty years ago. Look up when and where this essay was originally published. (As always, make note of your source and method for finding this information.) I wonder if you think that the text is completely outdated due to its publication date and historical context? In what ways does the author's argument remain relevant in the 21st century?

In the 1970s, critics worried over the possible deleterious effects of television on America's youth. Baker plays on these concerns near the opening of his essay, yet it's clear that concerns over television aren't central to his main argument. Baker makes subtle references to events that were taking place in and around New York City in the 1970s. He references teachers going on strike and desegregation efforts that involved bussing students from local neighborhoods to remote neighborhoods. What can you discern or figure out regarding these events from the way in which Baker references them? Why do you imagine that school districts were still undertaking desegregation efforts in the mid-1970s long after the Supreme Court's landmark 1954 decision in *Brown v. Board of Education of Topeka*? Why were desegregation efforts still taking place in 1975 if the court decision was made in 1954? What is happening these days in regard to school desegregation nationwide? Has the issue been resolved? School desegregation is not Baker's central theme, but a reader might find this topic interesting nonetheless. Moreover, understanding the context of this essay offers you an opportunity to learn and better understand important American history.

In order to understand this essay, it is also important to understand the *tone* of Baker's essay. How would you characterize his tone? Is it serious, sarcastic, or some combination of various tones? How can you tell when his tone is humorous or serious? How can you determine what the serious point is at the heart of Baker's essay?

## Questions to Consider

*Answer these questions as you read and annotate the text:*

- How does understanding the publication and/or historical context of this piece affect your understanding of the text? Mark passages where news events of the day seem to be playing a role or taking place.
- Describe the tone of Baker's essay. Mark words or phrases that indicate a certain tone.
- What is the difference, according to Baker, between "school" and "education"? How does the distinction between "school" and "education" relate to the main point that Baker is attempting to communicate?
- As you read, mark passages that seem to indicate the importance of socio-economic factors in the dynamic between "school" and "education." In your view, are these socio-economic factors central to the claims that Baker is making?

## Russell Baker, School vs. Education

By the age of six the average child will have completed the basic American education and be ready to enter school. If the child has been attentive in these preschool years, he or she will already have mastered many skills.

From television, the child will have learned how to pick a lock, commit a fairly elaborate bank holdup, prevent wetness all day long, get the laundry twice as white, and kill people with a variety of sophisticated armaments.

From watching his parents, the child, in many cases, will already know how to smoke, how much soda to mix with whiskey, what kind of language to use when angry, and how to violate the speed laws without being caught.

At this point, the child is ready for the second stage of education, which occurs in school. There, a variety of lessons may be learned in the very first days.

The teacher may illustrate the economic importance of belonging to a strong union by closing down the school before the child arrives. Fathers and mothers may demonstrate to the child the social cohesion that can be built on shared hatred by demonstrating their dislike for children whose pigmentation displeases them. In the latter event, the child may receive visual instruction in techniques of stoning buses, cracking skulls with a nightstick, and subduing mobs with tear gas. Formal education has begun.

During formal education, the child learns that life is for testing. This stage lasts twelve years, a period during which the child learns that success comes from telling testers what they want to hear.

Early in this stage, the child learns that he is either dumb or smart. If the teacher puts intelligent demands upon the child, the child learns he is smart. If the teacher expects little of the child, the child learns he is dumb and soon quits bothering to tell the testers what they want to hear.

At this point, education becomes more subtle. The child taught by school that he is dumb observes that neither he, she, nor any of the many children who are even dumber, ever fails to be promoted to the next grade. From this, the child learns that while everybody talks a lot about the virtue of being smart, there is very little incentive to stop being dumb.

What is the point of school, besides attendance? the child wonders. As the end of the first formal stage of education approaches, school answers this question. The point is to equip the child to enter college.

Children who have been taught they are smart have no difficulty. They have been happily telling testers what they want to hear for twelve years. Being artists at telling testers what they want to hear, they are admitted to college joyously, where they promptly learn that they are the hope of America.

Children whose education has been limited to adjusting themselves to their schools' low estimates of them are admitted to less joyous colleges which, in some cases, may teach them to read.

At this stage of education, a fresh question arises for everyone. If the point of lower education was to get into college, what is the point of college? The answer is soon learned. The point of college is to prepare the student—no longer a child now—to get into graduate school. In college the student learns that it is no longer enough simply to tell the testers what they want to hear. Many are tested for graduate school; few are admitted.

Those excluded may be denied valuable certificates to prosper in medicine, at the bar, in the corporate boardroom. The student learns that the race is to the cunning and often, alas, to the unprincipled.

Thus, the student learns the importance of destroying competitors and emerges richly prepared to play his role in the great simmering melodrama of American life.

Afterward, the former student's destiny fulfilled, his life rich with Oriental carpets, rare porcelain, and full bank accounts, he may one day find himself with the leisure and the inclination to open a book with a curious mind, and start to become educated.

## Questions for Comprehension

*Answer these questions as a comprehension reading quiz and/or for further clarification on the text:*

1. True or False. Baker claims, "During formal education, the child learns that life is for testing."

2. How does a child learn that he is either "dumb or smart," according to Baker?

3. How do concerns over the negative role of television in the lives of children seem similar to you to concerns over the role of the internet and social media in the lives of 21st century children? Are these valid concerns? Why or why not?

4. Who are the most successful students who end up in college, according to Baker's article?

5. In Baker's final sentence, why is the phrase "a curious mind" so important and a key to understanding the real intent of his essay?

"Two-thirds of kids will never get a four-year degree in the 21st century."
—John Hickenlooper, Governor of Colorado, *CBS Morning News, 6 Aug. 2017*

What if I told you that a primary data point to determine whether an entering first year college student will complete his or her degree has nothing to do with the individual abilities of the student? The most reliable single data point to determine whether a college student will complete on time, or at all, is this: Do the student's parents hold college degrees?

What do you think of that? It doesn't seem fair, does it? If the parents hold degrees, the kids are statistically speaking more likely to complete and to complete on time.

In the first decade of the 21st century, the National Endowment for the Arts undertook a study which, among other things, seemed to show the clear role early environment plays in someone's ability to engage in and enjoy literary reading later in life.[1] Rose also seems to consider the role of "nurture" that a student's environment can play. At the same time, I don't think any of us are willing to give up on the American dream of social, economic, and educational mobility. In this country we continue to believe that the individual and his or her free will can determine the person's destiny. In any case, knowledge is power, and it's good to know the statistics that you wish to defy.

What other themes can you identify in Rose's text?

As you read, note the author's most important phrases and sentences. Make notes for yourself in order to interpret his main themes and ideas. Again, an important primary task is to identify the author's thesis. We also want to identify meaningful language that will be suitable for quotation in our compositions.

## Questions to Consider

*Answer these questions as you read and annotate the text:*

- Why do some students "just wanna be average" and why does it bother Rose?
- What was Rose's neighborhood like and why in an essay on education does he spend so much space describing his neighbors and the neighborhoods of his classmates?
- What was wrong with Rose's early education?
- Rose argues that students will "float to the mark you set." What does this mean and do you agree?
- Note what Rose has to say regarding "vocational" track education. Are his observations valid? Why or why not? Do his observations remain relevant in the 21st century? Has anything changed in regard to vocational education?
- What ultimately enabled Rose to succeed academically?
- Under the "Further Inquiry" list below, you will find a news article entitled "Teachers expect less from Hispanic, black students, study shows." What connections can you find between the content of this news article and Rose's text?
- In general, what role do socio-economic factors play in Rose's experience? What, in your view, are the most important factors?

---

[1] "Reading at Risk: A Survey of Literary Reading in America." National Endowment for the Arts. https://www.arts.gov/publications/reading-risk-survey-literary-reading-america-0

## Mike Rose, "I Just Wanna Be Average"

It took two buses to get to Our Lady of Mercy. The first started deep in South Los Angeles and caught me at midpoint. The second drifted through neighborhoods with trees, parks, big lawns, and lots of flowers. The rides were long but were livened up by a group of South L.A. veterans whose parents also thought that Hope had set up shop in the west end of the county. There was Christy Biggars, who, at sixteen, was dealing and was, according to rumor, a pimp as well. There were Bill Cobb and Johnny Gonzales, grease-pencil artists extraordinaire, who left Nembutal-enhanced swirls of "Cobb" and "Johnny" on the corrugated walls of the bus. And then there was Tyrrell Wilson. Tyrrell was the coolest kid I knew. He ran the dozens[2] like a metric halfback, laid down a rap that outrhymed and outpointed Cobb, whose rap was good but not great—the curse of a moderately soulful kid trapped in white skin. But it was Cobb who would sneak a radio onto the bus, and thus underwrote his patter with Little Richard, Fats Domino, Chuck Berry, the Coasters, and Ernie K. Doe's mother-in-law, an awful woman who was "sent from down below." And so it was that Christy and Cobb and Johnny G. and Tyrrell and I and assorted others picked up along the way passed our days in the back of the bus, a funny mix brought together by geography and parental desire.

Entrance to school brings with it forms and releases and assessments. Mercy relied on a series of tests . . . for placement, and somehow the results of my tests got confused with those of another student named Rose. The other Rose apparently didn't do very well, for I was placed in the vocational track, a euphemism for the bottom level. Neither I nor my parents realized what this meant. We had no sense that Business Math, Typing, and English-Level D were dead ends. The current spate of reports on the schools criticizes parents for not involving themselves in the education of their children. But how would someone like Tommy Rose, with his two years of Italian schooling, know what to ask? And what sort of pressure could an exhausted waitress apply? The error went undetected, and I remained in the vocational track for two years. What a place.

My homeroom was supervised by Brother Dill, a troubled and unstable man who also taught freshman English. When his class drifted away from him, which was often, his voice would rise in paranoid accusations, and occasionally he would lose control and shake or smack us. I hadn't been there two months when one of his brisk, face-turning slaps had my glasses sliding down the aisle. Physical education was also pretty harsh. Our teacher was a stubby ex-lineman who had played old-time pro ball in the Midwest. He routinely had us grabbing our ankles to receive his stinging paddle across our butts. He did that, he said, to make men of us. "Rose," he bellowed on our first encounter; me standing geeky in line in my baggy shorts. "'Rose'? What the hell kind of name is that?"

"Italian, sir," I squeaked.

"Italian! Ho. Rose, do you know the sound a bag of shit makes when it hits the wall?"

"No, sir."

"*Wop!*"

Sophomore English was taught by Mr. Mitropetros. He was a large, bejeweled man who managed the parking lot at the Shrine Auditorium. He would crow and preen and list for us the stars he'd brushed against. We'd ask questions and glance knowingly and snicker, and all that fueled the poor

---

[2] A verbal game of African origin in which competitors try to top each other's insults.

guy to brag some more. Parking cars was his night job. He had little training in English, so his lesson plan for his day work had us reading the district's required text, *Julius Caesar,* aloud for the semester. We'd finished the play way before the twenty weeks was up, so he'd have us switch parts again and again and start again: Dave Snyder, the fastest guy at Mercy, muscling through Caesar to the breathless squeals of Calpurnia, as interpreted by Steve Fusco, a surfer who owned the school's most envied paneled wagon. Week ten and Dave and Steve would take on new roles, as would we all, and render a water-logged Cassius and a Brutus that are beyond my powers of description.

Spanish I—taken in the second year—fell into the hands of a new recruit. Mr. Montez was a tiny man, slight, five foot six at the most, soft-spoken and delicate. Spanish was a particularly rowdy class, and Mr. Montez was as prepared for it as a doily maker at a hammer throw. He would tap his pencil to a room in which Steve Fusco was propelling spitballs from his heavy lips, in which Mike Dweetz was taunting Billy Hawk, a half-Indian, half-Spanish, reed-thin, quietly explosive boy. The vocational track at Our Lady of Mercy mixed kids traveling in from South L.A. with South Bay surfers and a few Slavs and Chicanos from the harbors of San Pedro. This was a dangerous miscellany: surfers and hodads and South-Central blacks all ablaze to the metronomic tapping of Hector Montez's pencil.

One day Billy lost it. Out of the corner of my eye I saw him strike out with his right arm and catch Dweetz across the neck. Quick as a spasm, Dweetz was out of his seat, scattering desks, cracking Billy on the side of the head, right behind the eye. Snyder and Fusco and others broke it up, but the room felt hot and close and naked. Mr. Montez's tenuous authority was finally ripped to shreds, and I think everyone felt a little strange about that. The charade was over, and when it came down to it, I don't think any of the kids really wanted it to end this way. They had pushed and pushed and bullied their way into a freedom that both scared and embarrassed them.

Students will float to the mark you set. I and the others in the vocational classes were bobbing in pretty shallow water. Vocational education has aimed at increasing the economic opportunities of students who do not do well in our schools. Some serious programs succeed in doing that, and through exceptional teachers . . . students learn to develop hypotheses and troubleshoot, reason through a problem, and communicate effectively—the true job skills. The vocational track, however, is most often a place for those who are just not making it, a dumping ground for the disaffected. There were a few teachers who worked hard at education; young Brother Slattery, for example, combined a stern voice with weekly quizzes to try to pass along to us a skeletal outline of world history. But mostly the teachers had no idea of how to engage the imaginations of us kids who were scuttling along at the bottom of the pond.

And the teachers would have needed some inventiveness, for none of us was groomed for the classroom. It wasn't just that I didn't know things—didn't know how to simplify algebraic fractions, couldn't identify different kinds of clauses, bungled Spanish translations—but that I had developed various faulty and inadequate ways of doing algebra and making sense of Spanish. Worse yet, the years of defensive tuning out in elementary school had given me a way to escape quickly while seeming at least half alert. During my time in Voc. Ed., I developed further into a mediocre student and a somnambulant problem solver, and that affected the subjects I did have the wherewithal to handle: I detested Shakespeare; I got bored with history. My attention fitted here and there. I fooled around in class and read my books indifferently—the intellectual equivalent of playing with your food. I did what I had to do to get by, and I did it with half a mind.

But I did learn things about people and eventually came into my own socially. I liked the guys in Voc. Ed. Growing up where I did, I understood and admired physical prowess, and there was an abundance of muscle here. There was Dave Snyder, a sprinter and halfback of true quality. Dave's ability and his quick wit gave him a natural appeal, and he was welcome in any clique, though he always kept a little independent. He enjoyed acting the fool and could care less about studies, but he possessed a certain maturity and never caused the faculty much trouble. It was a testament to his independence that he included me among his friends—I eventually went out for track, but I was no jock. Owing to the Latin alphabet and a dearth of Rs and Ss, Snyder sat behind Rose, and we started exchanging one-liners and became friends.

There was Ted Richard, a much-touted Little League pitcher. He was chunky and had a baby face and came to Our Lady of Mercy as a seasoned street fighter. Ted was quick to laugh and he had a loud, jolly laugh, but when he got angry he'd smile a little smile, the kind that simply raises the corner of the mouth a quarter of an inch. For those who knew, it was an eerie signal. Those who didn't found themselves in big trouble, for Ted was very quick. He loved to carry on what we would come to call philosophical discussions: What is courage? Does God exist? He also loved words, enjoyed picking up big ones like *salubrious* and *equivocal* and using them in our conversations—laughing at himself as the word hit a chuckhole rolling off his tongue. Ted didn't do all that well in school—baseball and parties and testing the courage he'd speculated about took up his time. His textbooks were *Argosy* and *Field and Stream,* whatever newspapers he'd find on the bus stop—from the *Daily Worker* to pornography— conversations with uncles or hobos or businessmen he'd meet in a coffee shop, *The Old Man and the Sea.* With hindsight, I can see that Ted was developing into one of those rough-hewn intellectuals whose sources are a mix of the learned and the apocryphal, whose discussions are both assured and sad.

And then there was Ken Harvey. Ken was good-looking in a puffy way and had a full and oily ducktail and was a car enthusiast . . . a hodad. One day in religion class, he said the sentence that turned out to be one of the most memorable of the hundreds of thousands I heard in those Voc. Ed. years. We were talking about the parable of the talents, about achievement, working hard, doing the best you can do, blah-blah-blah, when the teacher called on the restive Ken Harvey for an opinion. Ken thought about it, but just for a second, and said (with studied, minimal affect), "I just wanna be average." That woke me up. Average? Who wants to be average? Then the athletes chimed in with the cliches that make you want to laryngectomize them, and the exchange became a platitudinous melee. At the time, I thought Ken's assertion was stupid, and I wrote him off. But his sentence has stayed with me all these years, and I think I am finally coming to understand it.

Ken Harvey was gasping for air. School can be a tremendously disorienting place. No matter how bad the school, you're going to encounter notions that don't fit with the assumptions and beliefs that you grew up with—maybe you'll hear these dissonant notions from teachers, maybe from the other students, and maybe you'll read them. You'll also be thrown in with all kinds of kids from all kinds of backgrounds, and that can be unsettling—this is especially true in places of rich ethnic and linguistic mix, like the L.A. basin. You'll see a handful of students far excel you in courses that sound exotic and that are only in the curriculum of the elite: French, physics, trigonometry. And all this is happening while you're trying to shape an identity, your body is changing, and your emotions are running wild. If you're a working-class kid in the vocational track, the options you'll have to deal with this will be constrained in certain ways: you're defined by your school as "slow"; you're placed in a curriculum that isn't designed to liberate you but to occupy you, or, if you're lucky, train you, though the training is for work the society does not esteem; other students are picking up the cues from your school and your curriculum and interacting with you in particular ways. If you're a kid like Ted Richard, you turn your back on all this and let your mind roam where it may. But youngsters like Ted are rare. What Ken and so many others do is protect themselves from such suffocating madness by taking on with a vengeance the identity implied in the vocational track. Reject the confusion and frustration by openly defining yourself as the Common

Joe. Champion the average. Rely on your own good sense. Fuck this bullshit. Bullshit, of course, is everything you—and the others—fear is beyond you: books, essays, tests, academic scrambling, complexity, scientific reasoning, philosophical inquiry.

The tragedy is that you have to twist the knife in your own gray matter to make this defense work. You'll have to shut down, have to reject intellectual stimuli or diffuse them with sarcasm, have to cultivate stupidity, have to convert boredom from a malady into a way of confronting the world. Keep your vocabulary simple, act stoned when you're not or act more stoned than you are, flaunt ignorance, materialize your dreams. It is a powerful and effective defense—it neutralizes the insult and the frustration of being a vocational kid and, when perfected, it drives teachers up the wall, a delightful secondary effect. But like all strong magic, it exacts a price.

My own deliverance from the Voc. Ed. world began with sophomore biology. Every student, college prep to vocational, had to take biology, and unlike the other courses, the same person taught all sections. When teaching the vocational group, Brother Clint probably slowed down a bit or omitted a little of the fundamental biochemistry, but he used the same book and more or less the same syllabus across the board. If one class got tough, he could get tougher. He was young and powerful and very handsome, and looks and physical strength were high currency. No one gave him any trouble.

I was pretty bad at the dissecting table, but the lectures and the textbook were interesting: plastic overlays that, with each turned page, peeled away skin, then veins and muscle, then organs, down to the very bones that Brother Clint, pointer in hand, would tap out on our hanging skeleton. Dave Snyder was in big trouble, for the study of life—versus the living of it—was sticking in his craw. We worked out a code for our multiple-choice exams. He'd poke me in the back: once for the answer under *A,* twice for *B,* and so on; and when he'd hit the right one, I'd look up to the ceiling as though I were lost in thought. Poke: cytoplasm. Poke, poke: methane. Poke, poke, poke: William Harvey. Poke, poke, poke, poke: islets of Langerhans. This didn't work out perfectly, but Dave passed the course, and I mastered the dreamy look of a guy on a record jacket. And something else happened. Brother Clint puzzled over this Voc. Ed. kid who was racking up 98s and 99s on his tests. He checked the school's records and discovered the error. He recommended that I begin my junior year in the College Prep program. According to all I've read since, such a shift, as one report put it, is virtually impossible. Kids at that level rarely cross tracks. The telling thing is how chancy both my placement into and exit from Voc. Ed. was; neither I nor my parents had anything to do with it. I lived in one world during spring semester, and when I came back to school in the fall, I was living in another.

Switching to College Prep was a mixed blessing. I was an erratic student. I was undisciplined. And I hadn't caught onto the rules of the game: why work hard in a class that didn't grab my fancy? I was also hopelessly behind in math. Chemistry was hard; toying with my chemistry set years before hadn't prepared me for the chemist's equations. Fortunately, the priest who taught both chemistry and second-year algebra was also the school's athletic director. Membership on the track team covered me; I knew I wouldn't get lower than a C. U.S. history was taught pretty well, and I did okay. But civics was taken over by a football coach who had trouble reading the textbook aloud—and reading aloud was the centerpiece of his pedagogy. College Prep at Mercy was certainly an improvement over the vocational program—at least it carried some status—but the social science curriculum was weak, and the mathematics and physical sciences were simply beyond me. I had a miserable quantitative background and ended up copying some assignments and finessing the rest as best I could. Let me try to explain how it feels to see again and again material you should once have learned but didn't.

You are given a problem. It requires you to simplify algebraic fractions or to multiply expressions containing square roots. You know this is pretty basic material because you've seen it for years. Once a teacher took some time with you, and you learned how to carry out these operations. Simple versions, anyway. But that was a year or two or more in the past, and these are more complex versions, and now you're not sure. And this, you keep telling yourself, is ninth-or even eighth-grade stuff.

Next it's a word problem. This is also old hat. The basic elements are as familiar as story characters: trains speeding so many miles per hour or shadows of buildings angling so many degrees. Maybe you know enough, have sat through enough explanations, to be able to begin setting up the problem: "If one train is going this fast. . ." or "This shadow is really one line of a triangle . . ." Then: "Let's see . . ." "How did Jones do this?" "Hmmmm." "No." "No, that won't work." Your attention wavers. You wonder about other things: a football game, a dance, that cute new checker at the market. You try to focus on the problem again. You scribble on paper for a while, but the tension wins out and your attention fits elsewhere. You crumple the paper and begin daydreaming to ease the frustration.

The particulars will vary, but in essence this is what a number of students go through, especially those in so-called remedial classes. They open their textbooks and see once again the familiar and impenetrable formulas and diagrams and terms that have stumped them for years. There is no excitement here. *No* excitement. Regardless of what the teacher says, this is not a new challenge. There is, rather, embarrassment and frustration and, not surprisingly, some anger in being reminded once again of long-standing inadequacies. No wonder so many students finally attribute their difficulties to something inborn, organic: 'That part of my brain just doesn't work.' Given the troubling histories many of these students have, it's miraculous that any of them can lift the shroud of hopelessness sufficiently to make deliverance from these classes possible.

Through this entire period, my father's health was deteriorating with cruel momentum. His arteriosclerosis progressed to the point where a simple nick on his shin wouldn't heal. Eventually it ulcerated and widened. Lou Minton would come by daily to change the dressing. We tried renting an oscillating bed—which we placed in the front room—to force blood through the constricted arteries in my father's legs. The bed hummed through the night, moving in place to ward off the inevitable. The ulcer continued to spread, and the doctors finally had to amputate. My grandfather had lost his leg in a stockyard accident. Now my father too was crippled. His convalescence was slow but steady, and the doctors placed him in the Santa Monica Rehabilitation Center, a sun-bleached building that opened out onto the warm spray of the Pacific. The place gave him some strength and some color and some training in walking with an artificial leg. He did pretty well for a year or so until he slipped and broke his hip. He was confined to a wheelchair after that, and the confinement contributed to the diminishing of his body and spirit.

I am holding a picture of him. He is sitting in his wheelchair and smiling at the camera. The smile appears forced, unsteady, seems to quaver, though it is frozen in silver nitrate. He is in his mid-sixties and looks eighty. Late in my junior year, he had a stroke and never came out of the resulting coma. After that, I would see him only in dreams, and to this day that is how I join him. Sometimes the dreams are sad and grisly and primal: my father lying in a bed soaked with his suppuration, holding me, rocking me. But sometimes the dreams bring him back to me healthy: him talking to me on an empty street, or buying some pictures to decorate our old house, or transformed somehow into someone strong and adept with tools and the physical.

Jack MacFarland couldn't have come into my life at a better time. My father was dead, and I had logged up too many years of scholastic indifference. Mr. MacFarland had a master's degree from Columbia and decided, at twenty-six, to find a little school and teach his heart out. He never took any credentialing courses, couldn't bear to, he said, so he had to find employment in a private system. He ended up at Our Lady of Mercy teaching five sections of senior English. He was a beatnik who was born too late. His teeth were stained, he tucked his sorry tie in between the third and fourth buttons of his shirt, and his pants were chronically wrinkled. At first, we couldn't believe this guy, thought he slept in his car. But within no time, he had us so startled with work that we didn't much worry about where he slept or if he slept at all. We wrote three or four essays a month. We read a book every two to three weeks, starting with the *Iliad* and ending up with Hemingway. He gave us a quiz on the reading every other day. He brought a prep school curriculum to Mercy High.

MacFarland's lectures were crafted, and as he delivered them he would pace the room jiggling a piece of chalk in his cupped hand, using it to scribble on the board the names of all the writers and philosophers and plays and novels he was weaving into his discussion. He asked questions often, raised everything from Zeno's paradox to the repeated last line of Frost's "Stopping by Woods on a Snowy Evening." He slowly and carefully built up our knowledge of Western intellectual history—with facts, with connections, with speculations. We learned about Greek philosophy, about Dante, the Elizabethan world view, the Age of Reason, existentialism. He analyzed poems with us, had us reading sections from John Ciardi's *How Does a Poem Mean*?, making a potentially difficult book accessible with his own explanations. We gave oral reports on poems Ciardi didn't cover. We imitated the styles of Conrad, Hemingway, and *Time* magazine. We wrote and talked, wrote and talked. The man immersed us in language.

Even MacFarland's barbs were literary. If Jim Fitzsimmons, hung over and irritable, tried to smart-ass him, he'd rejoin with a flourish that would spark the indomitable Skip Madison—who'd lost his front teeth in a hapless tackle—to flick his tongue through the gap and opine, "good chop," drawing out the single "0" in stinging indictment. Jack MacFarland, this tobacco-stained intellectual, brandished linguistic weapons of a kind I hadn't encountered before. Here was this *egghead*, for God's sake, keeping some pretty difficult people in line. And from what I heard, Mike Dweetz and Steve Fusco and all the notorious Voc. Ed. crowd settled down as well when MacFarland took the podium. Though a lot of guys groused in the schoolyard, it just seemed that giving trouble to this particular teacher was a silly thing to do. Tomfoolery, not to mention assault, had no place in the world he was trying to create for us, and instinctively everyone knew that. If nothing else, we all recognized MacFarland's considerable intelligence and respected the hours he put into his work. It came to this: the troublemaker would look foolish rather than daring. Even Jim Fitzsimmons was reading *On the Road* and turning his incipient alcoholism to literary ends.

There were some lives that were already beyond Jack MacFarland's ministrations, but mine was not. I started reading again as I hadn't since elementary school. I would go into our gloomy little bedroom or sit at the dinner table while, on the television, Danny McShane was paralyzing Mr. Mota with the atomic drop, and work slowly back through *Heart of Darkness,* trying to catch the words in Conrad's sentences. I certainly was not MacFarland's best student; most of the other guys in College Prep, even my fellow slackers, had better backgrounds than I did. But I worked very hard, for MacFarland had hooked me. He tapped my old interest in reading and creating stories. He gave me a way to feel special by using my mind. And he provided a role model that wasn't shaped on physical prowess alone, and something inside me that I wasn't quite aware of responded to that. Jack MacFarland established a literacy club, to borrow a phrase of Frank Smith's, and invited me—invited all of us—to join.

There's been a good deal of research and speculation suggesting that the acknowledgment of school performance with extrinsic rewards—smiling faces, stars, numbers, grades—diminishes the intrinsic satisfaction children experience by engaging in reading or writing or problem solving. While it's certainly true that we've created an educational system that encourages our best and brightest to become cynical grade collectors and, in general, have developed an obsession with evaluation and assessment, I must tell you that venal though it may have been, I loved getting good grades from MacFarland. I now know how subjective grades can be, but then they came tucked in the back of essays like bits of scientific data, some sort of spectroscopic readout that said, objectively and publicly, that I had made something of value. I suppose I'd been mediocre for too long and enjoyed a public redefinition. And I suppose the workings of my mind, such as they were, had been private for too long. My linguistic play moved into the world; . . . these papers with their circled, red B-pluses and A-minuses linked my mind to something outside it. I carried them around like a club emblem.

One day in the December of my senior year, Mr. MacFarland asked me where I was going to go to college. I hadn't thought much about it. Many of the students I teach today spent their last year in high school with a physics text in one hand and the Stanford catalog in the other, but I wasn't even aware of what "entrance requirements" were. My folks would say that they wanted me to go to college and be a doctor, but I don't know how seriously I ever took that; it seemed a sweet thing to say, a bit of supportive family chatter, like telling a gangly daughter she's graceful. The reality of higher education wasn't in my scheme of things: no one in the family had gone to college; only two of my uncles had completed high school. I figured I'd get a night job and go to the local junior college because I knew that Snyder and Company were going there to play ball. But I hadn't even prepared for that. When I finally said, "I don't know," MacFarland looked down at me—I was seated in his office—and said, "Listen, you can write."

My grades stank. I had A's in biology and a handful of B's in a few English and social science classes. All the rest were C's or worse. MacFarland said I would do well in his class and laid down the law about doing well in the others. Still, the record for my first three years wouldn't have been acceptable to any four-year school. To nobody's surprise, I was turned down flat by USC and UCLA. But Jack MacFarland was on the case. He had received his bachelor's degree from Loyola University, so he made calls to old professors and talked to somebody in admissions and wrote me a strong letter. Loyola finally accepted me as a probationary student. I would be on trial for the first year, and if I did okay, I would be granted regular status. MacFarland also intervened to get me a loan, for I could never have afforded a private college without it. Four more years of religion classes and four more years of boys at one school, girls at another. But at least I was going to college. Amazing.

In my last semester of high school, I elected a special English course fashioned by Mr. MacFarland, and it was through this elective that there arose at Mercy a fledgling literati. Art Mitz, the editor of the school newspaper and a very smart guy, was the kingpin. He was joined by me and by Mark Dever, a quiet boy who wrote beautifully and who would die before he was forty. MacFarland occasionally invited us to his apartment, and those visits became the high point of our apprenticeship: we'd clamp on our training wheels and drive to his salon.

He lived in a cramped and cluttered place near the airport, tucked away in the kind of building that architectural critic Reyner Banham calls a *dingbat.* Books were all over: stacked, piled, tossed, and crated, underlined and dog eared, well worn and new. Cigarette ashes crusted with coffee in saucers or spilling over the sides of motel ashtrays. The little bedroom had, along two of its walls, bricks and boards loaded with notes, magazines, and oversized books. The kitchen joined the living room, and there was a stack of German newspapers under the sink. I had never seen anything like it: a great flophouse of language furnished by City Lights and Cafe Le Metro. I read every title. I flipped through paperbacks and scanned jackets and memorized names: Gogol, *Finnegans Wake,* Djuna Barnes, Jackson Pollock, *A Coney Island of the Mind,* F. O. Matthiessen's *American Renaissance,* all sorts of Freud, *Troubled Sleep,* Man Ray, *The Education of Henry Adams,* Richard Wright, *Film as*

*Art,* William Butler Yeats, Marguerite Duras, *Red-burn,* A *Season in Hell, Kapital.* On the cover of Alain-Fournier's *The Wanderer* was an Edward Gorey drawing of a young man on a road winding into dark trees. By the hotplate sat a strange Kafka novel called *Amerika,* in which an adolescent hero crosses the Atlantic to find the Nature Theater of Oklahoma. Art and Mark would be talking about a movie or the school newspaper, and I would be consuming my English teacher's library. It was heady stuff. I felt like a Pop Warner athlete on steroids.

Art, Mark, and I would buy stogies and triangulate from MacFarland's apartment to the Cinema, which now shows X-rated films but was then L.A.'s premier art theater, and then to the musty Cherokee Bookstore in Hollywood to hobnob with beatnik homosexuals-smoking, drinking bourbon and coffee, and trying out awkward phrases we'd gleaned from our mentor's bookshelves. I was happy and precocious and a little scared as well, for Hollywood Boulevard was thick with a kind of decadence that was foreign to the South Side. After the Cherokee, we would head back to the security of MacFarland's apartment, slaphappy with hipness.

Let me be the first to admit that there was a good deal of adolescent passion in this embrace of the avant-garde: self-absorption, sexually charged pedantry, an elevation of the odd and abandoned. Still it was a time during which I absorbed an awful lot of information: long lists of titles, images from expressionist paintings, new wave shibboleths, snippets of philosophy, and names that read like Steve Fusco's misspellings—Goethe, Nietzsche, Kierkegaard. Now this is hardly the stuff of deep understanding. But it was an introduction, a phrase book, a travel guide to a vocabulary of ideas, and it *felt* good at the time to know all these words. With hindsight I realize how layered and important that knowledge was.

It enabled me to do things in the world. I could browse bohemian bookstores in far-off, mysterious Hollywood; I could go to the Cinema and see events through the lenses of European directors; and, most of all, I could share an evening, talk that talk, with Jack MacFarland, the man I most admired at the time. Knowledge was becoming a bonding agent. Within a year or two, the persona of the disaffected hipster would prove too cynical, too alienated to last. But for a time it was new and exciting: it provided a critical perspective on society, and it allowed me to act as though I were living beyond the limiting boundaries of South Vermont.

## Questions for Comprehension

*Answer these questions as a comprehension reading quiz and/or for further clarification on the text:*

1. Multiple choice, fill in the blank. "The _____ track, however, is most often a place for those who are just not making it, a dumping ground for the disaffected." A) academic, B) educational, C) vocational

2. Rose writes, "The tragedy is that you have to twist the knife in your own gray matter to make this defense work." What defense mechanism is he referencing? Explain it in your own words.

3. Name something unusual or outstanding that marked the kind of education that Rose received from Mr. MacFarland.

4. True or False. Rose grew up in Vermont.

5. In his final paragraph, what does Rose mean when he writes, "Knowledge was becoming a bonding agent"?

# Assignments

## Sentence Exercise #1

Use Isaac Asimov's "What Is Intelligence, Anyway?" as the basis to complete the following sentence exercises. See Notes for Composition at the end of the text.

Write three "clean copy" (that is, error-free) sentences (or combination of sentences) that could serve to introduce the text to an outside audience.

1. In his essay "What Is Intelligence, Anyway?" writer Isaac Asimov claims that _____ _____ .

2. Isaac Asimov makes an interesting argument in his essay "What Is Intelligence, Anyway?" He writes that _____ .

3. Isaac Asimov's brief essay "What Is Intelligence, Anyway?" encourages us to accept the notion that _____ .

4. **Correct This Faulty Sentence Structure:** In his essay "What Is Intelligence, Anyway?" argues that _____ .

5. **Improve This Weak Style:** In the essay "What Is Intelligence, Anyway?" it is argued that _____ .

## Suggested Evaluation Criterion and Point Values

| Exercise completed on deadline | 10 points |
|---|---|

## Sentence Exercise #2

Use Russell Baker's "School vs. Education" as the basis to complete the following sentence exercises. See Notes for Composition at the end of the text.

Write three "clean copy" (that is, error-free) sentences (or combination of sentences) that could serve to introduce the text to an outside audience.

**1.** In his essay "School vs. Education," writer Russell Baker implies that _____ _____ .

**2.** Russell Baker uses a tone of _____ in his essay "School vs. Education" in order to convey the idea that _____ .

**3.** Russell Baker's brief essay "School vs. Education" encourages us to consider the notion that _____ .

**4. Correct This Faulty Sentence Structure:** In his essay "School vs. Education" argues that _____ _____ .

**5. Improve This Weak Style:** In the article "School vs. Education," it is argued that _____ .

## Suggested Evaluation Criterion and Point Values

| Exercise completed on deadline | 10 points |
|---|---|

# Reader Response #1

See "Reader Response Guidelines" in Resources at the end of this unit.

Write a three paragraph reader response assignment on either Isaac Asimov's "What Is Intelligence, Anyway?" or Russell Baker's "School vs. Education." Do not write on both at the same time. Before you draft your assignment, make sure that you have solid responses to the discussion questions listed with each reading. You do not need to respond to these questions directly in your written response. Instead, focus your audience on your own interpretation and analysis of the reading. Follow the "Reader Response Guidelines." Review the "Introducing Texts" and "Quotation Integration" resource guidelines.

## Suggested Evaluation Criteria and Point Values

| | |
|---|---|
| Text Introduction<br>*The student demonstrates competence in formally introducing the text to an outside audience.* | 3 points |
| Quotation Integration<br>*The student demonstrates competence in appropriately integrating meaningful quotation selections using signal phrases and/or by other means.* | 3 points |
| Response<br>*The student offers a thoughtful response to the text.* | 3 points |
| Format and Voice<br>*The student follows proper MLA format or another standard as specified by the instructor. The student composes in standard written English.* | 1 point |

# Reader Response #2

*Reader Response #2 is a one to two page analysis and response paper presented in MLA format. This assignment helps you to develop draft material for Essay One.*

Respond to one of Mike Rose's main themes from his essay "I Just Wanna Be Average." Clearly identify and pursue this theme. Analyze the text by using direct quotations. Integrate quotations by using effective signal phrases and by other means.

*Consider the following prompts. Each prompt corresponds to an Essay One writing prompt:*

**1a.** Identify, analyze, and respond to a major theme that Rose hits upon either directly or indirectly: the psychology of disaffection, the role of an inspirational teacher, the importance of high expectations, education as empowerment, the role of socio-economic background in regard to education, or another theme which you may frame and interpret.

**1b.** What does Rose have to say regarding vocational education? Analyze and respond to his views on vocational education and the issues he associates with vocational education.

**1c.** What does the essay indicate to you in regard to the issue of college preparedness? Analyze and respond to the specific cognitive, mechanical, and other skills that Rose claims are necessary for academic success.

Suggested outline for this assignment:

- Paragraph one: Introduce the text to an outside audience. Focus on *one* of Rose's main points. Do not summarize his article. Offer a relevant quotation in order to focus your reader on the point or "theme" that you wish to explore.
- Paragraph two: Offer further quotations and examples from Rose's text in order to explore and illuminate your theme. Always use signal phrases and integrate quotations appropriately.
- Paragraph three: Offer your personal response to the essay. Have you experienced anything similar to what Rose describes? Maintain a clear focus on the theme you have selected while communicating your perspective to the outside audience.

See "Reader Response Guidelines" in Resources at the end of this unit. Review the "Introducing Texts" and "Quotation Integration" resource guidelines.

## Suggested Evaluation Criteria and Point Values

| | |
|---|---|
| Text Introduction<br>*The student demonstrates competence in formally introducing the text to an outside audience.* | 6 points |
| Quotation Integration<br>*The student demonstrates competence in appropriately integrating meaningful quotation selections using signal phrases and/or by other means.* | 6 points |
| Response<br>*The student offers a thoughtful response to the text.* | 6 points |
| Format and Voice<br>*The student follows proper MLA format or another standard as specified by the instructor. The student composes in standard written English.* | 2 points |

# Unit One Essay Topics

Length: about five pages (1000–1250 words)
*100 points*
*No matter which essay topic you choose to pursue (or your instructor chooses to assign), the basic assignment parameters and evaluation rubric remain the same. Be sure to study the Essay One evaluation criteria carefully prior to launching into a final essay draft.*

### 1a. Focused Analysis and Reflective Response to Rose

Offer a reflective response to a single aspect of Rose's essay. Do not summarize. We are learning to engage in a conversation or "public discourse." Focus, for example, on the influence of environment, the importance of challenging students, the psychology of failing students, the role of an inspirational teacher, or another single aspect of the text. Introduce and quote extensively from Rose's text for the benefit of your outside audience. Clarify and explore one of his main points and engage in a discourse that is relevant to your own education. Write an expository essay that makes a serious point about your own educational experience. Therefore, feel free to use "I" as appropriate to your task. However, "I" should never displace or come before the expert source material—in this case, Rose. Analyzing his text and its implications is your primary task. Then you can respond on a personal level. Students sometimes make the mistake of turning this expository essay assignment into a personal narrative. Writing a personal memoir is not the task at hand. Instead, this is an "analysis and reflective response" composition.

### 1b. Vocational Education

Ideas regarding "vocational education" or "trade school" alternatives have existed for decades in America. What does Mike Rose seem to have to say on this topic? What are the main arguments for and against vocational education as an alternative or substitute to a "traditional" two or four year college degree, or as an alternative to the traditional "college prep" high school curriculum? How has "vocational education" changed to adjust to a 21st century economy? Incorporate Rose's text and the additional resource listed below (or another resource that you find which meets your instructor's approval). Incorporate your source materials in meaningful ways as you join the conversation, that is, as you engage in a public discourse on this significant issue. Your primary task remains text analysis of source material.

 Reminder: Incorporate two sources for this topic.

## Further Reading for 1b:

Krupnich, Matt. "After decades of pushing bachelor's degrees, U.S. needs more tradespeople." *The Hechinger Report*. PBS Newshour. *PBS.org*. Aug. 29, 2017. http://www.pbs.org/newshour/updates/decades-pushing-bachelors-degrees-u-s-needs- tradespeople/

### 1c. College Preparedness and Success

In 2017, the California State University system took the controversial step of eliminating college "placement" exams, thereby reducing or eliminating remedial math courses for incoming freshmen, claiming that there is no evidence that math remediation helps struggling college students. Critics of the move say that the system is abandoning its obligation to fully educate these college students and is lowering its standards for obtaining a college degree. Some have even questioned why unprepared students are admitted to a college or university in the first place. On the other hand, advocates of the move claim that eliminating remedial math requirements is in the long-term best interest of the students, and that these students still must meet basic degree requirements. Study up on the issue using the Further Reading selections below and/or other resources approved by your instructor. You might also consider selections listed in "Further Inquiry & Research" at the end of this chapter.

How does Mike Rose's essay contribute to this conversation or "discourse" on remedial education in college? Incorporate Rose's text in a meaningful, significant way. Also incorporate two of the sources below or as approved by your instructor. Do not summarize your source material. Rather, integrate it as part of a larger conversation, an important public discourse on American higher education.

Reminder: Incorporate three sources for this topic.

## Further Reading for 1c:

Edley, Jr., Christopher. "At Cal State, algebra is a civil rights issue." *EdSource. edsource.org.* June 5, 2017. https://edsource.org/2017/at-cal-state-algebra-is-a-civil-rights-issue/582950

Hamilton, Elliott. "California State System Will No Longer Force Students To Know English And Math To Graduate: California paves the road to the dumbing down of America." *The DailyWire. www.dailywire.com.* Aug. 4, 2017. http://www.dailywire.com/news/19369/california-state-system-will-no-longer-force- elliott-hamilton#

Smith, Ashley A. "Cal State to End Placement Exams." *InsideHigherEd.com.* June 13, 2017. https://www.insidehighered.com/news/2017/06/13/california-state-university-looks- end-placement-exams

"University System Says Remedial Classes Aren't Helping Students." National Public Radio. *Here & Now. www.wbur.org.* August 16, 2017. http://www.wbur.org/hereandnow/2017/08/16/california-state-remedial-classes

## Scoring Criteria for Essay One

| | |
|---|---|
| Deadline and Word Count<br>*Turned in on deadline and meets mandatory word count range.* | 10 points |
| Holistic Assessment<br>*The student's writing appears thoughtful and descriptive; the essay focuses on and pursues one main theme or idea.* | 20 points |
| Text Introduction<br>*The main text (Rose) is effectively introduced to an "outside" audience not already familiar with the source material. See "Introducing Texts."* | 20 points |
| Handling of Quotations<br>*A bare minimum of (3) significant quotations from the Rose text are accurately presented and appropriately integrated. See "Quotation Integration."* | 20 points |
| Grammar/Usage/Syntax<br>*The student writes in complete, coherent sentences.* | 20 points |
| Format<br>*The student attempts to follow proper MLA format (or other format specified by instructor), including one inch margins, appropriate font style and size, and pagination. Student shows appropriate progress in regard to proper source citation.* | 10 points |

Resources

# Reader Response Guidelines

Reader responses are brief, formal compositions that require you to analyze and reflect upon the textbook readings. Use annotations, discussion notes, and your sentence exercises to form draft material. The recommended structure for a reader response is as follows:

*Paragraph One:* Introduce your source material to your audience. Introduce the reading to an educated "outside the classroom" audience who is not familiar with the reading and has not read the essay or article in question. See "Introducing Texts" for further information. Typically, you will also offer your interpretation of the author's main point or thesis. Provide an overview of the material without summarizing the article's content.

*Paragraph Two:* Analyze the reading by quoting important language. Select and appropriately integrate significant language in order to highlight important subject matter from the reading. Your quotation selections help you to focus your audience on whatever you view as the most significant and most relevant topics that appear in the reading. See "Quotation Integration."

*Paragraph Three:* Offer a personal response to the reading. Why is this reading selection important, and how is it relevant to our world? One ideal in composition involves coherence, meaning that your composition usually features one common theme, central focus, or idea (often referred to as your "thesis") from start to finish.

# Typical Reader Response Evaluation Criteria

| | |
|---|---|
| Text Introduction: *The student demonstrates competence in formally introducing the text to an outside audience.* | 30% |
| Quotation Integration: *The student demonstrates competence in appropriately integrating meaningful quotation selections using signal phrases and/or by other means.* | 30% |
| Response: *The student offers a thoughtful response to the text.* | 30% |
| Format and Voice: *The student follows proper MLA format or another standard as specified by the instructor. The student composes in standard written English.* | 10% |

# Why MLA?

There are many style guides. The Associated Press publishes a guidebook for journalists, for example. If you go to work for the famous magazine *The New Yorker*, you will follow the magazine's own particular formatting guidelines. In popular online web sites and journals and in hard copy printing in the arts and humanities, style guides tend to be similar if not exactly the same. Web and print editors of respectable publications favor straightforward prose and clear source citations.

In academia, that is, within colleges and universities, MLA or Modern Language Association style is favored in the liberal arts and humanities. APA or American Psychological Association style is favored in the social and behavioral sciences. Each academic discipline or field of study may have its own set of guidelines or preferences.

Style guides exist so that there is consistency nationally and internationally in how scholars present work to peers and to the public. It's also vital that academic critics and scholars cite their sources of information in a way so that if the reader wants to dig further into the topic or verify an author's claim, he or she can track down the author's source materials. If each person did things his or her own way, it would be difficult to share information and grow our collective knowledge. (As a side note, can you sense right now why your English teachers get frustrated with students who make use of "creative grammar" in their essays? It becomes very difficult to understand what a student is trying to say when the student composes outside the bounds of standard prose.)

The good news for you is that college composition courses use MLA, a fairly simple and straightforward format and citation style. You can master the basics of MLA with a little study and some practice.

Your reader response assignments are good opportunities for you to practice proper MLA formatting so that your essay assignments feature proper college formatting and citation style.

## Online Resources

The Purdue Online Writing Lab (OWL) is an excellent free web resource. Visit *https://owl.english.purdue .edu/* and see *https://owl.english.purdue.edu/owl/resource/747/01/.* You can study formatting, citation, and other essential composition skills at this site.

The Modern Language Association itself also publishes useful internet resources. See *https://style .mla.org/.*

## The Principle of Rising Rigor

I suggest that instructors use what I term the "Principle of Rising Rigor" as the course proceeds. For the first reader response, a student might earn 2.5 out of 3 or even 3 out of 3 for the skill of "Text Introduction" even though there is a significant error in the student's text introduction sentence such as a missing or misplaced comma. It is the student's responsibility to note the instructor's feedback for future reference. The same recurring error will cost the student more points down the line according to the Principle of Rising Rigor.

For example, if a student's performance for a certain composition skill in an essay or reader response receives 8.5 out of 10 (85% or "B") in week three of the semester, the same performance at semester's end might receive 6.5 out of 10 ("D") or even 5 out of 10 ("F") depending on the circumstances. Such decisions must be made at the discretion of the instructor with a holistic understanding of course objectives and the importance of the particular skill in question. Students, in my view, must be expected to show improvement and progress even as the assignments become more demanding and complicated. The progression of small to large assignments offers the opportunity for students to practice necessary composition skills.

### Point Values and Scoring

All of the assignments in this course come with *suggested* evaluation criteria. These rubrics are divided into categories with specific point values. I find that students favor reason over emotion when "points" are awarded instead of "grades." In any case, many of us, teachers and students alike, are well versed in "grades," so I offer the following general translation of point values for a ten (10) or a twenty (20) point category. Instructors may need to ponder the particular "grade" involved in assigning point values. As always, I offer the following in the spirit of helpful suggestion rather than mandate.☺

| 10 point category | 20 point category | = "Grade" |
|:---:|:---:|:---:|
| 10 | 20 | A |
| 8.5 | 17.5 | B |
| 7.5 | 15 | C |
| 6.5 | 13 | D |
| 5 | 10 | F |

## Introducing Texts or Sources for the Benefit of the "Outside" Audience

*The purpose of a "text introduction" is to introduce source material to an "outside" audience who is not already familiar with that source material. Why is it an "outside" audience? Let's say that your readers are not "inside" our classroom. Imagine writing your composition to an audience filled with your other instructors or to an assembly of college faculty. You are writing to instructors of math, sociology, psychology, anthropology, engineering, graphic design, et cetera, et cetera. Your reader is knowledgeable and educated but does not know your source materials or your topic. So you need to "introduce" your main texts or sources to your audience. Sometimes in composition we can simply acknowledge sources of information with citations. However, when your writing topic revolves around one or two central texts or sources, then you want to introduce those texts to your audience so that they can enjoy a full understanding of your discourse or discussion. Keep in mind that even though your audience is pretty sharp they don't know what you know about the topic at hand. They need basic information in order to follow your interpretations and analysis of the material.*

Do the following when you "introduce" a text:

- **Identify the author's full name and the full title of the source material.**
  - Use the author's full name on first reference; thereafter, use last name only, as per Modern Language Association (MLA) style.
  - Associated Press (AP) and other styles also favor the use of the last name only after the first reference.
  - Be sure to punctuate the title correctly according to MLA style: quotation marks for an "Article Title" or italics for a *Book Title*. Use capital letters for the first letters of the main words. This is not a text message to your bestie.
- **Clarify the authority of the author.**
  - Sometimes this can be done with a simple adjective: author X, journalist Y, or social psychologist Z.
  - Consider: Is the person an expert? Why is the person interested in the topic at hand? What does your outside audience need to know? What information can you share that will help with your interpretation, analysis, or argument?

- **Identify the author's thesis or main point.**
  - Give a brief overview of the main point of the text or your main focal point (that is, your interpretation of the author's thesis).
  - It is often helpful or necessary to provide historical or publication "context" or background information in order for your audience to understand your interpretation, analysis, or argument.
  - Sometimes you will want to clarify the author's tone and purpose. Sometimes it is helpful to provide some rhetorical analysis of the author's literary technique—for example, you might need to inform your audience that the author employs irony in order to make a point. Your audience does not have the benefit of the full original context. Your audience has only what you provide.
- **Whenever possible, incorporate significant language from the author in the form of an integrated quotation.**
- **You may need to touch upon the "Rhetorical Situation" of the text.** See Unit Five resources for further information.
- **Depending on the depth and complexity of your introduction and your composition assignment, the entire process can be done in one or two sentences or in one or two paragraphs.**
  - Good writing is clear and efficient. Aim for "clean copy" (error-free prose).
  - It is often useful for you to spend an entire paragraph introducing the text. Besides, it's an easy way to help you boost your word count.
  - Keep in mind the needs of your "outside" audience who has not read the source material.

EXAMPLE of a Text Introduction:

In his autobiographical essay "I Just Wanna Be Average," which is an excerpt from the author's book *Lives on the Boundary* (1989), educator Mike Rose reflects upon his school experiences. Rose describes disengaged students who were "bobbing in pretty shallow water" (12). The author appears to advocate a liberal arts education. He writes in praise of a demanding humanities teacher named Jack MacFarland. Rose believes that students "will float to the mark [that teachers] set" (15). If a teacher sets a high bar, the students will achieve more than if the teacher is comfortable with low expectations. For Rose, Jack MacFarland was an inspirational teacher who set high standards.

## Quotation Integration

Use your writer's handbook and other online resources to study signal phrases and quotation integration. For example, visit the Purdue Online Writing Lab (OWL) at https://owl.english.purdue.edu/owl/.

Your ability to "integrate" the author's language into your own prose is extremely important. Your ability to paraphrase appropriately and to properly integrate quotations demonstrates your capacity to analyze and to process the text material. Your goal is to "analyze" or "break down" the text—that is, to interpret accurately and respond appropriately to the source materials—rather than simply to summarize and respond to the text in a vague or generalized manner.

Look up the term "signal phrase." Be careful of where you find your definitions, of course. At the same time, take advantage of the amazing technology that is very likely at your disposal.

*An Important Factor in Assignment Evaluation*

In the Engaging Discourse suggested scoring rubrics, you will discover that the "ability to handle quotations" counts for a significant percentage of your written assignments. You can earn maximum points in this category by selecting meaningful quotations and properly integrating that language into your sentence structure using signal phrases and by other means.

## Three Effective Ways to Integrate Quotations

1. **The signal phrase (with a comma)**
   Example:
   Atwood claims, "[Pornography is] an educational tool and a powerful propaganda device" (34).
   See Notes for Composition at the end of the textbook.

2. **Whole sentence set up (with a colon)**
   Example:
   Atwood claims that pornography has a profound ability to sway its viewers' understandings of sex and sexual relationships: "It's also an educational tool and a powerful propaganda device" (34).

3. **The seamless transition (no punctuation)**
   Example:
   Atwood writes that pornography is "an educational tool and a powerful propaganda device" (34).

## Seamless Quotation Integration

*You can incorporate a word or phrase lifted from the source text instead of quoting a full sentence. Often, this form of quotation results in improved style.*

*Study the example below. Here, the writer uses quotation "excerpts" integrated within his own prose rather than relying on "complete sentences" lifted from the text. Often, quoted excerpts or phrases can more efficiently convey ideas and overall context to the audience. This sample also illustrates how to alter words within a quotation [indicated by brackets] in order to more effectively present the quotation to the reader.*

Rose describes a self-defense mechanism where students seek to "protect themselves from [the] suffocating madness [of school] by taking on" a mentality that values mediocrity above excellence (15). For Rose, this psychological condition explains why students such as Ken Harvey only want to be "average." The tragedy, Rose states, is that in order to make the defense work "you have to twist the knife in your own gray matter" (15). He means that some young people deny themselves the chance to succeed in order to feel OK about not succeeding in a "tremendously disorienting place" like school (14). It's a downward spiral that keeps students from encountering new ideas. They shield themselves by championing the average and by rejecting the "confusion and frustration" of academic scrambling, philosophical inquiry, and scientific reasoning (15).

# Suggested Outline for Essay One, Option 1a.

*Check with your instructor on his or her suggestions and preferences.*

The following is a basic outline of a possible essay. One of the key concepts in literacy is for you to take ownership of your thought processes and your compositions, so try to avoid getting in the habit of looking for a "key" or fundamental outline that will work in all circumstances. Writing doesn't function in the same manner at all times. Good writing habits involve the development of flexibility rather than rigidity.

1. Introduce the Rose text. Provide a full and complete context for your outside audience. Integrate a quotation or quoted phrase. Focus your interpretation of Rose's text on the theme or aspect that you have selected. Relate the theme in Rose's text to your own main theme or thesis. Perhaps your thesis is your response or personal angle on the text theme that you have identified. *250 words.*

2. Pursue your interpretation of Rose's text. Highlight the theme that you have decided to focus on. Integrate relevant quotations. Set up the quotations with appropriate signal phrases and explain the significance of the quotations to your readers. Clarify the points that you think Rose is trying to make. *250 words.*

3. Investigate the evidence and reasoning that Rose presents in his text in order to make his case. Integrate relevant quotations. Explain these quotations to your audience. Present your own analysis of Rose's argument. Clarify why you find his idea(s) persuasive or why you doubt the validity of his concept(s). *250 words.*

4. Transition from your analysis of Rose's text to your own experience. Using quoted language from Rose's text, show your readers how Rose's text is relevant to your own experience. Continue to integrate Rose's language as you present your own experience, always with a mind to expanding upon your analysis of the primary text, which is Rose. *250 words.*

5. In a concluding paragraph, present your final statement on the theme that you have identified in Rose's text. Don't repeat language that you have previously used. Move further into analysis and exploration of the subject matter. Has your interpretation and analysis of Rose's text left you with important questions that need to be answered or with important ideas that you can carry forward with you as you pursue your own education? In this sort of analysis/response essay, it seems appropriate to review the past but also to look forward to the potential future. Has your analysis of Rose's text given you any ideas for solutions to a problem that you have identified? Avoid cliché and trite language that will not seem authentic to your readers. *250 words.*

Remember that this is one possible outline for one option. The other two options provide opportunities to explore, in some sense, more immediate and pragmatic issues, and therefore the other two options also require you to study and incorporate the outside sources that have been provided. Even if you pursue one of the other topics, consider the outline above. It should prove to be a useful guide for you with topics 1b. and 1c. as well.

## Further Inquiry & Research

Edley, Jr., Christopher. "At Cal State, algebra is a civil rights issue." *EdSource. edsource.org*. June 5, 2017. https://edsource.org/2017/at-cal-state-algebra-is-a-civil-rights-issue/582950

Hamilton, Elliott. "California State System Will No Longer Force Students To Know English And Math To Graduate: California paves the road to the dumbing down of America." *The DailyWire. www.dailywire.com*. Aug. 4, 2017. http://www.dailywire.com/news/19369/california-state-system-will-no-longer-force- elliott-hamilton#

Krupnich, Matt. "After decades of pushing bachelor's degrees, U.S. needs more tradespeople." *The Hechinger Report*. PBS Newshour. *PBS.org*. Aug. 29, 2017. http://www.pbs.org/newshour/updates/decades-pushing-bachelors-degrees-u-s-needs- tradespeople/

Smith, Ashley A. "Cal State to End Placement Exams." *InsideHigherEd.com*. June 13, 2017. https://www.insidehighered.com/news/2017/06/13/california-state-university-looks- end-placement-exams

"University System Says Remedial Classes Aren't Helping Students." National Public Radio. *Here & Now. www.wbur.org*. August 16, 2017. http://www.wbur.org/hereandnow/2017/08/16/california-state-remedial-classes

# Additional Source Materials by Topic

## 21st Century Education

Clayton-Pedersen, Alma with O'Neill, Nancy. "Cirricula Designed to Meet 21st Century Expectations." *Educating the Net Generation,* Accessed via *Association of American Colleges and Universities,* 2005, https://www.educause.edu/research-and-publications/books/educating-net-generation/curricula-designed-meet-21st-century-expectations

Collier, Peter J. "What is the Purpose of 21st Century College Education." *Dr Peter J Collier Blog.* July 28, 2015, http://drpeterjcollier.com/blog/2015/07/28/tyjhhhh/

Miller, Abbey et al. "Access to Attainment: An Access Agenda for 21st Century College Students." *Institute for Higher Education.* Dec. 2014, https://files.eric.ed.gov/fulltext/ED558176.pdf

"Quality Higher Education for the 21st Century." *California Faculty Association White Paper,* https://www.csuchico.edu/futurepossibilities/documents/CFA_White_Paper_Quality_in_HE_for_21st_Century.pdf

Quardricos, Bernard Driskell. "The Reimagination of Higher Education in 21st Century America." *The Hill.* Jan. 10, 2018, http://thehill.com/blogs/congress-blog/education/368358-the-reimagination-of-higher-education-in-21st-century-america

Soffel, Jenny. "What are the 21st-century Skills Every Student Needs?" *World Economic Forum.* Mar. 10, 2016, https://www.weforum.org/agenda/2016/03/21st-century-skills-future-jobs-students/

Zinshteyn, Mikhail. "How to Help the 21st Century College Student." *Education Writers Association.* Sept. 9, 2014, https://www.ewa.org/blog-educated-reporter/how-help-21st-century-college-student

## Trade Education

"7 Benefits that Prove the Value of Education." *Trade Schools, Colleges and Universities.* Aug. 23, 2018, https://www.trade-schools.net/articles/value-of-education.asp

"Job-Ready Skills Needed for 21st Century Industries." *Rosedale Technical College Blog.* Jan. 25, 2016, https://www.rosedaletech.org/job-ready-skills-needed-for-21st-century-industries/

Morris-Sealey, Carrie. "Trades and Careers." *College Consensus.* N.d., https://www.collegeconsensus.com/major/trades-careers/

Pusser, Brian & Levin, John. "Re-imagining Community Colleges in the 21st Century." *Center for American Progress.* Dec. 2009, https://www.americanprogress.org/wp-content/uploads/issues/2009/12/pdf/community_colleges_reimagined.pdf

# UNIT TWO

# Feminism

## Suggested Timeline: Three to Four Weeks

I ask my students, "Who here would identify him- or herself as a feminist?" Typically, out of a class of two dozen, a couple of tentative hands rise up. I then ask, "Who supports the right for women to vote?" Amidst laughter, nearly every hand rises. I ask, "Who thinks it is legally possible for a husband to assault or rape his wife?" The laughter goes away, and the hands stay in the air. I ask, "Who supports equal pay for equal work?" Hands remain in the air. I ask, "Who here is a feminist?" All but a few hands go down.

What is it about the term "feminist" that seems to make people hesitate?

My contention, I tell my students, is that all of you are what we might call "first wave" feminists who support the political and legal enfranchisement of women. This is a well-established American value, it seems to me. By analyzing the readings in this unit, we can figure out a good deal about what it means to embrace or to reject "second wave" feminism. And likely you will come to your own conclusion whether you embrace or reject the values implied in the modern "feminist" label. You may also discover that some of your peers embrace what has been termed "third wave" feminism, which is the Millennial iteration of the Civil Rights Era feminist movement.

The ideas of "second wave" feminists like Susan Brownmiller, author of *Femininity* (1984), remain controversial and intriguing. Most of today's students clearly support, and probably take for granted, the feminist civil rights struggles of the 1960s, 1970s, and 1980s—for example, the right of a qualified candidate to be admitted to a college or university of one's choosing. Many of America's elite institutions of higher education admitted only men until as late as the 1970s. Earlier, even when a woman was accepted, she might only be able to apply to a program to study nursing or teaching. Second wave feminism won numerous important battles in regard to this sort of institutional sexism.

Second wave feminists attempted to focus attention on the notion that cultural concepts surrounding gender were often, in their view, sexist and proscriptive. Inspired by an earlier generation of language theorists, second wave feminists frequently tie together cultural concepts with the form and use of language. One idea here is that cultural biases are revealed through an analysis of language. Aileen Pace Nilsen, for example, sets out to reveal society's gender attitudes through a close examination of the English language dictionary. It's interesting, heady stuff, and I doubt you will find an English or composition teacher in

America who doesn't understand the intimate connection between the thoughts in a student's head, the words in his or her mouth, and the prose that he or she transfers to the page. Developing one's ability to connect and clarify this thought-to-page process is one of the most important learning objectives of this course.

Third wave, or Millennial, feminists seem to have more in common with Camille Paglia, who attacks academic feminists as being "lost in a fog of social constructionism." A major challenge for students in this unit will be to understand a conflict between the views of Brownmiller and Paglia that is indirect and off the page. They reveal very different attitudes toward "social constructionism." For example, these authors appear to have extremely different responses to the concept that society shapes the denotations and connotations of words like "femininity" and "masculinity." Brownmiller claims that patriarchal culture forms society's definition of "femininity," and that this definition bears real consequences for women. As a teacher, I simplify this concept by pointing out that Brownmiller makes a "nurture" argument; she emphasizes the importance of social environment in the development of our concepts of femininity. Paglia rejects such "social constructionism" and argues the role of "nature" in the formation of "masculinity," which she identifies as a creative cultural force that is "aggressive, unstable, [and] combustible."

It's not important to choose sides here. These authors aren't even arguing with each other directly, so why should we choose a side? Instead, let's analyze their attitudes in order to enlighten ourselves, so that we can participate in an engaging discourse on the complementary roles of nature and nurture in the formation of gender identity.

## Readings

Here is a list of the readings for this unit:

1. Judy Brady, "Why I Want A Wife" (1971)
2. Margaret Atwood, "Pornography" (1988)
3. Gloria Steinem, "Erotica and Pornography" (1972)
4. Wendy McElroy, "A Feminist Defense of Pornography" (1997)
5. Susan Brownmiller, "Femininity" (1984)
6. Camille Paglia, "Rape and Modern Sex War" (1991)

## Responsibilities

Associated **sentence exercises** (*20 points*) will lead to **Reader Responses #3 and #4** (*40 points)* which will help you to produce draft material for **Essay Two** (*100 points*).

## Objectives

The main objective of our second unit is for you to be able to participate in a public discourse (discussion) on two topics as seen through the lens of 20th century American feminism: 1) traditional masculine/feminine gender identity and 2) pornography.

✓ This unit aims to reinforce the development of sound critical and analytical thinking through the detailed evaluation of source materials.

✓ This unit challenges students to turn sound critical and analytical thinking on complex topics into clear prose.

✓ Students must produce writing with clear organization, appropriate logic, detailed text analysis, and solid support for their own views, with appropriately cited source information.

✓ Students will develop critical thinking, reading, and writing strategies in order to produce notes, drafts, and a final essay that exhibits synthetic connections between varied source materials.

## Resources

"Feminism": Denotation and Connotation
Purpose & Audience
Logos, Ethos, or Pathos?
The Definition of Pornography in America
Further Inquiry & Research
Additional Source Materials by Topic

## Editor's Note

I want to clarify a key point: you don't have to *like* any of these texts. And you certainly don't have to *agree* with them. You do have to *understand* them. You'll notice, of course, that the texts themselves feature major points of disagreement. Your job as a writer is to demonstrate your understanding of the texts by formally introducing them and explaining the authors' main points to an outside audience that is not already familiar with the source material. In doing so, you will also be able to formulate and express your own views. First and foremost, you must analyze the source material, which involves your ability to state an author's main idea—or to interpret a main supporting idea that is embedded within the text or implied by the text (critics sometimes call this process analyzing the *subtext*)—along with a detailed description of the reasoning and evidence that the author presents in support of his or her main idea.

Readings

## Judy Brady, "Why I Want a Wife" (1971)

As with Russell Baker's text in the first unit, it is imperative to understand the author's *tone* in order to understand the main idea or "thesis" that she expresses. As with the Baker and Asimov texts, Brady never directly expresses her thesis or main argument. She leaves it to the attuned reader to articulate the argument. And that is your challenge. While you may understand her main argument, the measurement in a composition course is whether you can express the author's main argument in clear prose that an outside audience (who has not read this article) can easily understand.

One interesting note to keep in mind is how easy it is to take for granted the social changes that the feminist movement has brought about. The majority of Americans these days, for example, agree that women, and mothers, ought to be free to pursue careers wherever their abilities can take them. Most Americans nowadays believe that women should have equal access to colleges and universities. When Brady's article was published in 1971, however, women could not take such attitudes for granted. Many major American universities, for example, did not admit women to their general undergraduate programs. As you read and annotate, infer what social attitudes may have prevailed at the time of publication. What is the target of Brady's social criticism? Brady is writing in a rich English language tradition of using sarcasm in order to expose an issue and to call for social change. Do you agree with her message? To what extent is her message relevant or no longer relevant in 21st century America?

## Questions to Consider

*Answer these questions as you read and annotate the text:*

- Dig around the internet or elsewhere to uncover the original publication context of this article. What can you find out about the magazine that originally published this article?
- As you read, make margin notes regarding specific social attitudes and behaviors that exist, according to the text. Have any of these attitudes or behaviors changed or gone away, in your view?
- What do the terms "wife" and "husband" mean, according to the text? Note specific language that clues you into these definitions. Have the definitions changed? Be prepared to justify your answer.

### Judy Brady, Why I Want a Wife

I belong to that classification of people known as wives. I am A Wife. And, not altogether incidentally, I am a mother.

Not too long ago a male friend of mine appeared on the scene fresh from a recent divorce. He had one child, who is, of course, with his ex-wife. He is looking for another wife. As I thought about him while I was ironing one evening, it suddenly occurred to me that I, too, would like to have a wife. Why do I want a wife?

I would like to go back to school so that I can become economically independent, support myself, and, if need be, support those de pen dent upon me. I want a wife who will work and send me to school. And while I am going to school I want a wife to take care of my children. I want a wife to keep track of the children's doctor and dentist appointments. And to keep track of mine, too.

_____

From *Ms. Magazine*, January 1972 by Judy (Syfers) Brady. Copyright © 1972 by Maia Syfers and Tanya Syfers. Reprinted by permission.

I want a wife to make sure my children eat properly and are kept clean. I want a wife who will wash the children's clothes and keep them mended. I want a wife who is a good nurturant attendant to my children, who arranges for their schooling, makes sure that they have an adequate social life with their peers, takes them to the park, the zoo, etc. I want a wife who takes care of the children when they are sick, a wife who arranges to be around when the children need special care, because, of course, I cannot miss classes at school. My wife must arrange to lose time at work and not lose the job. It may mean a small cut in my wife's income from time to time, but I guess I can tolerate that. Needless to say, my wife will arrange and pay for the care of the children while my wife is working.

I want a wife who will take care of my physical needs. I want a wife who will keep my house clean. A wife who will pick up after my children, a wife who will pick up after me. I want a wife who will keep my clothes clean, ironed, mended, replaced when need be, and who will see to it that my personal things are kept in their proper place so that I can find what I need the minute I need it. I want a wife who cooks the meals, a wife who is a good cook. I want a wife who will plan the menus, do the necessary grocery shopping, prepare the meals, serve them pleasantly, and then do the cleaning up while I do my studying. I want a wife who will care for me when I am sick and sympathize with my pain and loss of time from school. I want a wife to go along when our family takes a vacation so that someone can continue to care for me and my children when I need a rest and change of scene.

I want a wife who will not bother me with rambling complaints about a wife's duties. But I want a wife who will listen to me when I feel the need to explain a rather difficult point I have come across in my course of studies. And I want a wife who will type my papers for me when I have written them.

When I am through with school and have a job, I want my wife to quit working and remain at home so that my wife can more fully and completely take care of a wife's duties.

My God, who *wouldn't* want a wife?

## Questions for Comprehension

*Answer these questions as a comprehension reading quiz and/or for further clarification on the text:*

1. True or False. In this essay entitled "Why I Want a Wife," Judy Brady declares that she is a lesbian.

2. Brady writes, "I want a wife who will not bother me with rambling complaints about a wife's duties." What are a wife's duties, according to this text?

3. Brady writes, "If, by chance, I find another person more suitable as a wife than the wife I already have, I want the liberty to replace my present wife with another one. Naturally, I will expect a fresh, new life; my wife will take the children and be solely responsible for them so that I am left free." In this passage, what specific social attitudes does Brady criticize? Which of these attitudes has changed or remained the same?

# Margaret Atwood, "Pornography" (1988)

A friend of mine went to pick up his daughter after school let out. He noticed a group of 12-year-old girls huddled around a mobile phone. After the usual song and dance routine that children and parents bumble through, he saw that on the phone they had been watching an adult pornographic video. Despite his understanding of the healthy sense of curiosity on the part of young people, this was not, in my friend's view, harmless entertainment or informative sexual education. Most parents, it is safe to say, do not see the internet's unfiltered images and videos as any valid part of a child's healthy sexual development or education.

Pornography is a multi-billion dollar industry. With the advent of the internet, pornography has never been so widespread or so easily accessible. Yet a meaningful public discourse on the effects of pornography seems to be missing from the public and private lives of most Americans. We all know this billion-dollar industry is out there, but no one seems to have much to say about it. Meaningful public discourse on the topic seems absent.

Decades ago, in the 1970s and 1980s, second wave feminists thought it important to initiate a public discourse on the cultural meaning and impact of pornography. Second wave feminists such as Margaret Atwood and Gloria Steinem viewed pornography as a dangerous objectification of the female form. Pornography doesn't involve a woman, they argue, so much as it involves a female object, a dangerous fantasy portrayed from the male perspective.

It is a given, in the consensus view of second wave feminists, that pornography is not only harmful toward the women that it objectifies, but it may also prove harmful to the viewer or consumer of pornography. This is the viewpoint Atwood explains and explores in her article "Pornography" (1988).

Atwood urges us to move beyond binary understandings of the issue. (She references the "*You're-a-prude/You're-a-pervert* dialectic.") Similarly, she urges us to see beyond the "freedom of expression" argument and to think more deeply about the actual effects of pornography. In other words, she is not arguing about Larry Flint's right to publish *Hustler*, nor is she centrally concerned with a teenager's right to view the pictures therein. She asks us to consider the effects of pornography as an "educational tool." What does she mean by this?

Second wave feminists developed this public discourse at a time when pornography was, by our 21st century standards, fairly difficult to obtain. There were seedy adult theaters or that verboten aisle in the local video rental store. The porn viewer had to go somewhere to obtain the material. Now, in the age of the internet, literally thousands of pornographic images and outlets spring onto the screen with a few clicks of any keyboard. Studies of data traffic in the 1990s claimed that as much as half of all early internet traffic involved pornography, while contemporary studies vary widely in estimations, in the range of five to fifteen percent. Far from stimulating or expanding the public discourse that feminists believed was so important, the discourse seems to have largely vanished in the age of the internet.

The public discourse might seem more relevant than ever to Baby Boomers (born 1945–64), yet Millennials have largely dismissed second wave feminist doctrine when it comes to pornography. Millennial attitudes are often more closely aligned with Wendy McElroy, who in the journal *Free Inquiry* offers "A Feminist Defense of Pornography" (1997). She views pornography as a healthy outlet rather than a dangerous fantasy. Atwood describes pornography as "a powerful propaganda device," a substance that shapes unhealthy attitudes and habits.

Whatever one's view, it's hard to disagree that pornographic images are impactful. What does Atwood seem to argue in regard to *nature vs. nurture* when it comes to the question of healthy sexual development? It's impossible to disagree that porn is easily accessible. Therefore, despite possible discomfort and embarrassment (or is it just me?), it's a worthwhile public discourse.

## Questions to Consider

*Answer these questions as you read and annotate the text:*

- Why are Atwood's notions of pornography so disturbing, "death, messy, explicit and highly sadistic"? Where has she gotten this idea of pornography?
- Why is the word "pornography" nowadays like the word "Marxism" or "feminism"? What does she mean, and what point is she making?
- Atwood writes that "theoreticians theorize and speculators speculate." She does not take up the argument, but mentions the idea that the spread of pornography could be "a backlash against the women's movement by men who are threatened by uppity female behavior in real life." She does not follow up in depth on this line of thinking, but what can you glean regarding this "backlash" argument from what she does write?
- Do you agree with those who accuse Atwood (and other anti-porn feminists) of being "prudes"? Why or why not?
- Atwood writes, "The no-harm position is far from being proven." What does she mean?
- Atwood notes that "boys learn their concept of masculinity from other men." How does this sociological notion relate to the issue of pornography? In what other areas of life do you find this observation to be relevant?
- What is the effect of pornography on male/female relationships, according to Atwood? Why is it not just "harmless entertainment," according to her?
- Atwood proposes that porn consumption is related to a sense of satisfaction or dissatisfaction in people's sex lives. What is the relationship or dynamic, according to her argument? Do you find merit in this view? Why or why not?

### Margaret Atwood, Pornography

When I was in Finland a few years ago for an international writers' conference, I had occasion to say a few paragraphs in public on the subject of pornography. The context was a discussion of political repression, and I was suggesting the possibility of a link between the two. The immediate result was that a male journalist took several large bites out of me. Prudery and pornography are two halves of the same coin, said he, and I was clearly a prude. What could you expect from an Anglo-Canadian? Afterward, a couple of pleasant Scandinavian men asked me what I had been so worked up about. All "pornography" means, they said, is graphic depictions of whores, and what was the harm in that?

Not until then did it strike me that the male journalist and I had two entirely different things in mind. By "pornography," he meant naked bodies and sex. I, on the other hand, had recently been doing the research for my novel *Bodily Harm,* and was still in a state of shock from some of the material I had seen, including the Ontario Board of Film Censors' "outtakes." By "pornography," I meant women getting their nipples snipped off with garden shears, having meat hooks stuck into their vaginas, being disemboweled; little girls being raped; men (yes, there are some men) being smashed to a pulp and forcibly sodomized. The cutting edge of pornography, as far as I could see, was no longer simple old copulation, hanging from the chandelier or otherwise: it was death, messy, explicit and highly sadistic. I explained this to the nice Scandinavian men. "Oh, but that's just the United

States," they said. "Everyone knows they're sick." In their country, they said, violent "pornography" of that kind was not permitted on television or in movies; indeed, excessive violence of any kind was not permitted. They had drawn a clear line between erotica, which earlier studies had shown did not incite in more aggressive and brutal behavior toward women, and violence, which later studies indicated did.

Some time after that I was in Saskatchewan, where, because of the scenes in *Bodily Harm,* I found myself on an open-line radio show answering questions about "pornography." Almost no one who phoned in was in favor of it, but again they weren't talking about the same stuff I was, because they hadn't seen it. Some of them were all set to stamp out bathing suits and negligees, and, if possible, any depictions of the female body whatsoever. God, it was implied, did not approve of female bodies, and sex of any kind, including that practised by bumblebees, should be shoved back into the dark, where it belonged. I had more than a suspicion that *Lady Chatterley's Lover,* Margaret Laurence's *The Diviners,* and indeed most books by most serious modern authors would have ended up as confetti if left in the hands of these callers.

For me, these two experiences illustrate the two poles of the emotionally heated debate that is now thundering around this issue. They also underline the desirability and even the necessity of defining the terms. "Pornography" is now one of those catchalls, like "Marxism" and "feminism," that have become so broad they can mean almost anything, ranging from certain verses in the Bible, ads for skin lotion and sex texts for children to the contents of Penthouse, Naughty '90s postcards and films with titles containing the word *Nazi* that show vicious scenes of torture and killing. It's easy to say that sensible people can tell the difference. Unfortunately, opinions on what constitutes a sensible person vary.

But even sensible people tend to lose their cool when they start talking about this subject. They soon stop talking and start yelling, and the name-calling begins. Those in favor of censorship (which may include groups not noticeably in agreement on other issues, such as some feminists and religious fundamentalists) accuse the others of exploiting women through the use of degrading images, contributing to the corruption of children, and adding to the general climate of violence and threat in which both women and children live in this society; or, though they may not give much of a hoot about actual women and children, they invoke moral Standards and God's supposed aversion to "filth," "smut" and deviated *perversion,* which may mean ankles.

The camp in favor of total "freedom of expression" often comes out howling as loud as the Romans would have if told they could no longer bave innocent fun watching the lions eat up Christians. It too may include segments of the population who are not natural bedfellows: those who proclaim their God-given right to freedom, including the freedom to tote guns, drive when drunk, drool over chicken porn and get off on videotapes of women being raped and beaten, may be waving the same anticensorship banner as responsible liberals who fear the return of Mrs. Grundy, or gay groups for whom sexual emancipation involves the concept of "sexual theatre." *Whatever turns you on* is a handy motto, as is *A man's home is his castle* (and if it includes a dungeon with beautiful maidens strung up in chains and bleeding from every pore, that's his business).

Meanwhile, theoreticians theorize and speculators speculate. Is today's pornography yet another indication of the hatred of the body, the deep mind-body split, which is supposed to pervade Western Christian society? Is it a backlash against the women's movement by men who are threatened by uppity female behavior in real life, so like to fantasize about women done up like outsize parcels, being turned into hamburger, kneeling at their feet in slavelike adoration or sucking off guns? Is it a sign of collective impotence, of a generation of men who can't relate to real women at all but have to make do with bits of celluloid and paper? Is the current flood just a result of smart marketing and aggressive promotion by the money men in what has now become a multibillion-dollar industry? If they were selling movies about men getting their testicles stuck full of knitting needles by women with swastikas on their sleeves, would they do as well, or is this penchant somehow peculiarly male? If so, why? Is pornography a power trip rather than a sex one? Some say that those ropes, chains, muzzles and other restraining devices are an argument for the immense power female sexuality still wields in the male imagination: you don't put these things on dogs unless you're afraid of them. Others, more literary, wonder about the shift from the 19th-century Magic Women or Femme Fatale image to the lollipop-licker, airhead or turkey-carcass treatment of women in porn today. The proporners don't care much about theory: they merely demand product. The antiporners don't care about it in the final analysis either: there's dirt on the street, and they want it cleaned up, now.

It seems to me that this conversation, with its *You're-a-prude/You're-a-pervert* dialectic, will never get anywhere as long as we continue to think of this material as just "entertainment." Possibly we're deluded by the packaging, the format: magazine, book, movie, theatrical presentation. We're used to thinking of these things as part of the "entertainment industry," and we're used to thinking of ourselves as free adult people who ought to be able to see any kind of "entertainment" we want to. That was what the First Choice pay-TV debate was all about. After all, it's only entertainment, right? Entertainment means fun, and only a killjoy would be antifun. What's the harm?

This is obviously the central question: *What's the harm?* If there isn't any real harm to any real people, then the antiporners can tsk-tsk and/or throw up as much as they like, but they can't rightfully expect more legal controls or sanctions. However, the no-harm position is far from being proven.

(For instance, there's a clear-cut case for banning—as the federal government has proposed—movies, photos and videos that depict children engaging in sex with adults: real children are used to make the movies, and hardly anybody thinks this is ethical. The possibilities for coercion are too great.)

To shift the viewpoint, I'd like to suggest three other models for looking at "pornography"—and here I mean the violent kind.

Those who find the idea of regulating pornographic materials repugnant because they think it's Fascist or Communist or otherwise not in accordance with the principles of an open democratic society should consider that Canada has made it illegal to disseminate material that may lead to hatred toward any group because of race or religion. I suggest that if pornography of the violent kind depicted these acts being done predominantly to Chinese, to blacks, to Catholics, it would be off the market immediately, under the present laws. Why is hate literature illegal? Because whoever made the law thought that such material might incite real people to do real awful things to other real people. The human brain is to a certain extent a computer: garbage in, garbage out. We only hear about the extreme cases (like that of American multimurderer Ted Bundy) in which pornography has contributed to the death and/or mutilation of women and/or men. Although pornography is not the only factor involved in the creation of such deviance, it certainly has upped the ante by suggesting both a variety of techniques and the social acceptability of such actions. Nobody knows yet what effect this stuff is having on the less psychotic.

Studies have shown that a large part of the marker for all kinds of porn, soft and hard, is drawn from the 16-to-21-year-old population of young men. Boys used to learn about sex on the street, or (in Italy according to Fellini movies) from friendly whores, or, in more genteel surroundings, from girls, their parents, or, once upon a time, in school, more or less. Now porn has been added, and sex education in the schools is rapidly being phased out. The buck has been passed, and boys are being taught that all women secretly like to be raped and that real men get high on scooping out women's digestive tracts.

Boys learn their concept of masculinity from other men: is this what most men want them to be learning? If word gets around that rapists are "normal" and even admirable men, will boys feel that in order to be normal, admirable and masculine they will have to be rapists? Human beings are enormously flexible, and how they turn out depends a lot on how they're educated, by the society in which they're immersed as well as by their teachers. In a society that advertises and glorifies rape or even implicitly condones it, more women get raped. It becomes socially acceptable. And at a time when men and the traditional male role have taken a lot of flak and men are confused and casting around for an acceptable way of being male (and, in some cases, not getting much comfort from women on that score), this must be at times a pleasing thought.

It would be naïve to think of violent pornography as just harmless entertainment. It's also an educational tool and a powerful propaganda device. What happens when boy educated on porn meets girl brought up on Harlequin romances? The clash of expectations can be heard around the block. She wants him to get down on his knees with a ring, he wants her to get down on all fours with a ring in her nose. Can this marriage be saved?

Pornography has certain things in common with such addictive substances as alcohol and drugs: for some, though by no means for all, it induces chemical changes in the body, which the user finds exciting and pleasurable. It also appears to attract a "hard core" of habitual users and a penumbra of those who use it occasionally but aren't dependent on it in any way. There are also significant numbers of men who aren't dependent on it in any way. There are also significant numbers of men who aren't much interested in it, not because they're under-sexed but because real life is satisfying their needs, which may not require as many appliances as those of users.

For the "hard core," pornography may function as alcohol does for the alcoholic: tolerance develops, and a little is no longer enough. This may account for the short viewing time and last turnover in porn theatres. Mary Brown, chairwoman of the Ontario Board of Film Censors, estimates that for every one mainstream movie requesting entrance to Ontario, there is one porno flick. Not only the quantity consumed hut the quality of explicitness must escalate, which may account for the growing violence: once the big deal was breasts, then it was genitals, then copulation, then that was no longer enough and the hard users had to have more. The ultimate kick is death, and after that, as the Marquis de Sade so boringly demonstrated, multiple death.

The existence of alcoholism has not led us to ban social drinking. On the other hand, we do have laws about drinking and driving, excessive drunkenness and other abuses of alcohol that may result in injury or death to others.

This leads us back to the key question: what's the harm? Nobody knows, but this society should find out fast, before the saturation point is reached. The Scandinavian studies that showed a connection between depictions of sexual violence and increased impulse toward it on the pan of male viewers would he a starting point, but many more questions remain to be raised as well as answered. What, for instance, is die crucial difference between men who are users and men who are not? Does using affect a man's relationship with actual women, and, if so, adversely? Is there a clear line between erotica and violent pornography, or are they on an escalating continuum? Is this a "men versus women" issue, with all men secretly siding with the proporners and all women secretly siding against? (I think not; there *are* lots of men who don't think that running their true love through the Cuisinart is the best way they can think of to spend a Saturday night, and they're just as nauseated by films or someone else doing it as women are.) Is pornography merely an expression of the sexual confusion of this age or an active contributor to it?

Nobody wants to go back to the age of official repression, when even piano legs were referred to as "limbs" and had to wear pantaloons to be decent. Neither do we want to end up in George Orwell's *1984*, in which pornography is turned out by the State to keep the proles in a state of torpor, sex itself is considered dirty and the approved practise is only for reproduction. But Rome under the emperors isn't such a good model either.

If all men and women respected each other, if sex were considered joyful and life-enhancing instead of a wallow in germ-filled glop, if everyone were in love all the time, if, in other words, many people's lives were more satisfactory for them than they appear to be now, pornography might just go away on its own. But since this is obviously not happening, we as a society are going to have to make some informed and responsible decisions about how to deal with it.

## Questions for Comprehension

*Answer these questions as a comprehension reading quiz and/or for further clarification on the text:*

1. Atwood wrote this article in 1988. She claims that a large part of the pornographic market consists of "the 16-to-21-year-old population of young men." Do you think this is still the predominant portion of porn consumers? Why or why not? Since then, do more young women view pornography? What is your reasoning? On what ideas or evidence do you base your assumptions?

2. How might 21st century feminists draw a connection between Atwood's argument and the 2017 #metoo and the 2018 #timesup movements? Explain.

3. Atwood draws an analogy between porn use and alcohol use. What is it? Explain her analogy.

# Gloria Steinem, "Erotica and Pornography" (1972)

Here's a key question to keep in mind as you read this brief essay: Why is the issue of pornography so important to feminists, especially the so-called "second wave" feminists who came to national prominence in the 1970s and 1980s? Clearly, there were other important issues that feminists felt the need to address, including equal treatment in the workplace. Atwood and Steinem attempt to create a meaningful public discourse around the issue of pornography. As I noted earlier, if they had these concerns in an era when "porn" was relatively difficult to access, it's interesting to speculate how they might address the issue in the Internet Era when access is shockingly easy. Has easy accessibility heightened these feminist concerns?

Find reliable sources on the internet that can inform you regarding Gloria Steinem's life and background. How did she first rise to national prominence? Why is she an important figure in the American women's movement? Why does she qualify as a "second wave" feminist rather than a "first wave" or "third wave" feminist?

The major claim Steinem makes in this brief article essentially boils down to a distinction between two terms. Do you understand the distinction she is making? Articulate her major claim or "thesis." What means does she use to argue her main point? Do you find her argument persuasive and effective? Why or why not? What does Steinem imply in regard to *nature vs. nurture* when it comes to the question of defining the attitudes she associates with erotica and pornography?

## Questions to Consider

*Answer these questions as you read and annotate the text:*

- When it comes to sexuality, how are humans different from other animals, according to Steinem? Why is this concept important, or is it?
- Steinem cites a critic of the women's movement as having denounced the entire social movement as being "obscene." Why would a conservative critic of feminism have accused the movement of obscenity?
- Despite Steinem's frank discussion of sexuality, critics of feminism have sometimes accused feminists of being "prudes," even referring to feminists as being "anti-sex." Considering the readings in this unit, what is your view of whether it is accurate to characterize second wave feminists as "anti-sex"?
- What specific phrases does Steinem use in order to distinguish the differences she perceives in the terms "erotica" and "pornography"? Underline or mark these phrases (a pencil usually satisfies most bookstore and school book use policies) so that you have easy access to them for quotation later on.
- How do you understand Steinem's assertion that "rape is about violence, and not really about sexuality at all"?
- Do you find any common concerns expressed in this article and in Judy Brady's "Why I Want a Wife"?

## Gloria Steinem, Erotica and Pornography

Human beings are the only animals that experience the same sex drive at times when we can and cannot conceive.

Just as we developed uniquely human capacities for language, planning, memory, and invention along our evolutionary path, we siso developed sexuality as a form of expression; a way of communicating that is separable from our need for sex as a way of perpetuating ourselves. For humans alone, sexuality can be and often is primarily a way of bonding, of giving and receiving pleasure, bridging differetness, discovering sameness, and communicating emotion.

We developed this and other human gifts through our ability to change our environment, adapt physically, and, in the long run, affect our own evolution. But as an emotional result of this spiraling path away from other animals, we seem to alternate between periods of exploring our unique abilities to forge new boundaries, and feelings of loneliness in the unknown that we ourselves have created; a fear that sometimes sends us back to the comfort of the animal world by encouraging us to exaggerate our sameness with it.

The separation of "play" from "work," for instance, is a problem only in the human world. So is the difference between art and nature, or an intellectual accomplishment and a physical one. As a result, we celebrate play, art, and invention as leaps into the unknown; but any imbalance can send us back to nostalgia for our primate past and the conviction that the basics of work, nature, and physical labor are somehow more worthwhile or even more moral.

In the same way, we have explored our sexuality as separable from conception: a pleasurable, empathetic bridge to strangers of the same species. We have even invented contraception—a skill that has probably existed in some form since our ancestor figured out the process of birth—in order to extend this uniquely human difference. Yet we also have times of atavistic suspicion that sex is not complete—or even legal or intended-by-god—if it cannot end in conception.

No wonder the concepts of "erotica" and "pornography" can be so crucially different, and yet so confused. Both assume that sexuality can be separated from conception, and therefore can be used to carry a personal message. That's a major reason why, even in our current culture, both may be called equally "shocking" or legally "obscene," a word whose Latin derivative means "dirty, containing filth." This gross condemnation of all sexuality that isn't harnessed to childbirth and marriage has been increased by the current backlash against women's progress. Out of fear that the whole patriarchal structure might be upset if women really had the autonomous power to decide our reproductive futures (that is, if we controlled the most basic means of production—the production of human beings), right-wing groups are not only denouncing pro-choice abortion literature as "pornographic," but are trying to stop the sending of all contraceptive information through the mails by invoking obscenity laws. In fact, Phyllis Schlafly recently denounced the entire Women's Movement as "obscene."

Not surprisingly, this religious, visceral backlash has a secular, intellectual counterpart that relies heavily on applying the "natural" behavior of the animal world to humans. That application is questionable in itself, but these Lionel Tiger-ish studies make their political purpose even more clear in the particular animals they select and the habits they choose to emphasize. For example, some male primates (marmosets, titi monkeys, night monkeys) carry and/or generally "mother" their infants. Tiger types prefer to discuss chimps and baboons, whose behavior is very "male chauvinist."

---

The message is that females should accept their "destiny" of being sexually dependent and devote themselves to bearing and rearing their young.

Defending against such reaction in turn leads to another temptation; merely to reverse the terms, and declare that all nonprocreative sex is good. In fact, however, this human activity can be as constructive or destructive, moral or immoral, as any other. Sex as communication can send messages as different as life and death; even the origins of "erotica" and "pornography" reflect that fact After all, "erotica" is rooted in "eros" or passionate love, and thus in the idea of positive choice, free will, the yearning for a particular person. (Interestingly, the definition of erotica leaves open the question of gender.) 'Pornography" begins with a root "porno," meaning "prostitution" or "female captives," thus letting us know that the subject is not mutual love, or love at all, but domination and violence against women. (Though, of course, homosexual pornography may imitate this violence by putting a man in the "feminine" role of victim,) It ends with a root "graphos," meaning "writing about" or "description of," which puts still more distance between subject and object, and replaces a spontaneous yearning for closeness with objectification and voyeurism. The difference is clear in the words. It becomes even more so by example.

Look at any photo or film of people making love; really making love. The images may be diverse, but there is usually a sensuality and touch and warmth, an acceptance of bodies and nerve endings. There is always a spontaneous sense of people who are there because they want to be, out of shared pleasure.

Now look at any depiction of sex in which there is clear force, or an unequal power that spells coercion. It may be very blatant, with weapons of torture or bondage, wounds and bruises, some clear humiliation, or an adult's sexual power being used over a child. It may be much more subtle: a physical attitude of conqueror and victim, the use of race or class difference to imply the same thing, perhaps a very unequal nudity, with one person exposed and vulnerable while the other is clothed. In either case, there is no sense of equal choice or equal power.

The first is erotic: a mutually pleasurable, sexual expression between people who have enough power to be there by positive choice. It may or may not strike a sense-memory in the viewer, or be creative enough to make the unknown seem real; but it doesn't require us to, Rectify with a conqueror or a victim. It is truly sensuous, and may give us a contagion of pleasure.

The second is pornographic: its message is violence, dominance, and conquest. It is sex being used to reinforce some inequality, or to create one, or to tell us that pain and humiliation (ours or someone else's) are really the same as pleasure. If we are to feel anything, we must identify with conqueror or victim. That means we can only experience pleasure through the adoption of some degree of sadism or masochism. It also means that we may feel diminished by the role of conqueror, or enraged, humiliated, and vengeful by sharing identity with the victim.

Perhaps one could simply say that erotica is about sexuality, but pornography is about power and sex-as-weapon—in the same way we have come to understand that rape is about violence, and not really about sexuality at all.

Yes, it's true that there are women who have been forced by violent families and dominating men to confuse love with pain; so much so that they have become masochists. (A fact that in no way excuses those who administer such pain.) But the truth is that, for most women—and for men with enough humanity to imagine themselves in the predicament of women—pornography could serve as aversion-conditioning toward sex.

Of course, there will always be personal differences about what is and is not erotic, and there may be cultural differences for a long time to come. Many women feel that sex makes them vulnerable and therefore may continue to need more sense of personal connection and safety than men do before allowing any erotic feelings. Men, on the other hand, may continue to feel less vulnerable, and therefore more open to such potential danger as sex with strangers. Women now frequently find competence and expertise erotic in men, but that may pass as we develop those qualities in ourselves. As some men replace the need for submission from child-like women with the pleasure of cooperation from equals, they may find a partner's competence to be erotic, too.

Such group changes plus individual differences will continue to be reflected in sexual love between people of the same gender, as well as between women and men. The point is not to dictate sameness, but to discover ourselves and each other through a sexuality that is an exploring, pleasurable, empathetic part of our lives; a human sexuality that is unchained both from unwanted pregnancies and from violence.

But that is a hope, not a reality. At the moment, fear of change is increasing both the indiscriminate repression of all nonprocreative sex in the religious and "conservative" male-dominated world, and the pornographic vengeance against women's sexuality in the secular world of "liberal" or "radical" men. It's almost futuristic to debate what is and is not truly erotic, when many women are again being forced into compulsory motherhood, and the number of pornographic murders, tortures, and women-hating images are on the increase in both popular culture and real life.

Together, both of the above forms of repression perpetuate that familiar division: wife or whore; "good" woman who is constantly vulnerable to pregnancy or "bad" woman who is unprotected from violence. Both roles would be upset if we were to control our own sexuality. And that's exactly what we must do.

In spite of all our atavistic suspicions and training for the "natural" role of motherhood, we took up the complicated battle for reproductive freedom. Our bodies had borne the health burden of endless births and poor abortions, and we had a greater motive than men for separating sexuality and conception.

Now we have to take up the equally complex burden of explaining that all nonprocreative sex is not alike. We have a motive: our right to a uniquely human sexuality, and sometimes even to survival. As it is, our bodies have too rarely been enough our own to develop erotica in our own lives, much less in art and literature. And our bodies have too often been the objects of pornography and the woman-hating, violent practice that it preaches. Consider also our spirits that break a little each time we see ourselves in chains or full labial display for the conquering male viewer, bruised or on our knees, screaming a real or pretended pain to delight the sadist, pretending to enjoy what we don't enjoy, to be blind to the images of our sisters that really haunt us—humiliated often enough ourselves by the truly obscene idea that sex and the domination of women must be combined.

Sexuality is human, free, separate—and so are we.

But until we untangle the lethal confusion of sex with violence, there will be more pornography and less erotica. There will be little murders in our beds—and very little love.

# Questions for Comprehension

*Answer these questions as a comprehension reading quiz and/or for further clarification on the text:*

1. For Steinem, would the term "shared pleasure" describe erotica or pornography?

2. What connection is there between Gloria Steinem's and Margaret Atwood's concept of "pornography"?

3. Steinem writes, "We now find competence and expertise erotic in men, but that may pass as we develop those qualities in ourselves." In this sentence, who is "we"? Explain what you think she might mean by the phrase "develop those qualities in ourselves."

McElroy offers a defense of pornography by attempting to counter all of the mainstream second wave feminist arguments carried forward by writers such as Margaret Atwood, Gloria Steinem, and (elsewhere, in work outside of this textbook) Susan Brownmiller. McElroy calls herself a "pro-sex" feminist and claims, "Pornography benefits women, both personally and politically."

Just as we do not accept Atwood's or Steinem's claims without scrutiny, it is important to avoid the uncritical cognitive trap of 1) accepting McElroy's arguments without considering their validity, or 2) rejecting McElroy's arguments without considering their merit.

## Questions to Consider

*Answer these questions as you read and annotate the text:*

- Previously, we inquired why the question of pornography was important to mainstream or "academic" feminists. Let's inquire the same of McElroy. What does she say in regard to why the question of pornography is an important one?
- McElroy outlines three feminist positions on pornography. How does she describe the "academic" feminist position on pornography? How does the academic feminist view relate to the positions of Atwood and Steinem?
- Why does McElroy call herself "pro-sex"? What is your response to this label?
- McElroy makes an effort, in her words, to "peel. . . back the emotions" surrounding this issue. Does she succeed in relying on "logos" or critical reasoning to make her claims?
- Mark passages where McElroy's skepticism regarding the academic feminist position on pornography is apparent.
- McElroy references events surrounding the censorship of pornography that took place in Canada following a 1992 court decision. Try to describe what you understand took place. What's McElroy's point here?
- How does McElroy attempt to counter the academic feminist arguments that "Pornography is degrading to women" and that "Pornography leads to violence against women"? How might Atwood respond to these passages?
- While academic feminists decry pornography's tendency to play out so-called "rape fantasies," McElroy turns this argument on its head by describing pornography as a "safe" and "healthy" space in which to play out fantasies. How does Atwood address this issue in her essay?
- While academic feminists argue that pornography reinforces cultural stereotypes, McElroy claims that "pornography breaks cultural and political stereotypes." How are we to understand what exactly she means?

## Wendy McElroy, A Feminist Defense of Pornography

*The following article is from Free Inquiry magazine, Volume 17, Number 4.*

"Pornography benefits women, both personally and politically." This sentence opens my book *XXX: A Woman's Right to Pornography,* and it constitutes a more extreme defense of pornography than most feminists are comfortable with. I arrived at this position after years of interviewing hundreds of sex workers.

### Feminist Positions

Feminist positions on pornography currently break down into three rough categories. The most common one—at least, in academia—is that pornography is an expression of male culture through which women are commodified and exploited. A second view, the liberal position, combines a respect for free speech with the principle "a woman's body, a woman's right" and thus produces a defense of pornography along the lines of, "I don't approve of it, but everyone has the right to consume or produce words and images." A third view—a true defense of pornography—arises from feminists who have been labeled "pro-sex" and who argue that porn has benefits for women.

Little dialogue occurs between the three positions. Anti-pornography feminists treat women who disagree as either brainwashed dupes of patriarchy or as apologists for pornographers. In the anthology *Sexual Liberals and the Attack on Feminism* (1990), editor Dorchen Leidholdt claims that feminists who believe women make their own choices about pornography are spreading "a felicitous lie" (p. 131). In the same work, Sheila Jeffreys argues that "pro-sex" feminists are "eroticizing dominance and subordination." Wendy Stock accuses free speech feminists of identifying with their oppressors "much like . . . concentration camp prisoners with their jailors" (p. 150). Andrea Dworkin accuses them of running a "sex protection racket" (p. 136) and maintains that no one who defends pornography can be a feminist.

The liberal feminists who are personally uncomfortable with pornography tend to be intimidated into silence. Those who continue to speak out, like American Civil Liberties Union President Nadine Strossen (*Defending Pornography*) are ignored. For example, Catharine MacKinnon has repeatedly refused to share a stage with Strossen or any woman who defends porn. "Pro-sex" feminists-many of whom are current or former sex-workers-often respond with anger, rather than arguments.

Peeling back the emotions, what are the substantive questions raised by each feminist perspective?

### Anti-porn feminism

Page Mellish of Feminists Fighting Pornography has declared, "There's no feminist issue that isn't rooted in the porn problem." In her book *Only Words,* MacKinnon denies that pornography consists of words and images, both of which would be protected by the First Amendment. She considers pornography—in and of itself—to be an act of sexual violence. Why is pornography viewed as both the core issue of modern feminism and an inherent act of violence? The answer lies in radical feminist ideology, which Christina Hoff Sommers calls "gender feminism."

Gender feminism looks at history and sees an uninterrupted oppression of women by men that spans cultural barriers. To them, the only feasible explanation is that men and women are separate and antagonistic classes whose interests necessarily conflict. Male interests are expressed through and maintained by a capitalistic structure known as "patriarchy."

The root of the antagonism is so deep that it lies in male biology itself. For example, in the watershed book *Against Our Will*, Susan Brownmiller traces the inevitability of rape back to Neanderthal times when men began to use their penises as weapons. Brownmiller writes: "From prehistoric times to the present, I believe, rape has played a critical function. It is nothing more or less than a conscious process of intimidation by which all men keep all women in a state of fear." How Brownmiller acquired this knowledge of prehistoric sex is not known.

Another tenet of gender oppression is that sex is a social construct. Radical feminists reject what they call "sexual essentialism"-the notion that sex is a natural force based on biology that inclines women toward natural tendencies, such as motherhood. Even deeply felt sexual preferences, such as heterosexuality, are not biological. They spring from ideology.

Men construct women's sexuality through the words and images of society, which the French philosopher Foucault called the "texts" of society. After such construction, men commercialize women's sexuality and market it back in the form of pornography. In other words, through porn man defines woman sexually-a definition that determines every aspect of her role in society. To end the oppression, patriarchy and its texts must be destroyed.

## Liberal feminism

Liberal feminism is a continuation of 1960s feminism that called for equality with men, who were not inherent oppressors so much as recalcitrant partners to be enlightened. Equality did not mean destroying the current system, but reforming it through such measures as affirmative action. The liberal principle "a woman's body, a woman's right" underlay arguments ranging from abortion rights to lifestyle freedoms like lesbianism. The stress was upon the act of choosing, rather than upon the content of any choice.

Liberal feminists share the general liberal bias toward free speech, but they are in flux on pornography. Some liberal organizations like Feminists for Free Expression (FFE) have consistently opposed censorship in any form. Some liberal feminists like Sallie Tisdale (*Talk Dirty to Me*) have staunchly defended sexual freedom. But many liberal feminists commonly reason as follows: "As a woman I am appalled by Playboy . . . but as a writer I understand the need for free expression."

Such arguments are not pro-pornography. They are anticensorship ones based on several grounds, including: great works of art and literature would be banned; the First Amendment would be breached; political expression would be suppressed; and a creative culture requires freedom of speech.

Other liberal feminists, who have accepted many of the ideological assumptions of the anti-porn position, seem willing to sacrifice free speech for the greater good of protecting women. For example, they also condemn the free market for commercializing women as "body parts," which demeans women. In "A Capital Idea," an essay defending pornography, which sometimes seems to be an attack, Lisa Steel comments:

> Sexist representation of women . . . is all part of the same system that, in the service of profits, reduces society to "consumer groups." And marketing is every bit as conservative as the military . . . we pay dearly for the "rights" of a few to make profits from the rest of us.

Such muddled and ambivalent "defenses" often offend the sex workers they are intended to protect.

## Pro-sex feminism

Over the past decade, a growing number of feminists-labeled "pro sex"-have defended a woman's choice to participate in and to consume pornography. Some of these women, such as Nina Hartley, are current or ex-sex-workers who know firsthand that posing for pornography is an uncoerced choice that can be enriching. Pro-sex feminists retain a consistent interpretation of the principle "a woman's body, a woman's right" and insist that every peaceful choice a woman makes with her own body must be accorded full legal protection, if not respect.

Pro-sex arguments sometimes seem to overlap with liberal feminist ones. For example, both express concern over who will act as censor because subjective words, such as "degrading," will be interpreted to mean whatever the censor wishes.

The statute that banned Margaret Sanger because she used the words syphilis and gonorrhea is no different, in principle, than the one that interprets obscenity today. There will be no protection even for the classics of feminism, such as *Our Bodies, Ourselves*, which provided a generation of women with the first explicit view of their own biology. Inevitably, censorship will be used against the least popular views, against the weakest members of society . . . including feminists and lesbians. When the Canadian Supreme Court decided in 1992 to protect women by restricting the importation of pornography, one of the first victims was the lesbian/gay Glad Day Bookstore, which had been on a police hit list. Among the books seized by Canadian customs were two books by Andrea Dworkin, *Pornography: Men Possessing Women* and *Women Hating*. Such an event should not have surprised Dworkin who declared in *Take Back the Night*, "There is not a feminist alive who could possibly look to the male legal system for real protection from the systematized sadism of men" (p. 257).

On the dangers of censoring pornography, pro-sex and liberal feminists often agree. On the possible benefits of pornography to women, they part company.

## Dissecting Anti-Porn

Do the specific accusations hurled at pornography stand up under examination?

## Pornography is degrading to women.

Degrading is a subjective term. I find commercials in which women become orgasmic over soap-suds to be tremendously degrading. The bottom line is that every woman has the right to define what is degrading and liberating for herself.

The assumed degradation is often linked to the "objectification" of women: that is, porn converts them into sexual objects. What does this mean? If taken literally, it means nothing because objects don't have sexuality; only beings do. But to say that porn portrays women as "sexual beings" makes for poor rhetoric. Usually, the term sex objects means showing women as body parts, reducing them to physical objects. What is wrong with this? Women are as much their bodies as they are their minds or souls. No one gets upset if you present women as "brains" or as spiritual beings. If I concentrated on a woman's sense of humor to the exclusion of her other characteristics, is this degrading? Why is it degrading to focus on her sexuality?

## Pornography leads to violence against women.

A cause-and-effect relationship is drawn between men viewing pornography and men attacking women, especially in the form of rape. But studies and experts disagree as to whether any relationship exists between pornography and violence, between images and behavior. Even the pro-censorship Meese Commission Report admitted that the data connecting pornography to violence was unreliable.

Other studies, such as the one prepared by feminist Thelma McCormick in 1983 for the Metropolitan Toronto Task Force on Violence Against Women, find no pattern to connect porn and sex crimes. Incredibly, the Task Force suppressed the study and reassigned the project to a pro-censorship male, who returned the "correct" results. His study was published.

What of real-world feedback? In Japan, where pornography depicting graphic and brutal violence is widely available, rape is much lower per capita than in the United States, where violence in porn is severely restricted.

## Pornography is violence because women are coerced into pornography.

Not one of the dozens of women depicted in pornographic materials with whom I spoke reported being coerced. Not one knew of a woman who had been. Nevertheless, I do not dismiss reports of violence: every industry has its abuses. And anyone who uses force or threats to make a woman perform should be charged with kidnapping, assault, and/or rape. Any such pictures or films should be confiscated and burned because no one has the right to benefit from the proceeds of a crime.

## Pornography is violence because women who pose for porn are so traumatized by patriarchy they cannot give real consent.

Although women in pornography appear to be willing, anti-porn feminists know that no psychologically healthy woman would agree to the degradation of pornography. Therefore, if agreement seems to be present, it is because the women have "fallen in love with their own oppression" and must be rescued from themselves. A common characteristic of the porn actresses I have interviewed is a love of exhibitionism. Yet if such a woman declares her enjoyment in flaunting her body, anti-porn feminists claim she is not merely a unique human being who reacts from a different background or personality. She is psychologically damaged and no longer responsible for her actions. In essence, this is a denial of a woman's right to choose anything outside the narrow corridor of choices offered by political/sexual correctness. The right to choose hinges on the right to make a "wrong" choice, just as freedom of religion entails the right to be an atheist. After all, no one will prevent a woman from doing what he thinks she should do.

## A Pro-Sex Defense

As a "pro-sex" feminist, I contend: Pornography benefits women, both personally and politically. It provides sexual information on at least three levels:

- It gives a panoramic view of the world's sexual possibilities. This is true even of basic sexual information such as masturbation. It is not uncommon for women to reach adulthood without knowing how to give themselves pleasure.
- It allows women to "safely" experience sexual alternatives and satisfy a healthy sexual curiosity. The world is a dangerous place. By contrast, pornography can be a source of solitary enlightenment.
- It offers the emotional information that comes only from experiencing something either directly or vicariously. It provides us with a sense how it would "feel" to do something.

Pornography allows women to enjoy scenes and situations that would be anathema to them in real life. Take, for example, one of the most common fantasies reported by women-the fantasy of "being taken." The first thing to understand is that a rape fantasy does not represent a desire for the real thing. Why would a healthy woman daydream about being raped? Perhaps by losing control, she also sheds all sense of responsibility for and guilt over sex. Perhaps it is the exact opposite of the polite, gentle sex she has now. Perhaps it is flattering to imagine a particular man being so over-whelmed by her that he must have her. Perhaps she is curious. Perhaps she has some masochistic feelings that are vented through the fantasy. Is it better to bottle them up?

Pornography breaks cultural and political stereotypes, so that each woman can interpret sex for herself. Anti-feminists tell women to be ashamed of their appetites and urges. Pornography tells them to accept and enjoy them. Pornography can be good therapy. Pornography provides a sexual outlet for those who-for whatever reason-have no sexual partner. Perhaps they are away from home, recently widowed, isolated because of infirmity. Perhaps they simply choose to be alone. Couples also use pornography to enhance their relationship. Sometimes they do so on their own, watching videos and exploring their reactions together. Sometimes, the couples go to a sex therapist who advises them to use pornography as a way of opening up communication on sex. By sharing pornography, the couples are able to experience variety in their sex lives without having to commit adultery.

Pornography benefits women politically in many ways. Historically, pornography and feminism have been fellow travelers and natural allies. Although it is not possible to draw a cause-and-effect relationship between the rise of pornography and that of feminism, they both demand the same social conditions-namely, sexual freedom.

Pornography is free speech applied to the sexual realm. Freedom of speech is the ally of those who seek change: it is the enemy of those who seek to maintain control. Pornography, along with all other forms of sexual heresy, such as homosexuality, should have the same legal protection as political heresy. This protection is especially important to women, whose sexuality has been controlled by censorship through the centuries.

Viewing pornography may well have a cathartic effect on men who have violent urges toward women. If this is true, restricting pornography removes a protective barrier between women and abuse.

Legitimizing pornography would protect female sex-workers, who are stigmatized by our society. Anti-pornography feminists are actually undermining the safety of sex workers when they treat them as "indoctrinated women." Dr. Leonore Tiefer, a professor of psychology, observed in her essay "On Censorship and Women": "These women have appealed to feminists for support, not rejection. . . . Sex industry workers, like all women, are striving for economic survival and a decent life, and if feminism means anything it means sisterhood and solidarity with these women."

## The Purpose of Law

The porn debate is underscored by two fundamentally antagonistic views of the purpose of law in society.

The first view, to which pro-sex feminists subscribe, is that law should protect choice. "A woman's body, a woman's right" applies to every peaceful activity a woman chooses to engage in. The law should come into play only when a woman initiates force or has force initiated against her. The second view, to which both conservatives and anti-porn feminists subscribe, is that law should protect virtue. It should come into play whenever there has been a breach of public morality, or a breach of "women's class interests."

This is old whine in new battles. The issue at stake in the pornography debate is nothing less than the age-old conflict between individual freedom and social control.

# Questions for Comprehension

*Answer these questions as a comprehension reading quiz and/or for further clarification on the text:*

1. True/False. McElroy argues that women who support or participate in pornography are the victims of a false consciousness who do not understand their own oppression.

2. McElroy describes a split in the feminist or women's movement regarding the issue of free speech when it comes to pornography. Briefly state what this split entails or why it developed.

3. Take a moment to explore internet definitions of "second wave" feminism and "third wave" feminism. Be aware of the nature and quality of your internet sources. Understand that in looking up the general meaning of a word or phrase we are not engaging in actual research. A twentieth-century analogy might be looking up an encyclopedia article, which could possibly contain errors or unsubstantiated assertions. In what ways is McElroy's position more in line with "third wave" feminism rather than "second wave" feminism?

Brownmiller's brief, highly theoretical article may be difficult to follow. And you may sigh with exasperation when you see that my editorial prologue is almost as long as the article itself! Welcome to academia and the world of ideas!

All joking aside, it's important to realize that Brownmiller's brief article is actually an excerpt from the prologue to her book entitled *Femininity* (1984). (Note that the book title *Femininity* receives italics under MLA format, while the article title "Femininity" receives quotation marks under MLA format.) In the book format, she can more fully explore concepts that she simply touches upon in the prologue.

In many ways, Brownmiller is simply doing what Steinem did in her article: she is defining a term. In this case, the term is "femininity." My own 1989 *Webster's Encyclopedic Unabridged Dictionary of the English Language* defines "femininity" as "1) the quality of being feminine; womanliness: *She kept her femininity even in greasy overalls.*" *Def.*

Let's pause here a moment. What do you think of this definition? And, maybe more importantly, what do you think of the sentence example? Clearly, according to this example, it is unusual for someone in greasy overalls to bear the quality of "femininity." You might think, Well, since most mechanics are men, that makes sense; or you might react, Hold on, why should we think it unusual for a female mechanic to be feminine? I am not trying to persuade you to any particular line of thinking. I would like for you to share my enthusiasm and curiosity regarding the power, the effects, and the intricacies of language.

In my time teaching first semester college composition, I have seen the definition of the word "femininity" change before my eyes. One semester I went to a popular online dictionary site and showed my students a definition of "femininity" that read: "1) the quality of being female or womanly, as in wearing makeup and high heels." The following semester I went to the same site to seek out this same definition and discovered that it had changed. It now read: "1) the quality of being feminine; womanliness." The example of "makeup and high heels" had vanished. Why would it have disappeared? Was it "political correctness" gone awry? Or was there just cause for people to be concerned that the primary given example of "femininity" involved "makeup and high heels."

I do not know Susan Brownmiller. I do know, however, that she would not have been happy to see "as in wearing makeup and high heels" associated with the definition of the term "femininity."

Why would she recoil at this notion?

## Questions to Consider

*Answer these questions as you read and annotate the text:*

- Recall that words can be understood in two basic ways, by *denotation* and by *connotation*. "Denotations" are more precise definitions typically found in a dictionary, while "connotations" consist of less precise associations that society or culture gives to the word. According to Brownmiller, what are the connotations that society associates with the term "femininity"? Do you agree with her observations?
- What does Brownmiller mean when she writes that "femininity" is "a romantic sentiment, a nostalgic tradition of imposed limitations"? In what way is she using the word "romantic"? (Hint: visit *dictionary.com* to review the various meanings of the word.)
- As you read and write about Brownmiller's text, you must be careful not to confuse the terms "feminist" (one who advocates for women's rights) and "femininity" (the qualities associated with being female). I've found that, perhaps due to simple carelessness, a fair number of students tend to mix up these unrelated terms.

## Susan Brownmiller, Femininity

## Prologue

WE HAD A GAME in our house called "setting the table" and I was Mother's helper. Forks to the left of the plate, knives and spoons to the right. Placing the cutlery neatly, as I recall, was one of my first duties, and the event was alive with meaning. When a knife or a fork dropped to the floor, that meant a man was unexpectedly coming to dinner. A falling spoon announced the surprise arrival of a female guest. No matter that these visitors never arrived on cue, I had learned a rule of gender identification. Men were straight-edged, sharply pronged and formidable, women were softly curved and held the food in a rounded well. It made perfect sense, like the division of pink and blue that I saw in babies, an orderly way of viewing the world. Daddy, who was gone all day at work and who loved to putter at home with his pipe, tobacco and tool chest, was knife and fork. Mommy and Grandma, with their ample proportions and pots and pans, were grownup soup spoons, large and capacious. And I was a teaspoon, small and slender, easy to hold and just right for pudding, my favorite dessert.

Being good at what was expected of me was one of my earliest projects, for not only was I rewarded, as most children are, for doing things right, but excellence gave pride and stability to my childhood existence. Girls were different from boys, and the expression of that difference seemed mine to make clear. Did my loving, anxious mother, who dressed me in white organdy pinafores and Mary Janes and who cried hot tears when I got them dirty, give me my first instruction? Of course. Did my doting aunts and uncles with their gifts of pretty dolls and miniature tea sets add to my education? Of course. But even without the appropriate toys and clothes, lessons in the art of being feminine lay all around me and I absorbed them all: the fairy tales that were read to me at night, the brightly colored advertisements I pored over in magazines before I learned to decipher the words, the movies I saw, the comic books I hoarded, the radio soap operas I happily followed whenever I had to stay in bed with a cold. I loved being a little girl, or rather I loved being a fairy princess, for that was who I thought I was.

As I passed through a stormy adolescence to a stormy maturity, femininity increasingly became an exasperation, a brilliant, subtle esthetic that was bafflingly inconsistent at the same time that it was minutely, demandingly concrete, a rigid code of appearance and behavior defined by do's and don't-do's that went against my rebellions grain. Femininity was a challenge thrown down to the female sex, a challenge no proud, self-respecting young woman could afford to ignore, particularly one with enormous ambition that she nursed in secret, alternately feeding or starving its inchoate life in tremendous confusion.

"Don't lose your femininity" and "Isn't it remarkable how she manages to retain her femininity?" had terrifying implications. They spoke of a bottom-line failure so irreversible that nothing else mattered. The pinball machine had registered "tilt," the game had been called. Disqualification was marked on the forehead of a woman whose femininity was lost. No records would be entered in her name, for she had destroyed her birthright in her wretched, ungainly effort to imitate a man. She walked in limbo, this hapless creature, and it occurred to me that one day I might see her when I looked in the mirror. If the danger was so palpable that warning notices were freely posted, wasn't it possible that the small bundle of resentments I carried around in secret might spill out and place the mark on my own forehead? Whatever quarrels with femininity I had I kept to myself; whatever handicaps femininity imposed, they were mine to deal with alone, for there was no women's movement to ask the tough questions, or to brazenly disregard the rules.

Femininity, in essence, is a romantic sentiment, a nostalgic tradition of imposed limitations. Even as it hurries forward in the 1980s, putting on lipstick and high heels to appear well dressed, it trips on the ruffled petticoats and hoopskirts of an era gone by. Invariably and necessarily, femininity is something that women had more of in the past, not only in the historic past of prior generations, but in each woman's personal past as well—in the virginal innocence that is replaced by knowledge, in the dewy cheek that is coarsened by age, in the "inherent nature" that a woman seems to misplace so forgetfully whenever she steps out of bounds. Why should this be so? The XX chromosomal message has not been scrambled, the estrogen-dominated hormonal balance is generally as biology intended, the reproductive organs, whatever use one has made of them, are usually in place, the breasts of whatever size are most often where they should be. But clearly, biological femaleness is not enough.

Femininity always demands more. It must constantly reassure its audience by a willing demonstration of difference, even when one does not exist in nature, or it must seize and embrace a natural variation and compose a rhapsodic symphony upon the notes. Suppose one doesn't care to, has other things on her mind, is clumsy or tone-deaf despite the best instruction and training? To fail at the feminine difference is to appear not to care about men, and to risk the loss of their attention and approval. To be insufficiently feminine is viewed as a failure in core sexual identity, or as a failure to care sufficiently about oneself, for a woman found wanting will be appraised (and will appraise herself) as mannish or neutered or simply unattractive, as men have defined these terms.

We are talking, admittedly, about an exquisite esthetic. Enormous pleasure can be extracted from feminine pursuits as a creative outlet or purely as relaxation; indeed, indulgence for the sake of fun, or art, or attention, is among femininity's great joys. But the chief attraction (and the central paradox, as well) is the competitive edge that femininity seems to promise in the unending struggle to survive, and perhaps to triumph. The world smiles favorably on the feminine woman: it extends little courtesies and minor privilege. Yet the nature of this competitive edge is ironic, at best, for one works at femininity by accepting restrictions, by limiting one's sights, by choosing an indirect route, by scattering concentration and not giving one's all as a man would to his own, certifiably masculine, interests. It does not require a great leap of imagination for a woman to understand the feminine principle as a grand collection of compromises, large and small, that she simply must make in order to render herself a successful woman. If she has difficulty in satisfying femininity's demands, if its illusions go against her grain, or if she is criticized for her shortcomings and imperfections, the more she will see femininity as a desperate strategy of appeasement, a strategy she may not have the wish or the courage to abandon, for failure looms in either direction.

It is fashionable in some quarters to describe the feminine and masculine principles as polar ends of the human continuum, and to sagely profess that both polarities exist in all people. Sun and moon, yin and yang, soft and hard, active and passive, etcetera, may indeed be opposites, but a linear continuum does not illuminate the problem. (Femininity, in all its contrivances, is a very active endeavor.) What, then, is the basic distinction? The masculine principle is better understood as a driving ethos of superiority designed to inspire straightforward, confident success, while the feminine principle is composed of vulnerability, the need for protection, the formalities of compliance and the avoidance of conflict—in short, an appeal of dependence and good will that gives the masculine principle its romantic validity and its admiring applause.

Femininity pleases men because it makes them appear more masculine by contrast; and, in truth, conferring an extra portion of unearned gender distinction on men, an unchallenged space in which to breathe freely and feel stronger, wiser, more competent, is femininity's special gift. One could say that masculinity is often an effort to please women, but masculinity is known to please by displays of mastery and competence while femininity pleases by suggesting that these concerns, except in small matters, are beyond its intent. Whimsy, unpredictability and patterns of thinking and behavior that are dominated by emotion, such as tearful expressions of sentiment and fear, are thought to be feminine precisely because they lie outside the established route to success.

If in the beginnings of history the feminine woman was defined by her physical dependency, her inability for reasons of reproductive biology to triumph over the forces of nature that were the tests of masculine strength and power, today she reflects both an economic and emotional dependency that is still considered "natural," romantic and attractive. After an unsettling fifteen years in which many basic assumptions about the sexes were challenged, the economic disparity did not disappear. Large numbers of women—those with small children, those left high and dry after a mid-life divorce—need financial support. But even those who earn their own living share a universal need for connectedness (call it love, if you wish). As unprecedented numbers of men abandon their sexual interest in women, others, sensing opportunity, choose to demonstrate their interest through variety and a change in partners. A sociological fact of the 1980s is that female competition for two scarce resources—men and jobs—is especially fierce.

So it is not surprising that we are currently witnessing a renewed interest in femininity and an unabashed indulgence in feminine pursuits. Femininity serves to reassure men that women need them and care about them enormously. By incorporating the decorative and the frivolous into its definition of style, femininity functions as an effective antidote to the unrelieved seriousness, the pressure of making one's way in a harsh, difficult world. In its mandate to avoid direct confrontation and to smooth over the fissures of conflict, femininity operates as a value system of niceness, a code of thoughtfulness and sensitivity that in modern society is sadly in short supply.

There is no reason to deny that indulgence in the art of feminine illusion can be reassuring to a woman, if she happens to be good at it. As sexuality undergoes some dizzying revisions evidence that one is a woman "at heart" (the inquisitor's question) is not without worth. Since an answer of sorts may be furnished by piling on additional documentation, affirmation can arise from such identifiable but trivial feminine activities as buying a new eyeliner, experimenting with the latest shade of nail color, or bursting into tears at the outcome of a popular romance novel. Is there anything destructive in this? Time and cost factors, a deflection of energy and an absorption in fakery spring quickly to mind, and they need to be balanced, as in a ledger hook, against the affirming advantage.

Throughout this book I have attempted to trace significant feminine principles to basic biology, for feminine expression is conventionally praised as an enhancement of femaleness, or the raw materials of femaleness shaped and colored to perfection. Sometimes I found that a biological connection did exist, and sometimes not, and sometimes I had to admit that many scientific assumptions about the nature of femaleness were unresolved and hotly debated, and that no sound conclusion was possible before all the evidence was in. It was more enlightening to explore the origins of femininity in borrowed affectations of upper-class status, and in the historic subjugation of women through sexual violence, religion and law, where certain myths about the nature of women were put forward as biological fact. It was also instructive to approach femininity from the angle of seductive glamour, which usually does not fit smoothly with aristocratic refinement, accounting for some contradictory feminine messages that often appear as an unfathomable puzzle.

The competitive aspect of femininity, the female-against-female competition produced by the effort to attract and secure men, is one of the major themes I have tried to explore. Male-against-male competition for high rank and access to females is a popular subject in anthropology, in the study of animals as well as humans, but few scholars have thought to examine the pitched battle of females for ranking and access to males. Yet the struggle to approach the feminine ideal, to match the femininity of other women, and especially to outdo them, is the chief competitive arena (surely it is the only sanctioned arena) in which the American woman is wholeheartedly encouraged to contend. Whether or not this absorbing form of competition is a healthy or useful survival strategy is a critical question.

Hymns to femininity, combined with instruction, have never been lacking. Several generations of us are acquainted with sugar and spice, can recite the job description for "The Girl That I Marry" (doll-size, soft and pink, wears lace and nail polish, gardenia in the hair), or wail the payoff to "Just Like a Woman" ("She breaks like a little girl"). My contribution may be decidedly unmusical, but it is not a manual of how-not-to, nor a wholesale damnation. Femininity deserves some hard reckoning, and this is what I have tried to do.

A powerful esthetic that is built upon a recognition of powerlessness is a slippery subject to grapple with, for its contradictions are elusive, ephemeral and ultimately impressive. A manner that combines a deferential attitude with ornaments of the upper class and an etiquette composed in equal parts of modesty and exhibition are paradoxes that require thoughtful interpretation. A strategy of survival that is based on overt concession and imposed restrictions deserves close study, for what is lost and what is gained is not always apparent. By organizing my chapters along pragmatic lines—body, hair, clothes, voice, etcetera—I have attempted a rational analysis that is free of mystification. Coming down hard on certain familiar aspects while admitting a fond tolerance for some others has been unavoidable in my attempt to give an honest appraisal of the feminine strategies as I have myself practiced or discarded them, I do not mean to project my particular compromises and choices as the better way, or the final word, nor do I mean to condemn those women who practice the craft in ways that are different from mine. I offer this book as a step toward awareness, in the hope that one day the feminine ideal will no longer be used to perpetuate inequality between the sexes, and that exaggeration will not be required to rest secure in biological gender.

SUSAN BROWNMILLER
*New York City*
*September 1983*

# Questions for Comprehension

*Answer these questions as a comprehension reading quiz and/or for further clarification on the text:*

1. True/False. When Brownmiller writes, "The feminine principle is composed of vulnerability [and] the need for protection," she is expressing her view that "feminine" women are incapable of taking care of themselves.

2. Brownmiller expresses the view that "Femininity always demands more." Explain what she means.

I hope we can all agree with author and professor Camille Paglia's opening statement: "Rape is an outrage that cannot be tolerated in civilized society." It is a despicable crime, and society's growing awareness of the various facets of this crime (one form of which was once termed "date rape" and then "acquaintance rape" and finally, sensibly, simply "rape") can only be gauged as a good thing. Paglia agrees that awareness of a danger is a good thing. Instead of debating the merits of Paglia's provocative surface argument—that young women need to be wary of young men who are by nature a sexual threat to young women—I would like to look beyond her surface argument to the larger worldview that she announces in this essay and elsewhere.

Clearly, Paglia positions herself in disagreement with "academic" or "second wave" feminists like Susan Brownmiller. She engages in a provocative discourse with these fellow feminists, positioning herself as a dissident who expresses pointed skepticism regarding feminist dogma. For example, she writes, "Academic feminism is lost in a fog of social constructionism. It believes we are totally the product of our environment. This idea was invented by Rousseau. He was wrong." The idea that "we are totally the product of our environment" I would characterize, and perhaps simplify, as a viewpoint that emphasizes the importance of *nurture*. It is true that feminists like Brownmiller emphasize the role of "nurture" or environment in the development of one's concept of "femininity." Culture and society play a large role, argue these second wave feminists, in creating and maintaining the definition of "femininity." Paglia, on the other hand, emphasizes the role of *nature* when it comes to sexual identity. Her comments in this essay concern "masculinity" rather than femininity. For example, she claims that masculinity is "aggressive, unstable, [and] combustible."

I wonder if you think that the development of one's sense of "femininity" and "masculinity" has more to do with *nurture* or *nature*?

## Questions to Consider

*Answer these questions as you read and annotate the text:*

- Can you determine the "historical context" of this essay based on what Paglia writes? In other words, what issue prompted her to write this opinion piece for *New York Newsday* in 1991? (Hint: this same issue, unfortunately, has once again surfaced on college campuses in recent years.)
- Paglia observes, "Men become masculine only when other men say they are." Do you agree? Why or why not? Does this observation underscore the role of *nature* or *nurture* in the development of masculinity? Do women become feminine when other women say they are? What does Paglia say and what do you say?
- How exactly have academic feminists failed young women, according to Paglia?
- Feminist dogma, writes Paglia, teaches its disciples that rape is a crime of violence and not of sex. She calls this idea "sugar-coated Shirley Temple nonsense." (Feel free to Google "Shirley Temple" if you don't understand the pop culture reference.) What do you make of the argument that rape is a crime of violence and not of sex?
- Paglia claims, "Aggression and eroticism . . . are deeply intertwined." Do you agree? Why or why not?
- Paglia criticizes "militant feminism" and "academic feminism" for not being able to "understand preverbal or nonverbal communication." What does she mean, and why does she argue that it's a problem?
- What evidence does Paglia provide throughout her essay that young men are sexually dangerous and that young women must exercise self-awareness and self-control? Do you find her argument persuasive? Do you agree that for men there is a "fun element in rape, especially the wild, infectious delirium of gang rape"?

## Camille Paglia, Rape and Modern Sex War

Rape is an outrage that cannot be tolerated in civilized society. Yet feminism, which has waged a crusade for rape to be taken more seriously, has put young women in danger by hiding the truth about sex from them.

In dramatizing the pervasiveness of rape, feminists have told young women that before they have sex with a man, they must give consent as explicit as a legal contract's. In this way, young women have been convinced that they have been the victims of rape. On elite campuses in the Northeast and on the West Coast, they have held consciousness-raising sessions, petitioned administrations, demanded inquests. At Brown University, outraged, panicky "victims" have scrawled the names of alleged attackers on the wails of women's rest rooms. What marital rape was to the '70s, "date rape" is to the '90s.

The incidence and seriousness of rape do not require this kind of exaggeration. Real acquaintance rape is nothing new. It has been a horrible problem for women for all of recorded history. Once, father and brothers protected women from rape. Once, the penalty for rape was death. I come from a fierce Italian tradition where, not so long ago in the motherland, a rapist would end up knifed, castrated, and hung out to dry.

But the old clans and small rural communities have broken down. In our cities, on our campuses far from home, young women are vulnerable and defenseless. Feminism has not prepared them for this. Feminism keeps saying the sexes are the same. It keeps telling women they can do anything, go anywhere, say anything, wear anything. No, they can't. Women will always be in sexual danger.

One of my male students recently slept overnight with a friend in a passageway of the Great Pyramid in Egypt. He described the moon and sand, the ancient silence and eerie echoes. I am a woman. I will never experience that. I am not stupid enough to believe I could ever be safe there. There is a world of solitary adventure I will never have. Women have always known these somber truths. But feminism, with its pie-in-the-sky fantasies about the perfect world, keeps young women from seeing life as it is.

We must remedy social injustice whenever we can. But there are some things we cannot change. There are sexual differences that are based in biology. Academic feminism is lost in a fog of social constructionism. It believes we are totally the product of our environment. This idea was invented by Rousseau. He was wrong. Emboldened by dumb French language theory, academic feminists repeat the same hollow slogans over and over to each other. Their view of sex is naive and prudish. Leaving sex to the feminists is like letting your dog vacation at the taxidermist's.

The sexes are at war. Men must struggle for identity against the overwhelming power of their mothers. Women have menstruation to tell them they are women. Men must do or risk something to be men. Men become masculine only when other men say they are. Having sex with a woman is one way a boy becomes a man.

College men are at their hormonal peak. They have just left their mothers and are questing for their male identity. In groups, they are dangerous. A woman going to a fraternity party is walking into Testosterone Flats, full of prickly cacti and blazing guns. If she goes, she should be armed with resolute alertness. She should arrive with girlfriends and leave with them. A girl who lets herself get dead drunk at a fraternity party is a fool. A girl who goes upstairs alone with a brother at a fraternity party is an idiot. Feminists call this "blaming the victim." I call it common sense.

For a decade, feminists have drilled their disciples to say, "Rape is a crime of violence but not of sex." This sugar-coated Shirley Temple nonsense has exposed young women to disaster. Misled by feminism, they do not expect rape from the nice boys from good homes who sit next to them in class.

Aggression and eroticism are deeply intertwined. Hunt, pursuit and capture are biologically programmed into male sexuality. Generation after generation, men must be educated, refined, and ethically persuaded away from their tendency toward anarchy and brutishness. Society is not the enemy, as feminism ignorantly claims. Society is woman's protection against rape. Feminism, with its solemn Carry Nation repressiveness, does not see what is for men the eroticism or fun element in rape, especially the wild, infectious delirium of gang rape. Women who do not understand rape cannot defend themselves against it.

The date-rape controversy shows feminism hitting the wall of its own broken promises. The women of my '60s generation were the first respectable girls in history to swear like sailors, get drunk, stay out all night—in short, to act like men. We sought total sexual freedom and equality. But as time passed, we woke up to cold reality. The old double standard protected women. When anything goes, it's women who lose.

Today's young women don't know what they want. They see that feminism has not brought sexual happiness. The theatrics of public rage over date rape are their way of restoring the old sexual rules that were shattered by my generation. Yet nothing about the sexes has really changed. The comic film *Where the Boys Are* (1960), the ultimate expression of '50s man-chasing, still speaks directly to our time. It shows smart, lively women skillfully anticipating and fending off the dozens of strategies with which horny men try to get them into bed. The agonizing date-rape subplot and climax are brilliantly done. The victim, Yvette Mimieux, makes mistake after mistake, obvious to the other girls. She allows herself to be lured away from her girlfriends and into isolation with boys whose character and intentions she misreads. *Where the Boys Are* tells the truth. It shows courtship as a dangerous game in which the signals are not verbal but subliminal.

Neither militant feminism, which is obsessed with politically correct language, nor academic feminism, which believes that knowledge and experience are "constituted by" language, can understand preverbal or nonverbal communication. Feminism, focusing on sexual politics, cannot see that sex exists in and through the body. Sexual desire and arousal cannot be fully translated into verbal terms. This is why men and women misunderstand each other.

Trying to remake the future, feminism cut itself off from sexual history. It discarded and suppressed the sexual myths of literature, art and religion. Those myths show us the turbulence, the mysteries and passions of sex. In mythology we see men's sexual anxiety, their fear of woman's dominance. Much sexual violence is rooted in men's sense of psychological weakness toward women, It takes many men to deal with one woman. Woman's voracity is a persistent motif. Clara Bow, it was rumored, took on the USC football team on weekends. Marilyn Monroe, singing "Diamonds Are a Girl's Best Friend," rules a conga line of men in tuxes. Half-clad Cher, in the video for "If I Could Turn Back Time," deranges a battleship of screaming sailors and straddles a pink-lit cannon. Feminism, coveting social power, is blind to woman's cosmic sexual power.

To understand rape, you must study the past. There never was and never will be sexual harmony. Every woman must take personal responsibility for her sexuality, which is nature's red flame. She must be prudent and cautious about where she goes and with whom. When she makes a mistake, she must accept the consequences and, through self-criticism, resolve never to make that mistake again. Running to mommy and daddy on the campus grievance committee is unworthy of strong women. Posting lists of guilty men in the toilet is cowardly infantile stuff.

The Italian philosophy of life espouses high-energy confrontation. A male student makes a vulgar remark about your breasts? Don't slink off to whimper and simper with the campus shrinking violets. Deal with it. On the spot. Say,

"Shut up, you jerk! And crawl back to the barnyard where you belong!" In general, women who project this take-charge attitude toward life get harassed less often. I see too many dopey, immature, self-pitying women walking around like melting sticks of butter. It's the Yvette Mimieux syndrome: make me happy. And listen to me weep when I'm not.

The date-rape debate is already smothering in propaganda churned out by the expensive Northeastern colleges and universities, with their over-concentration of boring, uptight academic feminists and spoiled, affluent students. Beware of the deep manipulativeness of rich students who were neglected by their parents. They love to turn the campus into hysterical psychodramas of sexual transgression, followed by assertions of parental authority and concern. And don't look for sexual enlightenment from academe, which spews out mountains of books but never looks at life directly.

As a fan of football and rock music, I see in the simple, swaggering masculinity of the jock and in the noisy posturing of the heavy-metal guitarist certain fundamental, unchanging truths about sex. Masculinity is aggressive, unstable, combustible. It is also the most creative cultural force in history. Women must reorient themselves toward the elemental powers of sex, which can strengthen or destroy.

The only solution to date rape is female self-awareness and self-control. A woman's number-one line of defense against rape is herself. When a real rape occurs, she should report it to the police. Complaining to college committees because the courts "take too long" is ridiculous. College administrations are not a branch of the judiciary. They are not equipped or trained for legal inquiry. Colleges must alert incoming students to the problems and dangers of adulthood. Then colleges must stand back and get out of the sex game.

## Questions for Comprehension

*Answer these questions as a comprehension reading quiz and/or for further clarification on the text:*

1. True/False. Paglia claims that when it comes to the issue of rape, society is not the enemy of women.

2. Provide one example from the essay of Paglia's idea of "simple, swaggering masculinity."

3. Team "Stereotype" or Team "Reality"? Engage in a class debate, each side chosen randomly (or draft a couple of impromptu paragraphs), in which you take up the argument of "Stereotype" or "Reality" when it comes to Paglia's depiction of masculinity.

## Sentence Exercise #3

Use Margaret Atwood's "Pornography" as the basis to complete the following sentence exercises.

Write three "clean copy" (that is, error-free) sentences (or combination of sentences) that serve to integrate significant language from the text in the form of paraphrases and quotations. See Notes for Composition at the end of the text.

1. Atwood's claim that _____ becomes more clear when she writes, "_____" (xx).

2. Atwood offers supporting evidence for her idea that _____ in the form of _____.

3. One of Atwood's main points is that _____. She notes, "_____" (xx). In writing this, she attempts to draw awareness to her concept that _____.

## Suggested Evaluation Criterion and Point Values

| Exercise completed on deadline | 10 points |
|---|---|

## Reader Response #3

Consult the "Reader Response Guidelines" in Unit One. Draft and revise one to two pages in MLA format. Be aware of any specific directions or requirements that your instructor may offer.

It might be OK to stick with an ABC response structure: paragraph A) introduce the text and focus your audience on a theme or thesis, paragraph B) analyze the text with properly integrated quotations, and paragraph C) respond to the text. Suggested outlines can be useful. However, you always want to structure your compositions according to your purpose. Your primary purpose in first semester college composition is typically "to analyze the text." "Analyze" literally means "to break down." You want to break apart the author's argument into small, comprehensible segments for the benefit of your outside readers. You do not need to offer a comprehensive summary of the article. Your instructor will have useful tips in regard to structure, purpose, and audience.

Select *either* Margaret Atwood's essay "Pornography" *or* Gloria Steinem's essay "Erotica and Pornography." (*Do not select both unless your instructor asks you to do so.*) Identify the author's thesis or main idea. Quote extensively in order to portray the author's argument accurately and highlight her most important points. Characterize her evidence and means of persuasion. Respond to the author's argument. As always, your composition and tone must address an "outside-our-classroom" academic audience. The recognition of your audience will help you with diction (word choice) and with other essential matters of composition, such as quotation selection and presentation.

## Suggested Scoring Criteria and Point Values

| | |
|---|---|
| Proper text introduction and article overview | 4 points |
| Ability to select and integrate quotations | 8 points |
| Effective syntax and usage (follows the conventions of standard written English) | 4 points |
| Format and Deadline | 4 points |

## Paragraph Exercise #1

In college composition, once you have introduced a text to an outside audience, you next need to engage in a process of text analysis in order to underscore your points of focus. Practice this skill using Susan Brownmiller's article and the four-sentence template outlined below. Let's say you have already introduced the text and now you are ready to compose a new paragraph. You wish to address the question: If, in portions of her composition, Susan Brownmiller is not stating her own point of view directly, whose point of view is she attempting to describe?

Using the template sentences below, or ones your instructor develops, or ones you develop on your own, write a four-sentence paragraph clarifying Brownmiller's viewpoint and rhetorical strategy. Feel free to change the verbs to make them more fitting or effective (e.g., "believes" might become "argues" or "claims").

Feminists, in general, believe that _____. Brownmiller implies that she believes _____ when she observes _____. She writes, "_____." It is clear that she wants her reader to understand that _____.

## Suggested Scoring Criteria and Point Values

| | |
|---|---|
| Four-sentence paragraph accurately reflects the author's viewpoints, turned in on deadline | 10 points |
| Coherency, including proper grammar, usage, and syntax | 10 points |

## Reader Response #4

One or two pages in MLA format

Option #1: Respond to Camille Paglia's attitudes regarding "masculinity." Also focus on her criticisms of "social constructionism," that is, the feminist belief that masculine and feminine identity are largely matters of social or cultural construction (and not strictly the result of nature or biology). Why or how does Paglia emphasize the role of "nature" and "biology" rather than "nurture" and social environment?

Option #2: Respond to Susan Brownmiller's concept that "femininity" is a social construction.

Option #3: Recount a relevant selection of Judy Brady's grievances from her 1971 article. Analyze her concerns. To what extent do her grievances, especially regarding home and work, remain relevant for women in 21st century America?

Unless you have a better strategy, stick with the ABC paragraph response structure: A) introduce the text and focus your audience on a theme, thesis, or the author's major claim; B) analyze the text with properly integrated quotations; and C) respond to the text. The same scoring criteria apply for each option.

## Suggested Scoring Criteria and Point Values

| Proper text introduction and article overview | 4 points |
|---|---|
| Ability to select and integrate quotations | 8 points |
| Effective syntax and usage (composed in standard written English) | 4 points |
| Format and Deadline | 4 points |

# Unit Two Essay Topics

*See suggested assignment requirements, parameters, and scoring criteria below.*

Expand upon the topic that you selected for one of your Unit Two reader responses. Expand your composition in order to engage in an in-depth analysis of the chosen topic.

OPTION #1: Write a critical essay that reflects on how or if (or to what degree) our concepts of "femininity" and "masculinity" are social rather than biological constructions. Brownmiller's "Femininity" and Paglia's "Rape and Modern Sex War" comment on issues surrounding traditional feminine and masculine identity. What, for example, are the distinctions between "biological femaleness" and "femininity"? What about "maleness" and "masculinity"? Focus on the texts themselves prior to any exploration of your own concepts. Quotation selection, integration, and explanation are key components to your composition. You will need to be especially careful to place quotations and other text references in a context that your outside audience can understand.

OPTION #2: Margaret Atwood poses the question, "What happens when boy educated on porn meets girl brought up on Harlequin romances?" Gloria Steinem poses similar questions, at least by implication. Analyze Atwood's and Steinem's concerns. Compare and contrast these concerns to Wendy McElroy's arguments in "A Feminist Defense of Pornography." At a minimum, you must analyze and incorporate Atwood's and McElroy's texts. Incorporating Steinem's text may be helpful to you in clarifying concepts for your outside audience.

OPTION #3: Connect second wave feminist concerns regarding pornography with the 2017 #metoo and the 2018 #timesup social movements. Keep in mind that your primary goal is to analyze the source texts, so focus on quotation selection and integration as you focus your audience on your topic. Placing quotations in a clear context for your audience as well as explaining the meaning and significance of the quotations are key components. Analyze the primary source texts before you develop connections to these current social movements that seek to end sexual harassment in the workplace and elsewhere.

OPTION #4: Analyze the concerns expressed in Judy Brady's text. Use Brady's text and at least two other sources under Unit Two "Further Inquiry & Research" (or elsewhere, as approved by your instructor) in order to develop a composition that compares the feminist concerns expressed in Brady's 1971 essay and feminist concerns in 21st century America.

OPTION #5: Using sources under Unit Two "Further Inquiry & Research" (or elsewhere, as approved by your instructor), propose a topic of your own. Your topic must involve analysis of a minimum of two sources and must conform to the requirements and parameters described below. You must present your topic proposal in a formal page of writing to your instructor for approval well ahead of deadline. If your instructor does not approve your topic, do not move forward with the composition.

Requirements and Parameters:

Compose an analytical essay that incorporates at least two sources from the *Engaging Discourse* reader. Seek to establish a significant synthetic connection between these sources, and treat your sources in such a way that your outside reader or outside audience can follow your analysis.

Length: Four or five pages (plus Works Cited) in MLA format (about 1,000 to 1,500 words). Include a Word Count (e.g., Word Count: 1250) at the top left along with your name, date, etc.

*Tutoring and/or workshop is a suggested requirement for this assignment.*

## Suggested Scoring Criteria and Point Values

| | |
|---|---|
| Holistic Assessment<br>*The essay features thoughtful, relevant analysis with an appropriate academic tone maintained throughout; it addresses a significant topic in a meaningful way, meets length requirements, and is turned in on deadline.* | 20 points |
| Audience<br>*The essay is written for an appropriate audience, not for our classroom but for an outside audience.* | 10 points |
| Text Introductions<br>*Proper, effective text introductions of at least two (2) major texts/sources, including a paraphrase or quotation of an author's main idea, a main point or thesis in order to focus the audience on a theme or topic.* | 20 points |
| Quotations<br>*A bare minimum of four (4) significant quotations, two (2) from each major source, properly and effectively integrated. Quoted material constitutes no more than about 10% of paper.* | 20 points |
| Explanatory Remarks<br>*Writer comments explicitly on the quotations, explaining, clarifying, contextualizing, or sensibly challenging the authors' idea(s).* | 10 points |
| Voice<br>*The writer makes appropriate use of SWE (standard written English) (i.e., effective grammar/usage/syntax).* | 10 points |
| Format<br>*The writer presents the composition in proper Modern Language Association (MLA) format, including a proper Works Cited page, or in another standard format as indicated by the instructor.* | 10 points |

Resources

# "Feminism": Denotation and Connotation

What does the term "feminism" mean? What does it imply? If you follow the "dictionary definition" of a word (or term), you are investigating the word's *denotation*. When you investigate the unstated social or cultural implications of a word (or term), you are dealing with *connotation*. An understanding of both the denotation and the connotation of a word or term are essential if you want to develop a complete understanding of the concepts and social attitudes that surround the label in question.

Arguably, a great many Americans are "feminists" by the strict denotation of the term. Americans support the right of women to own property, to vote, and to enjoy equal protection under the law. We have largely adopted the values of our country's 19th century "first wave" feminists, women like Elizabeth Cady Stanton who argued in the Seneca Falls Declaration (1848) that "all men and women are created equal."

At the same time, a great many Americans resist the term "feminist" due to its connotations. I am not a feminist, said a famous American actress during a 2014 *Time* interview, "because I love men, and I think the idea of 'raise women to power, take the men away from the power' is never going to work out because you need balance." Critics blasted her for misunderstanding and misrepresenting feminism, which, they said, does not mean tearing down men. Later, the actress backed off of the "take the men away from the power" aspect of her comment but maintained that the label "feminist" was too divisive for her to embrace. Later yet, she said that she "would today consider myself a feminist."

Articles from a wide array of media outlets, including *NPR* and *National Review*, indicate an increasing aversion in Millennials to the "feminist" label. Why do you think this might be so? What are your own feelings on the matter? You can investigate these questions under this unit's "Further Inquiry & Research" section.

If you're unsure of your own feelings regarding the term "feminism," hunt around the internet to get a general idea of the denotation and connotation of the term as well as the history of the social movement.

- If **first wave feminists** (19th and early 20th century) called for fundamental political rights such as the right to vote, what did **second wave feminists** (1960s to 1990s) call for?
- What do Millennials seem to think of feminism?
- Would Millennial feminists mostly consider themselves **third wave** feminists (1990s)? Or **fourth** wave feminists (21st century)? What does "third wave" (or "fourth wave") feminism mean, and how is it a distinct social movement from second wave feminism?

Of course, sweeping labels such as "feminist" and "feminism" are inadequate to describe unique individuals. As you'll discover, it's entirely possible for Camille Paglia and Susan Brownmiller, who both consider themselves feminists, to disagree entirely on fundamental issues.

Martha Rampton writes, "An aspect of third wave feminism that mystified the mothers of the earlier feminist movement was the readoption by young feminists of the very lip-stick, high-heels, and cleavage proudly exposed by low cut necklines that the first two phases of the movement identified with male oppression." A distinct aspect of third wave feminism involves the idea of sexuality as empowerment. Some "fourth wave" feminists, according to Rampton, have trouble with the very word "feminism" which seems to imply to them "for women only."

# Purpose & Audience

Whenever you sit down to write, you must keep these two things in mind. Determining purpose and audience dictates how you must write. You have to consider your "purpose" and your "audience."

You go to the grocery store. What is your purpose? To get food for yourself or your family. Who is your audience? You yourself are the audience. So you can scribble out a simple list and use as many obscure symbols and emoticons as you would like.

You wish to write an email to your history professor in order to clarify an essay question so that you can achieve a better score. Your professor is your audience. He or she needs appropriate details—not vague statements—in order to respond meaningfully to your email. An education professional will likely appreciate a certain level of formality in your note. You will probably minimize the use of improper grammar and slang, and you will have to make a judgment call before incorporating any emoticons. Is he or she the sort of instructor who would appreciate the implied intimacy and informality of the emoticon, or will it simply alienate you from your intended audience?

You write a formal college essay. The concept of "audience" is not as simple as it may seem. Some instructors in some disciplines may want you to simply address "insiders" within that field. For example, your anthropology professor may want you to compose as though you are addressing other anthropologists. Generally speaking, in composition classes, we want you to compose as though you are addressing a general outside audience, an educated audience that is not familiar with the inside information contained within the sources and texts that you are analyzing. In general, in composition classes, your purpose involves analyzing the texts in question. Your specific purpose may vary from assignment to assignment, and you will always want to make sure that your writing addresses your primary purpose.

As frightening as it may seem, I ask my students to imagine a roomful of their *other* professors besides me—your math instructor, your political science professor, etc.—who are interested in your composition and want to read your work and maybe even partake in the discourse that you develop in your writing. In other words, pretend that your other instructors need to be able to read and understand your essay.

Don't let "purpose and audience" inhibit you early on. Even for professionals, writing is a multistage process. No published writer ever wants to present an editor with an early draft. The consequences in the so-called "real world" are worse than a "D" grade. You can lose respect and even payment. So allow yourself to take on compositions in stages. At first, maybe you don't worry too much about purpose and audience. Simply get your thoughts down on paper. As you draft, revise, and edit, develop a clear purpose as you write for an "outside" audience, an audience that is not familiar with the source material and an audience that may not necessarily share your own beliefs and values.

When analyzing a text, it's also useful to ask yourself, *What is the writer's purpose? Who is the writer's audience?* And, finally, *what is the writer's tone?* Does his/her tone shift over the course of the text or is it consistent? The answers to these basic questions can often solve problems you might otherwise have on your mission to "analyze the text."

Be sure to stay "close to the text" when you analyze. Use signal phrases (*She writes*), attributions (*Her supporting evidence consists of. . .*), and quotations to express the main ideas of the text, and use the text itself to help you to express your own point of view. Oftentimes, as you express agreement, disagreement, or shades in between, you will also be figuring out and developing your own point of view.

# Logos, Ethos, or Pathos?

Your instructor may or may not wish for you to engage in a "rhetorical analysis" of these articles. A "rhetorical analysis" essay asks you to break a nonfiction work into parts in order to explain the collective effect of the sum of the parts—for example, to make a certain claim, to persuade the audience toward a certain perspective, to entertain, or simply to inform.

Most of the essays that we deal with in first semester college composition, of course, engage in argument. Typically, these essays make a specific claim, although, as we have seen, at times the reader must do some work in order to be able to articulate the specific claim at hand. In other words, oftentimes the art of *interpretation* is called for.

Traditional means of argument and persuasion in Western culture stem back to a foundation established in ancient Greek culture and to the great Roman orators such as Cicero. Medieval "scholastics" carried on the tradition of argument in early European universities. A millennium later, composition teachers still find useful the basic vocabulary that Aristotle described in his treatise *The Art of Rhetoric*. The famous philosopher defines "rhetoric" as the ability to observe in any given case the means of persuasion being used. He goes on to describe three basic means of persuasion: *logos, pathos,* and *ethos*. Here's how these concepts have come to be understood over the centuries:

- "Logos" involves using reasoning and logic to persuade the audience; it involves citing expert authorities and avoiding so-called logical fallacies or thinking errors.
- "Pathos" involves the use of emotional persuasion.
- "Ethos" relies mainly on the established authority (think "ethical authority") of the speaker/ writer who is making the appeal.

As you learn to become an independent, critical reader, you will learn to engage in "rhetorical analysis" as you read. Your *annotations* or margin notes will reflect this thought process. As you read Margaret Atwood, for example, do you find that she relies mostly on logos, pathos, or ethos as a means of persuasion? Very likely she relies a bit on all three, as good writers tend to do. Find specific examples of her use of logical persuasion, emotional appeal, and ethical authority in her essay "Pornography" (1988).

## The Definition of Pornography in America

In 1959, the manager of a movie theater in Ohio was convicted under a state obscenity law for showing the French film *Les Amants* (*The Lovers*, 1958). By 21st century standards, the film might not even qualify as "racy." U.S. Supreme Court Justice Potter Stewart (1915—1985), in reviewing the case in 1964, agreed that the film did not qualify as "obscene." In his majority decision, Stewart wrote that he could not precisely define what constitutes "hard-core pornography" but that a reasonable person could use an "I know it when I see it" litmus test to determine whether a movie or other art form has pornographic intent.

Under current judicial rulings, sexually explicit material is protected under the First Amendment unless it is deemed "obscene" or involves children. It strikes some commentators as odd that explicit hard-core pornography could be understood as anything other than "obscene," yet the government has hesitated in the past half century to attempt to ban porn or prosecute purveyors of pornography. Over the years, the Supreme Court has taken different stances on the issue of obscenity and pornography. In 1952, striking down a law allowing film censorship, the Court ruled that films were like speech and therefore protected under the First Amendment. In 1957, the United States Supreme Court ruled that "obscene" expressions do not qualify for free speech protection under the First Amendment. A 1973 standard dictated that "contemporary community standards" (that is, local public opinion) were a key factor in deciding whether material may be considered obscene. A pertinent factor is whether the material is publicly or privately accessible. It would seem that the internet represents the public sphere, but the federal government has rarely prosecuted or attempted to enforce "obscenity" standards in recent decades, particularly in regard to internet pornography. No case, it appears, has definitively tested whether the government has the right to shut down pornographic web sites. Despite the arguments of anti-porn opponents, the issue seems mostly marked by a general lack of interest. Many Americans are hesitant to involve the government in any kind of censorship effort, even if it involves an attempt to ban obscene materials. America's anti-censorship attitudes stem from more than two centuries of broad judicial interpretations regarding our rights of free speech under the First Amendment to the U.S. Constitution.

Questions of legality and censorship may become a part of the conversation in the classroom or in online forums. When it comes to the actual essay topics for this unit, however, unless your instructor directs you otherwise, *Engaging Discourse* does not ask you to examine questions of legality, censorship, or whether people have a right to own or view pornography. Instead, the main issues are:

- What are the effects of pornography viewing, if any?
- What, if any, are the greater social and cultural impacts of pornography, especially in regard to perceptions and attitudes toward women?
- Does pornography function in our society as an "educational tool"?
- What effect, if any, does pornography have on shaping perceptions of gender and sexuality?

## Further Inquiry & Research

Bennett, Morgan. "The New Narcotic." *Public Discourse*, Oct. 9, 2013, http://www.thepublicdiscourse.com/ 2013/10/10846/.

Bennett, Morgan. "Internet Pornography & the First Amendment." *Public Discourse,* Oct. 10, 2013, http://www .thepublicdiscourse.com/2013/10/10998/.

Castleman, Michael. "Dueling Statistics: How Much of the Internet is Porn?" *Psychology Today*, Nov. 3, 2016, *www.psychologytoday.com, https://www.psychologytoday.com/blog/all-about- sex/201611/dueling-statistics-how-much-the-internet-is-porn.*

Cummins, Denise. "Column: Why Millennial Women Don't Want to Call Themselves Feminists." *PBS News Hour, Feb. 12, 2016, www.pbs.org, https://www.pbs.org/newshour/economy/column-why-millennial-women-dont-want-to-call- themselves-feminists.*

Donahue, Rosemary. "Shailene Woodley Is a Feminist Now, But Seems Confused About What That Means." *Allure,* Aug. 22, 2017, *www.allure.com, https://www.allure.com/story/shailene- woodley-confused-feminist.*

"Feminism: A Collection of TED Talks (and more) on the Topic of Feminism." TED: Ideas Worth Spreading, *www.ted.com, https://www.ted.com/topics/feminism.*

Mac, Juno. "The Laws That Sex Workers Really Want." TED: Ideas Worth Spreading. TEDxEastEnd, Jan. 16, 2016, *www.ted.com, https://www.ted.com/talks/juno_mac_the_laws_that_sex_workers_really_want.*

McDonough, Katie. "Camille Paglia Thinks Rape Is Intrinsic To Men's Nature—And A Lot of Men Are Like, 'This Is Awesome!'" *Salon,* Sept. 30, 2014, *www.salon.com, https://www.salon.com/2014/09/30/camille_paglia_thinks_rape_is_intrinsic_to_mens_nature_an d_a_lot_of_men_are_like_this_is_awesome/.*

Orenstein, Peggy. "What Young Women Believe About Their Own Sexual Pleasure." TED: Ideas Worth Spreading. TEDWomen, Oct. 2016, *www.ted.com, https://www.ted.com/talks/peggy_orenstein_what_young_women_believe_about_their_own_sexual_pleasure.*

Rampton, Martha. "Four Waves of Feminism." Pacific University Oregon, Oct. 25, 2015, www.pacific.edu, https://www.pacificu.edu/about/media/four-waves-feminism.

## Additional Source Materials by Topic

### 21st Century Feminism

"100 Women: What is 21st Century Feminism". *BBC News.* Oct. 25, 2013, http://www.bbc.com/news/av/world-24672368/100-women-what-is-21st-century-feminism

Bianco, Marcie. "New Research: Millenials Passionate about Feminism." *Women's Media Center,* Sept. 7, 2017, http://www.womensmediacenter.com/news-features/new-research-millennials-passionate-about-feminism

Cochrane, Kira. "Nine Inspiring Lessons the Suffragettes can Teach Feminists Today". *The Guardian.* May 29, 2013, https://www.theguardian.com/world/2013/may/29/nine-lessons-suffragettes-feminists

Cosslett, L. and Baxter, H. "The Five Main Issues Facing Modern Feminism". *New Statesman America.* May 20, 2013, https://www.newstatesman.com/v-spot/2013/05/five-main-issues-facing-modern-feminism

German, Lindsey. "21st Century Feminism". *Socialist Review.* Oct. 2009, http://socialistreview.org.uk/340/21st-century-feminism

Herman, Emmanuelle. "Celebrating 21st-Century Feminism and Why it Matters". *Huffington Post.* April 17, 2015, https://www.huffingtonpost.com/emmanuelle-herman/celebrating-21st-century-feminism-and-why-it-matters_b_7085080.html

Isomäki, Mari. "Why We Still Need Feminism in the 21st Century" Mar. 7, 2016, https://www.hercampus.com/school/helsinki/why-we-still-need-feminism-21st-century

Leach, Samantha. "Empowerment – Just Don't Call Them Feminists". *Glamour.* Aug 4, 2017, https://www.glamour.com/story/conservative-millennial-women-and-feminism

Morgan, Robin. "Feminism is a 21st Century Word". *Time.* Nov. 17, 2014, http://time.com/3588846/time-apologizes-feminist-word-poll-robin-morgan/

Pringle, Brendan. "As Millennials Postpone Marriage, Feminists are Turning the Tables". *Washington Examiner.* Feb. 14, 2018, https://www.washingtonexaminer.com/as-millennials-postpone-marriage-feminists-are-turning-the-tables

Rapp, Alyssa. "Feminism in the Era of Millenials: It's about Leaping Versus Leaning." *Forbes,* Feb. 14, 2017, https://www.forbes.com/sites/yec/2017/02/14/feminism-in-the-era-of-millennials-its-about-leaping-versus-leaning/#2032ca2a8a17

Ross, India et al. "The Meaning of the F-word – Feminism in Five Voices". *Financial Times.* Oct. 19, 2017, https://www.ft.com/content/0284b792-b522-11e7-aa26-bb002965bce8

Tani, Ellen Yoshi. "What Makes Contemporary Art Feminist? An Art Genome Project Case Study". *Artsy.* Jan. 16, 2015, https://www.artsy.net/article/theartgenomeproject-what-makes-contemporary-art-feminist-an-art

Wilcox, W and Sturgeon, S. "Why Would Millennial Men Prefer Stay-at-home Wives? Race and Feminism." *The Washington Post.* April 5, 2017, https://www.washingtonpost.com/posteverything/wp/2017/04/05/why-would-millennial-men-prefer-stay-at-home-wives-race-and-feminism/

Yancey, Mel. "Celebrating 21st Century Feminism and Why it Matters". *Caya Blog.* May 11, 2016, http://caya.us.com/2016/05/11/celebrating-21st-century-feminism-and-why-it-matters/

## Millennials and Pornography

Bahrampour, Tara. "'There isn't Really Anything Magical about it': Why More Millennials are Avoiding Sex". *The Washington Post.* Aug. 2, 2016, https://www.washingtonpost.com/local/social-issues/there-isnt-really-anything-magical-about-it-why-more-millennials-are-putting-off-sex/2016/08/02/e7b73d6e-37f4-11e6-8f7c-d4c723a-2becb_story.html

Copland, Simon. "The Many Reasons that People are Having Less Sex". *BBC.* May 9, 2017, http://www.bbc.com/future/story/20170508-the-many-reasons-that-people-are-having-less-sex

Doré, Louis. "How Porn Habits of Millennials Differ from Their Parents' Generation". *Indy100.* 2015, https://www.indy100.com/article/how-porn-habits-of-millennials-differ-from-their-parents-generation--WJZWzpLofe

ElHage, Alysse. "Millennials, Infidelity, and Porn". *Institute for Family Studies.* Aug. 2, 2016, https://ifstudies.org/blog/millennials-infidelity-and-porn

Fiens, Hans. "Why it's Terrible News That Millennials are Having Less Sex". Feb. 10, 2017, https://illinoisfamily.org/marriage/terrible-news-millennials-less-sex/

Hanbury, Aaron Cline. "Porn Addiction is Now Threatening an Entire Generation". *Relevant.* Sept. 1, 2016, https://relevantmagazine.com/current/porn-addiction-now-threatening-entire-generation-2017

Johnston, Ian. "Millennial Generation Turning their Backs on Sex in Highest Numbers Since the 1920s". *Independent.* Aug. 2, 2016, https://www.independent.co.uk/news/science/sex-millennials-study-young-people-turning-back-on-sexual-intercourse-in-record-numbers-a7167946.html

Pullmann, Joy. "Why are Millennials Having so Much Less Sex than Their Grandparents Did?". *The Federalist.* Mar. 15, 2017, http://thefederalist.com/2017/03/15/millennials-much-less-sex-grandparents/

Tijerina, Joshua. "Millennials & Pornography: Are we Preventing or Perpetuating Sexual Violence?". *Medium.* Feb 16, 2016, https://medium.com/@HalcyonMovement/millennials-pornography-are-we-preventing-or-perpetuating-sexual-violence-2ea4a9e2cfa3

## Feminism and Pornography

Bindel, Julie. "Without Porn, the World would be a Better Place". *The Guardian.* Oct. 24, 2014, https://www.theguardian.com/commentisfree/2014/oct/24/pornography-world-anti-porn-feminist-censorship-misogyny

Blake, Pandora. "Don't ask if Porn 'empowers' Women – Instead, ask if your Feminism Does". *New Statesman America.* Mar. 10, 2015, https://www.newstatesman.com/voices/2015/03/dont-ask-if-porn-empowers-women-instead-ask-if-your-feminism-does

Bronstein, Carolyn. "The Origins of Anti-Pornography Feminism". *Cambridge Blog.* Aug. 10, 2011, http://www.cambridgeblog.org/2011/08/the-origins-of-anti-pornography-feminism-by-carolyn-bronstein/

Bryden, David. "Between Two Constitutions: Feminism and Pornography". 1985. https://conservancy.umn.edu/bitstream/handle/11299/164525/02_01_Bryden.pdf;sequence=1

Ellis, K., O'Dair, B. & Tallmer, A. "Feminism and Pornography". *Feminist Review (1990) 36: 15*, https://link.springer.com/article/10.1057%2Ffr.1990.41

Ellis, K., O'Dair, B. & Tallmer, A.. "Feminism and Pornography". *Feminist Review (1990) 36: 15*, https://www.jstor.org/stable/pdf/1395105.pdf?refreqid=excelsior%3A35167c905b693ea97d2dda665cef60b5

Jagger, Erica. "How I can be a Feminist and Still Like Porn". *Huffington Post.* Dec. 1, 2014, https://www.huffingtonpost.com/erica-jagger/women-and-porn_b_6239550.html

James, Samuel D. "Pornography is Worse than Feminism". *First Things.* Sept. 29, 2017, https://www.firstthings.com/web-exclusives/2017/09/pornography-is-worse-than-feminism

Purcell, Natalie. "Feminism and Pornography: Building Sensitive Research and Analytic Approaches". *Electronic Journal of Human Sexuality.* May 11, 2009, http://www.ejhs.org/Volume12/Feminism%20and%20Porn.htm

# UNIT THREE

# Political Correctness

## Suggested Timeline: Two Weeks

When I was young, parents taught their children this rhyme: *Sticks and stones may break my bones / But words will never hurt me.* The idea, of course, was for kids to ignore mean words and insults. The problem, of course, is that the rhyme isn't true: Words do hurt. There is a growing recognition nationwide of the real dangers associated with online bullying, for example. It would be ideal if all children understood how to deal with unkind words. The fact is, however, that most kids are not well equipped to deal with the "sticks and stones" of cruel language.

The social movement termed "political correctness" doesn't actually have much to do with children bullying and picking on one another. It is a social movement that recognizes the power of language to shape thought and cultural attitudes. With its origins in American colleges and universities of the 1970s and 1980s, the social movement has often been viewed with suspicion by the mainstream populace. "Political correctness," or "PC," is often viewed, especially by conservative critics, as a leftwing academic concoction that indulges the hypersensitivities of minority groups. Rather than encouraging mainstream unity, political correctness encourages fringe isolation and stifles true public discourse. So runs the criticism.

Just as the term "feminist" may have a negative cultural connotation even while the feminist movement itself has clearly changed social attitudes in regard to women in the home and in the workplace, so does the term "political correctness" carry a negative connotation even while the movement itself has effected real social change in regard to attitudes about the use of language. Words that were once acceptable in the mainstream are no longer acceptable. Most "waitresses" prefer to be called "servers" these days, and you will be hard pressed to find a "stewardess" on your next plane flight. Whether these are silly or serious examples is really up to you to decide.

The issues that underscore people's sensitivities are serious. The word "retarded" is no longer acceptable to describe someone with an intellectual disability. (Many of you, I hope and presume, will find it baffling and even alarming that the term was ever deemed socially acceptable.) The misunderstood and misused term "Oriental" was once a synonym for "Asian" and is now no longer acceptable. If people are physically disabled, they are not "cripples."

These changes have come about, in large part, due to political correctness. Most people would agree that these are positive changes.

Yet to be called "politically correct" has become an insult. No one wants to stand up and declare, "I am politically correct!" It would be like admitting, "I have no sense of humor!" or "I am obsessed with monitoring other people's words!"

When presidential candidate Donald Trump declared on multiple occasions, "I do not have time for total political correctness" and "This country does not have time for political correctness," he could be sure to enjoy a rousing cheer from his audience. When journalist Megan Kelly challenged the presidential candidate on his use of derogatory language in regard to women, the candidate responded, "I think the big problem this country has is being politically correct." The audience applauded his response. "I've been challenged by so many people, I don't frankly have time for total political correctness. And to be honest with you, this country doesn't have time either."

Political liberals tend to see political correctness as an appropriate response to our increasingly diverse democracy, while conservatives have often associated "political correctness" with the Orwellian specter of "thought police" who monitor our every word.

As we have seen with the term "feminist," sometimes the label and the values behind the label are separate matters. My claim in the prior unit was that few people want to be labeled "feminist," yet most Americans embrace the values of first wave feminism (i.e., political enfranchisement and legal protection for women). My similar claim in regard to "PC" is that many people who are suspicious of the label "politically correct" are, in essence, politically correct. We, as a society, understand and accept many of the basic tenets of political correctness. Yet we don't want to be called "PC."

I propose this argument to my college classroom which is filled, year after year, with the most open-minded, tolerant, and sympathetic generation in human history. This generation of young people is aware of the power of language in regard to cyber bullying. Millennials have clearly accepted key elements underpinning "political correctness" even while they too cannot embrace the label.

In the 1970s and 1980s, nutritionists told my Generation X, "You are what you eat." In other words, there is a direct connection between food and health. (We ate way too much junk food, evidently.) It seems common sense, yes?

In the 1980s and 1990s, proponents of political correctness (often feminists) told the public, "You are what you say." In other words, you *are* the words that you use. Is this also common sense? If you only use courteous language in public, and embrace offensive language in private, then are you actually a courteous person?

If you go around speaking offensive language, it likely reveals your offensive thoughts. Or is this line of reasoning simply leftist dogma gone too far? When does the pressure to "adjust" our language (and, hence, our thoughts) become an onerous impingement on our freedom of speech and our freedom of thought akin to the pressures exerted by Big Brother in George Orwell's iconic novel *1984*? When does political correctness go too far in curbing our capacities to engage in meaningful public discourse?

At the same time, to what extend *must* we remain politically correct in a functioning democracy where we do not share a common ethnic or religious heritage? How can we engage in meaningful and inclusive public discourse when one group uses language that is offensive to another group?

# Readings

Here is a list of readings for this unit:

1. Alleen Pace Nilsen, "Sexism in English: Embodiment and Language" (1990)
2. George Orwell, "Politics and the English Language" (1946)
3. Jonathan Chait, "Not a Very P.C. Thing to Say: How the Language Police Are Perverting Liberalism" (2015)

# Responsibilities

Critiquing three sample compositions may help you to produce your own **Essay Three** (*100 points*).

# Objectives

The main objective of our third unit is for you to be able to participate in a public discourse (discussion) on the broad topic of political correctness.

✓ This unit aims to reinforce the development of sound critical and analytical thinking through the detailed evaluation of source materials.
✓ This unit challenges students to turn sound critical and analytical thinking on complex topics into clear prose.
✓ Students must produce writing with clear organization, appropriate logic, detailed text analysis, and solid support for their own views, with appropriately cited source information.
✓ Students will develop critical thinking, reading, and writing strategies in order to produce notes, drafts, and a final essay that exhibits synthetic connections between varied source materials.

# Resources

Students can develop their own research topics and begin to dig into word histories using the source materials listed under "Further Inquiry & Research."

Definition of "Politically Correct"
Definition of "Social Justice Warrior"
PC in the Classroom
The Importance of Attribution
Drawing Synthetic Connections
The "N" Word
An Exercise in Peer Critical Analysis
Further Inquiry & Research
Additional Source Materials by Topic

# Readings

# Alleen Pace Nilsen, "Sexism in English: Embodiment and Language" (1990)

Alleen Pace Nilsen seems to spell out the agenda of "political correctness" when she writes, "I'm one of those linguists who believes that new language customs will cause a new generation of speakers to grow up with different expectations. This is why I'm happy about people's efforts to use inclusive language, to say *he or she* or *they* when speaking about individuals whose names they do not know. I'm glad that leading publishers have developed guidelines to help writers use language that is fair to both sexes, and I'm glad that most newspapers and magazines list women by their own names instead of only by the husbands' names and that educated and thoughtful people no longer begin their business letters with 'Dear Sir' or 'Gentlemen.'"

Nilsen's article provides a bridge between the concerns of feminism—specifically, second wave feminists inspired by the work of Simone de Beauvoir and other language theorists—and the concerns of political correctness. In her seminal work *The Second Sex*, the French philosopher Beauvoir argues that historically "man" has been the default for humanity and so "woman" is viewed as a secondary "Other." Second wave feminists used Beauvoir's work as an intellectual foundation for America's women's movement in the 1960s and in subsequent decades. An early concern of second wave feminism involves society's use of language. In language, these feminists observe, one can discern the predominant underlying attitudes of society and culture. Political correctness shares this supposition.

To a certain extent, this insight appears to be common sense. For example, if in a given historical era, it was socially acceptable for a public figure to use racist language, then a cultural critic can assert with justification that the society in which the public figure resided held racist values, either consciously or unconsciously. The public figure's use of language reveals social values. One of the claims, or observations, that Nilsen makes in her article is that language, which changes slowly, contains the attitudes that our ancestors held.

Using outdated language can get a person in trouble, of course, when that language strikes others as being offensive. Even people who claim to hate "political correctness" are honed in on the word choices of others in matters of personal and public discourse, especially, I find, in online environments. In the 21st century, we appear to live in a world where people rely less and less on sound judgment and genuine intellectual curiosity when it comes to understanding others' viewpoints and more and more on knee-jerk assumptions and emotional intuition.

Twenty-first century online "social justice warriors," who question the rights of others to use certain terms in public discourse, are the inheritors of a late 20th century tradition of political correctness as well as a mid-20th century tradition of second wave feminism. Beauvoir's assertion that "One is not born but rather becomes a woman," for example, might represent the first moment in modern Western culture where an intellectual distinguishes between "sex" and "gender." There is much more to political correctness, though, than a rancorous debate over the proper terms to use for men and women. The concepts that underlie political correctness as a social movement cut to the heart of America's so-called "culture wars" even while political correctness itself continues to be simultaneously misunderstood and weaponized.

## Questions to Consider

*Answer these questions as you read and annotate the text:*

- What is the point of the anecdote that Nilsen conveys regarding her time in Afghanistan?
- How would you characterize Nilsen's dictionary project? Would you say it's an academic study? A scientific analysis? Something else?

- "Language and society," Nilsen writes, "are as intertwined as a chicken and an egg." What does she mean? Do you agree with her? Why or why not?
- What examples of "Women Are Sexy; Men Are Successful" stand out to you?
- What examples of "Women Are Passive; Men Are Active" do you find convincing or unconvincing?
- Is it true that "Women Are Connected with Negative Connotations; Men with Positive Connotations"? Which examples sway you one way or another?
- How does Nilsen's penultimate paragraph which begins "I embarked on my study . . ." relate to the ideology known as political correctness?
- To what extent is the final paragraph metaphor of "Language is like an X-ray" apt and effective in regard to Nilsen's thesis or main points? To what extent is this an inapt metaphor?
- In the 21st century, the idea of a "1990s update" might strike us as quaint or antiquated. To what extent does this article remain relevant in regard to the American English language in the 21st century? At what specific points does the article or the author's examples strike you as outdated?

## Alleen Pace Nilsen, Sexism in English: Embodiment and Language

During the late 1960s, I lived with my husband and three young children in Kabul, Afghanistan. This was before the Russian invasion, the Afghan civil war, and the eventual taking over of the country by the Taleban Islamic movement and its resolve to return the country to a strict Islamic dynasty, in which females are not allowed to attend school or work outside their homes.

But even when we were there and the country was considered moderate rather than extremist, I was shocked to observe how different were the roles assigned to males and females. The Afghan version of the *chaderi* prescribed for Moslem women was particularly confining. Women in religious families were required to wear it whenever they were outside their family home, with the result being that most of them didn't venture outside.

The household help we hired were made up of men, because women could not be employed by foreigners. Afghan folk stories and jokes were blatantly sexist, as in this proverb: "If you see an old man, sit down and take a lesson; if you see an old woman, throw a stone."

But it wasn't only the native culture that made me question women's roles, it was also the American community within Afghanistan.

Most of the American women were like myself—wives and mothers whose husbands were either career diplomats, employees of USAID, or college professors who had been recruited to work on various contract teams. We were suddenly bereft of our traditional roles. The local economy provided few jobs for women and certainly none for foreigners; we were isolated from former friends and the social goals we had grown up with. Some of us became alcoholics, others got very good at bridge, while still others searched desperately for ways to contribute either to our families or to the Afghans.

When we returned in the fall of 1969 to the University Of Michigan in Ann Arbor, I was surprised to find that many other women were also questioning the expectations they had grown up with. Since I had been an English major when I was in college, I decided that for my part in the feminist movement I could study the English language and see what it could tell me about sexism. I started reading a desk dictionary and making note cards on every entry that seemed to tell something different about male and female. I soon had a dog-eared dictionary, along with a collection of note cards filling two shoe boxes.

The first thing I learned was that I couldn't study the language without getting involved in social issues. Language and society are as intertwined as chicken and an egg. The language a culture uses is telltale evidence of the rules and beliefs of that culture. And because there is a lag in how fast a language changes—new words can easily be introduced, but it takes a long time for old words and usages to disappear—a careful look at English will reveal the attitudes that our ancestors held and that we as a culture are therefore predisposed to hold. My note cards revealed three main points. While friends have offered the opinion that I didn't need to read a dictionary to learn such obvious facts, the linguistic evidence lends credibility to the sociological observations.

## 1. Women Are Sexy; Men Are Successful

First, in American culture a woman is valued for the attractiveness and sexiness of her body, while a man is valued for his physical strength and accomplishments. A woman is sexy. A man is successful.

A persuasive piece of evidence supporting this view are the eponyms—words that have come from someone's name—found in English. I had a two-and-a-half-inch stack of cards taken from men's names but less than a half-inch stack from women's names, and most of those came from Greek mythology. In the words that came into American English since we separated from Britain, there are many eponyms based on the names of famous American men: Bartlett pear, boysenberry, Franklin stove; Ferris wheel, Gatling gun, mason jar, sideburns, sousaphone, Schick test, and Winchester rifle. The only common eponyms that I found taken from American women's names are Alice blue (after Alice Roosevelt Longworth), bloomers (after Amelia Jenks Bloomer), and Mae West jacket (after the buxom actress), Two out of the three feminine eponyms relate closely to a woman's physical anatomy, while the masculine eponyms (except far "sideburns" after General Burnsides) have nothing to do with the namesake's body, but, insead, honor the man for an accomplishment of some kind.

In Greek mythology women played a bigger role than they did in the biblical stories of the Judeo-Christian cultures, and so the names of goddesses are accepted part of the language in such place names as Pomona, from the goddess of fruit, and Athens, from Athens, and in such common words as cereal from Ceres, *psythology* from Psyche, and *arachnoid* from Arachne. However there is the same tendency to think of women inrelation to sexuality as shown through the eponyms "aphrodisiac" from Aphrodite, the Greek name for the goddess of love and beauty, and "venereal disease" from Venus, the Roman name for Aphrodite.

Another interesting word from Greek mythology is *Amazon* According to Greek folk etymology, the *a*-means "without," as in *atypical* or *amoral,* while-*mazon* comes from "mazos," meaning "breast," as still seen in *mastectomy.* In the Greek legend, Amazon women cut off their right breasts so they could better shoot their bows. Apparently, the storytellers had a feeling that for women to play the active, "masculine" role the Amazons adopted for themselves, they had to trade in part of their femininity.

This preoccupation with women's breasts is not limited to the Greeks; it's what inspired the definition and the name for "mammals" (from Indo-European "mammae" for "breasts"). As a volunteer for the University of Wisconsin's *Dictionary of American Regional English* (DARE), I read a western trapper's diary from the 1830s. I was to make notes of any unusual usages or language patterns. My most interesting finding was that the trapper referred to a range of mountains as "The Teats," a metaphor based on the similarity between the shapes of the mountains and women's breasts. Because today we use the French wording "The Grand Tetons" the metaphor isn't as obvious, but I wrote to mapmakers and found the following listings: Nipple Top and Little Nipple Top near Mount Marcy in the Adirondacks; Nipple Mountain in Archuleta County, Colorado; Nipple Peak in Coke County, Texas; Nipple Butte in Pennington, South Dakota; Squaw Peak in Placer County, California (and many other locations); Maiden's Peak and Squaw Tit (they're the same mountain) in the Cascade Range in Oregon; Mary's Nipple near Salt Lake City, Utah; and Jane Russell Peaks near Stark, New Hampshire.

Except for the movie star Jane Russell, the women being referred to are anonymous—it's only a sexual part of their body that is mentioned. When topographical features are named after men, it's probably not going to be to draw attention to a sexual part of their bodies but instead to honor individuals for an accomlishment.

Going back to what I learned from my dictionary cards, I was surprised to realize how many pairs of words we have in which the feminine word has acquired sexual connotations while the masculine word retains a serious businesslike aura. For example, a callboy is the person who calls actors when it is time for them to go on stage, but a callgirl is a prostitute. Compare sir and madam. *Sir* is a term of respect, while *madam* has acquired the specialized meaning of a brothel manager. Something similar has happened to master and mistress. Would you rather have a painting "by an old master" or "by an old mistress"?

It's because the word *woman* had sexual connotations, as in "She's his woman," that people began avoiding its use, hence such terminology as ladies' room, lady of the house, and girl's school or school for young ladies. Those of us who in the 1970s began asking that speakers use the term *women* rather than *girl* or *lady* were rejecting the idea that *woman* is primarily a sexual term.

I found two hundred pairs of words with masculine and feminine forms; for example, *heir-heiress, hero-heroine, steward-stewardess, usher-usherette*. In nearly all such pairs, the masculine word is considered the base, with some kind of a feminine suffix being added. The masculine form is the one from which compounds are made; for example, from king/queen comes kingdom but not queendom, from sportsman/sportslady comes sportsmanship but not sportsladyship. There is one—and only one—semantic area in which the masculine word is not the base or more powerful word. This is in the area dealing with sex, marriage, and motherhood. When someone refers to a virgin, a listener will probably think of a female unless the speaker specifies male or uses a masculine pronoun. The same is true for prostitute.

In relation to marriage, linguistic evidence shows that weddings are more important to women than to men. A woman cherishes the wedding and is considered a bride for a whole year, but a man is referred to as a groom only on the day of the wedding. The word *bride* appears in *bridal attendant, bridal gown, bridesmaid, bridal shower*, and even *bridegroom*. *Groom* comes from the Middle English *grom*, meaning "man," and in that sense is seldom used outside of the wedding. With most pairs of male/female words, people habitually put the masculine word first: *Mr. and Mrs., his and hers, boys and girls, men and women, kings and queens, brothers and sisters, guys and dolls*, and *host and hostess*. But it is the bride and groom who are talked about, not the groom and bride.

The importance of marriage to a woman is also shown by the fact that when a marriage ends in death the woman gets the title of widow. A man gets the derived title of widower. This term is not used in other phrases or contexts, but widow is seen in widowhood, widow's peak, and widow's walk. A widow in a card game is an extra hand of cards, while in typesetting it is a leftover line of type.

Changing cultural ideas bring changes to language, and since I did my dictionary study three decades ago the word *singles* has largely replaced such gender-specific and value-laden terms as *bachelor*, *old maid*, *spinster*, *divorcee*, *widow*, and *widower*. In 1970 I wrote that when people hear a man called "a professional," they visually think of him as a doctor or a lawyer, but when people hear a woman referred to as "a professional," they are likely to think of her as a prostitute. That's not as true today because so many women have become doctors and lawyers, it's no longer incongruous to think of women in those professional roles.

Another change that has taken place is in wedding announcements. They used to be sent out from the bride's parents and did not even give the name of the groom's parents. Today, most couples choose to list either all or none of the parents' names. Also it is now much more likely that both the bride and groom's picture will be in the newspaper, while twenty years ago only the bride's picture was published on the "Women's" or the "Society" page. In the weddings I have recently attended, the official has pronounced the couple "husband and wife" instead of the traditional "man and wife," and the bride has been asked if she promises to "love, honor, and cherish," instead of to "love, honor, and obey."

## 2. Women Are Passive; Men Are Active

However, other wording in the wedding ceremony relates to a second point that my cards showed, which is that women are expected to play a passive or weak role while men plan an active or strong role. In the traditional ceremony, the official asks, "Who gives the bride away?" and the father answers, "I do." Some fathers answer, "Her mother and I do," but that doesn't solve the problem inherent in the question. The idea that a bride is something to be handed over from one man to another bothers people because it goes back to the days when a man's servants, his children, and his wife were all considered to be his property. They were known by his name because they belonged to him, and he was responsible for their actions and their debts.

The grammar used in talking or writing about weddings as well as other sexual relationships shows the expectation of men playing the active role. Men *wed* women while women *become* brides of men. A man possesses a woman; he *deflowers* her; he *performs*; he *scores*; he *takes away* her virginity. Although a woman can *seduce* a man, she cannot offer him her virginity. When talking about virginity, the only way to make the woman the actor in the sentence is to say that "she lost her virginity," but people lose thmgs by accident rather than by purposeful actions, and so she's only the grammatical, not the real-life, actor.

The reason that women brought the term Ms. into the language to replace *Miss* and *Mrs.* relates to this point. Many married women resent being identified in the "Mrs. Husband" form. The dictionary cards showed what appeared to be an attitude on the part of the editors that it was almost indecent to let a respectable woman's name march unaccompanied across the pages of a dictionary. Women were listed with male names whether or not the male contributed to the woman's reason for being in the dictionary or whether or not in his own right he was as famous as the woman. For example:

Charlotte Brontë = Mrs. Arthur B. Nicholls
Amelia Earhart = Mrs. George Palmer Putnam
Helen Hayes = Mrs. Charles MacArthur
Jenny Lind = Mme. Otto Goldschmit

Cornelia Otis Skinner = daughter of Otis
Harriet Beecher Stowe = sister of Henry Ward Beecher
Dame Edith Sitwell = sister of Osbert and Sacheverell

Only a small number of rebels and crusaders got into the dictionary without the benefit of a masculine escort: temperance leaders Frances Elizabeth Caroline Willard and Carry Nation, women's rights leaders Carrie Chapman Catt and Elizabeth Cady Stanton, birth control educator Margaret Sanger, religious leader Mary Baker Eddy, and slaves Harriet Tubman arid Phillis Wheatley.

Etiquette books used to teach that if a woman had Mrs. in front of her name, then the husband's name should follow because Mrs. is an abbreviated form of Mistress and a woman couldn't be a mistress of herself. As with many arguments about "correct" language usage, this isn't very logical because Miss is also an abbreviation of Mistress. Feminists hoped to simplify matters by introducing Ms. as an alternative to both Mrs. and Miss, but what happened is that Ms. largely replaced Miss to become a catch-all business title for women. Many married women still prefer the title Mrs., and some even resent being addressed with the term Ms. As on frustrated newspaper reporter complained, "Before I can write about a woman I have to know not only her marital status but also her political philosophy." The result of such complications may contribute to the demise of titles, which are already being ignored by many writers who find it more efficient to simply use names; for example, in a business letter. "Dear Joan Garcia," instead of "Dear Mrs. Joan Garcia," "Dear Ms. Garcia," or "Dear Mrs. Louis Garcia,"

Titles given to royalty show how males can be disadvantaged by the assumption that they always play the more powerful role. In British royalty, when a male holds a title, his wife is automatically given the feminine equivalent. But the reverse is not true. For example, a count is a high political officer with a countess being his wife. The same pattern holds true for a duke and a duchess and a king and a queen. But when a female holds the royal title, the man she marries does not automatically acquire the matching title. For example, Queen Elizabeth's husband has the title of prince rather than king, but when Prince Charles married Diana, she became Princess Diana. If they had stayed married and he had ascended to the throne, then she would have become Queen Diana. The reasoning appears to be that since masculine words are stronger, they are reserved for true heirs and withheld from males coming into the royal family by marriage. If Prince Phillip were called "King Phillip," British subjects might forget who had inherited the right to rule.

The names that people give their children show the hopes and dreams they have for them, and when we look at the differences between male and female names in a culture, we can see the cumulative expectations of that culture. In our culture girls often have names taken from small, aesthetically pleasing items; for example, Ruby, Jewel, and Pearl. Esther and Stella mean "star," and Ada means "ornament." One of the few women's names that refers to strength is Mildred, and it means "mild strength." Boys often have names with meanings of power and strength; for example, Neil means "champion"; Martin is from Mars, the God of war; Raymond means "wise protection"; Harold means "chief of the army"; Ira means "vigilant"; Rex means "king"; and Richard means "strong king."

We see similar differences in food metaphors. Food is a passive substance just sitting there waiting to be eaten. Many people have recognised this and so no longer feel comfortable describing women as "delectable morsels." However, when I was a teenager, it was considered a compliment to refer to a girl (we didn't call anyone a "woman" until she was middle-aged) as a cute tomato, a peach, a dish, a cookie, honey, sugar, or sweetie-pie. When being affectionate, women will occasionally call a man honey or sweetie, but in general, food metaphors are used much less often with men than with women. If a man is called "a fruit," his masculinity is being questioned. But it's perfectly acceptable to use a food metaphor if the food is heavier and more substantive than that used for women. For example, pin-up pictures of women have long been known as "cheesecake," but when Burt Reynolds posed for a nude centerfold the picture was immediately dubbed "beefcake," that is, a hunk of meat. That such sexual references to men have come into the language is another reflection of how society is beginning to lessen the differences between their attitudes toward men and women.

Something similar to the fruit metaphor happens with references to plants. We insult a man by calling him a "pansy," but it wasn't considered particularly insulting to talk about a girl being a wall-flower, a clinging vine, or a shrinking violet, or to give girls such names as Ivy, Rose, Lily, Iris, Daisy, Camelia, Heather, and Flora. A positive plant metaphor can be used with a man only if the plant is big and strong; for example, Andrew Jackson's nickname of Old Hickory. Also, the phrases *blooming idiots* and *budding geniuses* can be used with either sex, but notice how they are based on the most active thing a plant can do, which is to bloom or bud.

Animal metaphors also illustrate the different expectations for males and females. Men are referred to as studs, bucks, and wolves, while women are referred to with such metaphors as kitten, bunny, beaver, bird, chick, and lamb. In the 1950s we said that boys went "tom catting," but today it's just "catting around," and both boys and girls do it. When the term foxy, meaning that someone was sexy, first became popular it was used only for females, but now someone of either sex can be described as a fox. Some animal metaphors that are used predominantly with men have negative connotations based on the size and/or strength of the animals; for example, beast, bull-headed, jack-ass, rat, loanshark, and vulture. Negative metaphors used with women are based on smaller animals; for example, social butterfly, mousey, catty, and vixen. The feminine terms connote action, but not the same kind of large scale action as with the masculine terms.

### 3. Women Are Connected with Negative Connotations; Men with Positive Connotations

The final point that my note cards illustrated was how many positive connotations are associated with the concept of masculinity, while there are either trivial or negative connotations connected with the corresponding feminine concept. An example from the animal metaphors makes a good illustration. The word *shrew* taken from the name of a small but especially vicious animal was defined in my diction-ary as "an ill-tempered scolding woman," but the word *shrewd* taken from the same foot was defined as "marked by clever discerning awareness" and was illustrated with the phrase "a shrewd businessman."

Early in life, children are conditioned to the superiority of the masculine role. As child psychologists point out, little girls have much more freedom to experiment with sex roles than do little boys. If a little girl acts like a tomboy, most parents have mixed feelings, being at least partially proud. But if their little boy acts like a sissy (derived from *sister*), they call a psy-chologist. It's perfectly acceptable for a little girl to sleep in the crib that was purchased for her brother, to wear his hand-me-down jeans and shirts, and to ride the bicycle that he has outgrown. But few parents would put a boy baby in a white-and-gold crib decorated with frills and lace, and virtually no parents would have their little boy wear his sister's hand-me-down dresses, nor would they have their son ride a girl's pink bicycle with a flower-bedecked basket. The proper names given to girls and boys show this same attitude. Girls can have "boy" names—Cris, Craig, Jo, Kelly, Shawn, Teri, Toni, and Sam—but it doesn't work the other way around. A couple of generations ago, Beverly, Frances, Hazel, Marion, and Shirley were common boys' names. As parents gave these names to more and more girls, they fell into disuse for males, and some older men who have these names prefer to go by their initials or by such abbreviated forms as Haze or Shirl.

When a little girl is told to be a lady, she is being told to sit with her knees together and to be quiet and dainty. But when a little boy is told to be a man, he is being told to be noble, strong, and virtuous—to have all the qualities that the speaker looks on as desirable. The concept of manliness has such positive connotations that it used to be a compliment to call someone a he-man, to say that he was doubly a man. Today many people are more ambivalent about this term and respond to it much as they do to the word *macho*. But calling someone a manly man or a virile man is nearly always meant as a compliment. Virile comes, from the Indo-European *vir*, meaning "man," which is also the basis of *virtuous*. Consider the positive connotations of both virile and virtuous with the negative connotations of hysterical. The Greeks took this latter word from their name for uterus (as still seen in *hysterectomy*). They thought that women were the only ones who experienced uncontrolled emotional outbursts, and so the condition must have something to do with a part of the body that only women have. But how word meanings change is regularly shown at athletic events where thousands of *virtuous* women sit quietly beside their *hysterical* husbands.

Differences in the connotations between positive male and negative female connotations can be seen in several pairs of words that differ denotatively only in the matter of sex. Bachelor as compared to spinster or old maid has such positive connotations that women try to adopt it by using the term *bachelor-girl* or *bachelorette*. Old maid is so negative that it's the basis for metaphors; pretentious, and fussy old men are called "old maids," as are the leftover kernels of unpopped popcorn and the last card in a popular children's card game.

Patron and matron (Middle English for "father" and "mother") have such different levels of prestige that women try to borrow the positive masculine connotations with the word *patroness*, literally "female father." Such a peculiar term came about because of the high prestige attached to patron in such phrases as *a patron of the arts* or *a patron saint*. Matron is more apt to be used in talking about a woman in charge of a jail or a public restroom.

When men are doing jobs that women often do, we apparently try to pay the men extra by giving them fancy titles. For example, a male cook is more likely to be called a "chef" while a male seamstress will get the title of "tailor." The armed forces have a special problem in that they recruit under such slogans as "The Marine Corps builds men!" and "Join the Army! Become a Man." Once the recruits are enlisted, they find themselves doing much of the work that has been traditionally thought of as "women's work." The solution to getting the work done and not insulting anyone's masculinity was to change the titles as shown below:

waitress = orderly
nurse = medic or corpsman
secretary = clerk-typist
assistant = adjutant
dishwasher = KP (kitchen police) or kitchen helper

Compare *brave* and *squaw*. Early settlers in America truly admired Indian men and hence named them with a word that carried connotations of youth, vigor, and courage. But for Indian women they used an Algonquin slang term with negative-sexual connotations that are almost opposite to those of brave. Wizard and witch contrast almost as much. The masculine *wizard* implies skill and wisdom combined with magic, while the feminine *witch* implies evil intentions combined with magic. When witch is used for men, as in witch-doctor, many mainstream speakers feel some carry-over of the negative connotations.

Part of the unattractiveness of both witch and squaw is that they have been used so often to refer to old women, something with which our culture is particularly uncomfortable, just as the Afghans were. Imagine my surprise when I ran across the phrases *grandfatherly advice* and *old wives' tales* and realized that the underlying implication is the same as the Afghan proverb about old men being worth listening to while old women talk only foolishness.

Other terms that show how negatively we view old women as compared to young women are *old nag* as compared to *filly, old crow* or *old bat* as compared to *bird,* and being *catty* as compared to being *kittenish.* There is no matching set of metaphors for men. The chicken metaphor tells the whole story of a woman's life. In her youth she is a chick. Then she marries and begins feathering her nest. Soon she begins feeling cooped up, so she goes to hen parties where she cackles with her friends. Then she has her brood, begins to henpeck her husband, and finally turns into an old biddy.

I embarked on my study of the dictionary not with the intentions of prescribing language change but simply to see what the language would tell me about sexism. Nevertheless; I have been both surprised and pleased as I've watched the changes that have occurred over the past three decades. I'm one of those linguists who believes that new language customs will cause a new generaon of speakers to grow up with different expectations. This is why I'm happy about people's efforts to use inclusive languages, to say "he or she" or "they" when speaking about individuals whose names they do not know. I'm glad that leading publishers have developed guidelines to help writers use language that is fair to both sexes. I'm glad that most newspapers and magazines list women by their own names instead of only by their husbands' names. And am so glad that educated and thoughtful people no longer begin their business letters with "Dear Sir" or "Gentlemen," but instead use a memo form or begin with such salutations as "Dear Colleagues," "Dear Reader," or "Dear Committee Members." I'm also glad that such words as *poetess, authoress, conductress,* and *aviatrix* now sound quaint and old-fashioned and that *chairman* is giving way to *chair* or *head, mailman* to *mail carrier, clergyman* to *clergy,* and *stewardess* to *flight attendant.* I was also pleased when the National Oceanic and Atmospheric Administration bowed to feminist complaints and in the late 70s began to alternate men's and women's names for hurricanes. However, I wasn't so pleased to discover that the change did not immediately erase sexist thoughts from everyone's mind, as shown by a headline about Hurricane David in a 1979 New York tabloid, "David Rapes Virgin Islands." More recently a similar metaphor appeared in a headline in the *Arizona Republic* about Hurricane Charlie, "Charlie Quits Carolinas, Flirts with Virginia."

What these incidents show is that sexism is not something existing independently in American English or in the particular dictionary that I happened to read. Rather, it exists in people's minds. Language is like an X-ray in producing visible evidence of invisible thoughts. The best thing about people being interested in and discussing sexist language is that as they make conscious decisions about what pronouns they will use, what jokes they will tell or laugh at, how they will write their names, or how they will begin their letters, they are forced to think about the underlying issue of sexism. This is good because as a problem that begins in people's assumptions and expectations, it's a problem that will be solved only when a great many people have given it a great deal of thought.

## Questions for Comprehension

*Answer these questions as a comprehension reading quiz and/or for further clarification on the text:*

1. Fill in the blank. In her article, Nilsen writes, "Language is like an X-ray in providing visible evidence of invisible _____."

2. Nilsen quips that her friends told her that she didn't need to read the dictionary in order to ascertain such "obvious facts." What obvious facts does she mean?

3. True/False. Nilsen asserts that there is a cause and effect relationship between language and thoughts. She argues that sexist language causes sexist thinking. Justify your answer.

## Definition of "Politically Correct"

**politically correct**, *adjective*
    : conforming to a belief that language and practices which could offend political sensibilities (as in matters of sex or race) should be eliminated
    political correctness, *noun*
    —Merriam-Webster Dictionary, *www.merriam-webster.com*

## Definition of "Social Justice Warrior"

**"Social Justice Warrior,"** *noun*

1. *Disparaging.* a person who advocates a progressive orthodoxy, often on the Internet, especially involving the treatment of ethnic, racial,gender, or gender-identity minorities. Abbreviation: SJW. Origin of "social justice warrior": 1990–1995
    —*Dictionary.com*

## PC in the Classroom

What obligation do teachers have to use inclusive language and to avoid alienating language? Why is it important, in your view, that they do so? On the other hand, what obligation do teachers have to use language that challenges students into new ways of thinking? If teachers only use "safe" and acceptable language, can that task still be accomplished?

Review the "Our Classroom" statement at the beginning of the textbook. How do the goals and ambitions set forth in that piece of writing tie into the subject of "political correctness"? Is there a difference, in your view, between conversation that goes on in a classroom and conversation that goes on between friends, or between co-workers, or between family members, or between citizens at a public gathering? Does "PC" in the classroom get in the way of real learning? Can it actually enhance the learning environment? Why are words themselves sometimes more important than the intentions behind the words?

## The Importance of Attribution

I favor a form of attribution which places the author's last name first and foremost as the active subject of a sentence. For example, I favor this form of sentence construction: "Taylor deconstructs the political agenda of the academics who lead the movement." I do not favor the following: "The political agenda of the academics who lead the movement is called into question." Who calls it into question? The former sentence is constructed in *active* voice, while the latter is constructed in *passive* voice. George Orwell, by the way, agrees with me on this matter. See his guidelines for better writing in "Politics and the English Language."

Beyond the advantages associated with clear sentence constructions, there are other considerations when it comes to the importance of attribution. In a world of increasing information complexities, it is useful to be able to "attribute" your sources of information as you compose. Can you hear your reader thinking, "Where does he get *that* idea from?" We can also reduce the level of unhelpful emotional response in our audience when we attribute information. Imagine that a friend of mine posts a provocative article or concept on a controversial topic. I disagree with him. Rather than saying, "Hey, I disagree," I write, "That's an interesting perspective. Here a link to an article that I find even more persuasive. There's some pretty solid evidence there, I think. Let me know what you think." (Remember that our hypothetical scenario here takes place online. I'm not modeling formal composition.)

You are probably familiar, at least on an introductory level, with citation and documentation requirements, that is, with the need to cite your sources and document those sources with a full bibliographic entry at the end of your paper. This source list is called a "Works Cited" page in Modern Language Association (MLA) format. Other academic or professional styles may call this page a "Bibliography."

*Attribution* is different from bibliographic documentation. Attribution takes place within your actual sentences. Attribution is a skill that is distinct from citation as well. While citation is associated most closely with quotation, attribution is linked more closely with paraphrase (restating someone else's words or concept in your own words). When you need to convey a great deal of information in limited space, attribution can help. For example:

> Knobel and Lankshear argue that developing new teaching strategies to address a wide range of emerging digital literacies should be a primary goal in secondary education.

I have attributed the argument to the authors Knobel and Lankshear. My reader, if he or she chooses, can go to my Works Cited page to view the full bibliographic information. Since I am paraphrasing an entire claim rather than quoting specific language or identifying a particular detail from their text, I do not need to cite a specific page number. If I wanted to paraphrase a detail, I would attribute and cite too:

> Knobel and Lankshear claim that the emphasis on single authorship and the production of so-called "original" work does not recognize or value the practice of remixing items to produce valuable new cultural creations (99).

Here I am paraphrasing a specific point, so I must cite page 99. Again, if my reader is interested, he or she can go to the Works Cited page in order to find the information necessary to track down the article.

Oftentimes, attributions like the ones above can be used as topic sentences in order to indicate the organization of the paragraph to follow. The job of focusing and informing your outside reader becomes more manageable with clear attribution strategies.

Take a moment to notice the actual content—the meaning—of the latter attribution example above. The Knobel and Lankshear article is cited under the Unit Four "Further Inquiry & Research" bibliography. The specific point regarding the authors' skepticism toward the emphasis on the production of "original" work might strike you as ironic coming in a section on the importance of source attribution. It is true, in my opinion, that schools, colleges, and universities do not necessarily value the necessary process of emulation and blending as a positive aspect of creativity and cultural contribution. Sometimes, these institutions and the instructors in these institutions label such efforts as "plagiarism." Besides the benefits of attribution mentioned above, here's another benefit: proper attribution protects you from charges of stealing, unfairly co-opting, or improperly appropriating the work of others. With attribution, you subtly inform your reader that you are making the insightful connections which form the foundation of cognition and creativity.

# George Orwell, "Politics and the English Language" (1946)

What would George Orwell have thought of "political correctness"?

In fact, we cannot know what British novelist and political activist Eric Blair (George Orwell was his penname) would have thought of "political correctness." "PC" didn't exist in its current iteration until long after his passing, so we cannot claim that Orwell is concerned with "political correctness" at all.

Orwell would have associated the term "political correctness" with the political oppressions of Stalinist Communism. It is very clear, though, to anyone who has studied Orwell's life and his literary work that he was fascinated by the connections between social ideology, personal thought, and language. Modern day "PC" draws our attention to these same connections.

Orwell's premise that language is an "instrument which we shape for our own purposes" and his plea for us to avoid the "vagueness and sheer incompetence" which is "the most marked characteristic of modern English prose, and especially of any kind of political writing" clearly reveals an attentiveness to the subtleties and impact of language that is a common concern of those who insist on the use of "politically correct" language in public discourse.

As a writer, Orwell understood the power of language. The iconic dystopia he created in his novel *1984* (written in 1948, published in 1949) reveals not only the political omnipotence of the authoritarian state called "Big Brother" but also speaks to how the authoritarian state wields public discourse as a mechanism of political control. If the state controls the language, then the state controls the thoughts of its citizenry as well. Or so *1984* warns us. Big Brother uses "Doublespeak" language as a weaponized tool of thought control in *1984*.

Clearly, one tenet of the "politically correct" movement rests upon the belief that language, as Orwell writes, is an "instrument which we shape for our own purposes." A corollary premise of "political correctness" involves the concept that people's word choices reveal their attitudes, both conscious and unconscious. As you have seen, Alleen Pace Nilsen has a great deal to say on this matter in her essay "Sexism in English: A 1990s Update."

"Politically correct" is an adjective that means, according to *Merriam-Webster.com*, "conforming to a belief that language and practices which could offend political sensibilities (as in matters of sex or race) should be eliminated."

The idea of "eliminating" any sort of language may have disturbed Orwell. We can't know what he would have thought. We can only speculate.

Orwell's well-known essay "Politics and the English Language" draws a direct connection between thought and language. Such a belief in the connection of thought, language, and cultural values is a hallmark of political correctness as well as second wave feminism.

Orwell was acutely sensitive to the power of language in public discourse. He calls for people to take control of their language. He argues that the English language becomes "ugly and inaccurate because our thoughts are foolish, but the slovenliness of our language makes it easier for us to have foolish thoughts." In other words, sloppy thought processes produce sloppy language even while sloppy language makes it easy for us to engage in sloppy thought processes. Pause a moment to consider what Orwell is claiming here. We need to be careful in our use of language, Orwell warns us, or we risk becoming fools who are in the habit of indulging foolish thoughts. It's really a profound declaration. Would Orwell agree with the notion, *You are the language that you use*?

Orwell tells us that political language covers up the truth more often than it reveals the truth. Anyone who listens closely to most presidential candidates can agree with that assertion. He also tells us that "it is broadly true that political writing is bad writing." But if that's the case, then why are we so often so deeply moved by the oratory of these same politicians?

Finally, Orwell argues that you can improve your writing. He even offers specific tips. Pay attention. More than seventy years after he created this list, most American newspaper and magazine editors continue to demand that their writers follow Orwell's advice. It's amazing when you step back to think about it. Look at his specific tips and do please get rid of your clunky adverbs, but don't miss the subtext either. Orwell is saying, Get the unnecessary words out of the way so that we can read what you are *really thinking*. Good advice.

## Drawing Synthetic Connections

How does Alleen Pace Nilsen's observation that "Language is like an X-ray in providing visible evidence of invisible thoughts" align with George Orwell's concept that "the slovenliness of our language makes it easier for us to have foolish thoughts"?

## Questions to Consider

*Answer these questions as you read and annotate the text:*

- How does Orwell persuade you, or fail to persuade you, that language is "an instrument which we shape for our own purposes"?
- Who develops language, individuals or the society? Do individuals control language, according to Orwell?
- What are the two most grievous faults of modern writing, according to Orwell? Do you believe that these same faults apply to contemporary 21st century prose?
- Orwell covers some technical matters of usage, grammar, and syntax. Which technical details make sense to you? Which leave you confused?
- Note the examples Orwell cites of "meaningless words." What 21st century examples of meaningless words would you add to his list and why?
- What is the point of Orwell's reiteration of the Biblical passage from *Ecclesiastes*? Does his point seem relevant to you in the 21st century? Why or why not?
- What is wrong, in Orwell's opinion, with "gumming together long strips of words which have already been set in order by someone else"?
- What is wrong, in Orwell's view, with a cliché like "leave no stone unturned"? How difficult is it to avoid such clichés, in your experience?
- Restate the elementary rules of better prose which Orwell enumerates. Which of these do you understand, and which require the clarification of your instructor?
- To what extent does Orwell's plea for you to use the "correct" words bear any relevance to the mandate of "political correctness" that we should find the "correct" word and avoid "incorrect" words that may cause offense?

## George Orwell, Politics and the English Language

Most people who bother with the matter at all would admit that the English language is in a bad way, but it is generally assumed that we cannot by conscious action do anything about it. Our civilization is decadent and our language—so the argument runs—must inevitably share in the general collapse. It follows that any struggle against the abuse of language is a sentimental archaism, like preferring candles to electric light or hansom cabs to aeroplanes. Underneath this lies the half-conscious belief that language is a natural growth and not an instrument which we shape for our own purposes.

Now, it is clear that the decline of a language must ultimately have political and economic causes: it is not due simply to the bad influence of this or that individual writer. But an effect can become a cause, reinforcing the original cause and producing the same effect in an intensified form, and so on indefinitely. A man may take to drink because he feels himself to be a failure, and then fail all the more completely because he drinks. It is rather the same thing that is happening to the English language. It becomes ugly and inaccurate because our thoughts are foolish, but the slovenliness of our language makes it easier for us to have foolish thoughts. The point is that the process is reversible. Modern English, especially written English, is full of bad habits which spread by imitation and which can be avoided if one is willing to take the necessary trouble. If one gets rid of these habits one can think more clearly, and to think clearly is a necessary first step toward political regeneration: so that the fight against bad English is not frivolous and is not the exclusive concern of professional writers. I will come back to this presently, and I hope that by that time the meaning of what I have said here will have become clearer. Meanwhile, here are five specimens of the English language as it is now habitually written.

These five passages have not been picked out because they are especially bad—I could have quoted far worse if I had chosen—but because they illustrate various of the mental vices from which we now suffer. They are a little below the average, but are fairly representative examples. I number them so that I can refer back to them when necessary:

1. I am not, indeed, sure whether it is not true to say that the Milton who once seemed not unlike a seventeenth-century Shelley had not become, out of an experience ever more bitter in each year, more alien *[sic]* to the founder of that Jesuit sect which nothing could induce him to tolerate. Professor Harold Laski (Essay in *Freedom of Expression*)

2. Above all, we cannot play ducks and drakes with a native battery of idioms which prescribes egregious collocations of vocables as the Basic *put up with* for *tolerate*, or *put at a loss* for *bewilder*. Professor Lancelot Hogben (*Interglossia*)

3. On the one side we have the free personality: by definition it is not neurotic, for it has neither conflict nor dream. Its desires, such as they are, are transparent, for they are just what institutional approval keeps in the forefront of consciousness; another institutional pattern would alter their number and intensity; there is little in them that is natural, irreducible, or culturally dangerous. But *on the other side*, the social bond itself is nothing but the mutual reflection of these self-secure integrities. Recall the definition of love. Is not this the very picture of a small academic? Where is there a place in this hall of mirrors for either personality or fraternity? Essay on psychology in *Politics* (New York)

4. All the 'best people' from the gentlemen's clubs, and all the frantic fascist captains, united in common hatred of Socialism and bestial horror at the rising tide of the mass revolutionary movement,

have turned to acts of provocation, to foul incendiarism, to medieval legends of poisoned wells, to legalize their own destruction of proletarian organizations, and rouse the agitated petty-bourgeoise to chauvinistic fervor on behalf of the fight against the revolutionary way out of the crisis.
    Communist pamphlet

5. If a new spirit is to be infused into this old country, there is one thorny and contentious reform which must be tackled, and that is the humanization and galvanization of the B.B.C. Timidity here will bespeak canker and atrophy of the soul. The heart of Britain may be sound and of strong beat, for instance, but the British lion's roar at present is like that of Bottom in Shakespeare's *A Midsummer Night's Dream*—as gentle as any sucking dove. A virile new Britain cannot continue indefinitely to be traduced in the eyes or rather ears, of the world by the effete languors of Langham Place, brazenly masquerading as 'standard English'. When the Voice of Britain is heard at nine o'clock, better far and infinitely less ludicrous to hear aitches honestly dropped than the present priggish, inflated, inhibited, school-ma'amish arch braying of blameless bashful mewing maidens!
    Letter in *Tribune*

Each of these passages has faults of its own, but, quite apart from avoidable ugliness, two qualities are common to all of them. The first is staleness of imagery; the other is lack of precision. The writer either has a meaning and cannot express it, or he inadvertently says something else, or he is almost indifferent as to whether his words mean anything or not. This mixture of vagueness and sheer incompetence is the most marked characteristic of modern English prose, and especially of any kind of political writing. As soon as certain topics are raised, the concrete melts into the abstract and no one seems able to think of turns of speech that are not hackneyed: prose consists less and less of *words* chosen for the sake of their meaning, and more and more of *phrases* tacked together like the sections of a prefabricated hen-house. I list below, with notes and examples, various of the tricks by means of which the work of prose-construction is habitually dodged.

DYING METAPHORS. A newly invented metaphor assists thought by evoking a visual image, while on the other hand a metaphor which is technically 'dead' (e. g. iron resolution) has in effect reverted to being an ordinary word and can generally be used without loss of vividness. But in between these two classes there is a huge dump of worn-out metaphors which have lost all evocative power and are merely used because they save people the trouble of inventing phrases for themselves. Examples are: *Ring the changes on, take up the cudgel for, toe the line, ride roughshod over, stand shoulder to shoulder with, play into the hands of, no axe to grind, grist to the mill, fishing in troubled waters, on the order of the day, Achilles' heel, swan song, hotbed.* Many of these are used without knowledge of their meaning (what is a 'rift', for instance?), and incompatible metaphors are frequently mixed, a sure sign that the writer is not interested in what he is saying. Some metaphors now current have been twisted out of their original meaning without those who use them even being aware of the fact. For example, *toe the line* is sometimes written as *tow the line*. Another example is *the hammer and the anvil*, now always used with the implication that the anvil gets the worst of it. In real life it is always the anvil that breaks the hammer, never the other way about: a writer who stopped to think what he was saying would avoid perverting the original phrase.

OPERATORS OR VERBAL FALSE LIMBS. These save the trouble of picking out appropriate verbs and nouns, and at the same time pad each sentence with extra syllables which give it an appearance of symmetry. Characteristic phrases are *render inoperative, militate against, make contact with, be subjected to, give rise to, give grounds for, have the effect of, play a leading part (role) in, make itself felt, take effect, exhibit a tendency to, serve the purpose of*, etc., etc. The keynote is the elimination of simple verbs. Instead of being a single word, such as *break, stop, spoil, mend, kill*, a verb becomes a *phrase*, made up of a noun or adjective tacked on to some general-purpose verb such as *prove, serve, form, play, render*. In addition, the passive voice is wherever possible used in preference to the active, and noun constructions are used instead of gerunds (*by examination of* instead of *by examining*). The range of verbs is further cut down by means of the *-ize* and *de-* formations, and the banal statements are given an appearance of profundity by means of the *not un-* formation. Simple conjunctions and prepositions are replaced by such phrases as *with respect to, having regard to, the fact that, by dint of, in view of, in the interests of, on the hypothesis that*; and the ends of sentences are saved by anticlimax by such resounding commonplaces as *greatly to be desired, cannot be left out of account, a development to be expected in the near future, deserving of serious consideration, brought to a satisfactory conclusion*, and so on and so forth.

PRETENTIOUS DICTION. Words like *phenomenon, element, individual (as noun), objective, categorical, effective, virtual, basic, primary, promote, constitute, exhibit, exploit, utilize, eliminate, liquidate*, are used to dress up a simple statement and give an air of scientific impartiality to biased judgements. Adjectives like *epoch-making, epic, historic, unforgettable, triumphant, age-old, inevitable, inexorable, veritable*, are used to dignify the sordid process of international politics, while writing that aims at glorifying war usually takes on an archaic colour, its characteristic words being: *realm, throne, chariot, mailed fist, trident, sword, shield, buckler, banner, jackboot, clarion*. Foreign words and expressions such as *cul de sac, ancien regime, deus ex machina, mutatis mutandis, status quo, gleichschaltung, weltanschauung*, are used to give an air of culture and elegance. Except for the useful abbreviations *i. e., e. g.* and *etc.*, there is no real need for any of the hundreds of foreign phrases now current in the English language. Bad writers, and especially scientific, political, and sociological writers, are nearly always haunted by the notion that Latin or Greek words are grander than Saxon ones, and unnecessary words like *expedite, ameliorate, predict, extraneous, deracinated, clandestine, subaqueous*, and hundreds of others constantly gain ground from their Anglo-Saxon numbers(1). The jargon peculiar to Marxist writing (*hyena, hangman, cannibal, petty bourgeois, these gentry, lackey, flunkey, mad dog, White Guard*, etc.) consists largely of words translated from Russian, German, or French; but the normal way of coining a new word is to use Latin or Greek root with the appropriate affix and, where necessary, the size formation. It is often easier to make up words of this kind (*deregionalize, impermissible, extramarital, non-fragmentary* and so forth) than to think up the English words that will cover one's meaning. The result, in general, is an increase in slovenliness and vagueness.

MEANINGLESS WORDS. In certain kinds of writing, particularly in art criticism and literary criticism, it is normal to come across long passages which are almost completely lacking in meaning(2). Words like *romantic, plastic, values, human, dead, sentimental, natural, vitality*, as used in art criticism, are strictly meaningless, in the sense that they not only do not point to any discoverable object, but are hardly ever expected to do so by the reader. When one critic writes, 'The outstanding feature of Mr. X's work is its living quality', while another writes, 'The immediately striking thing about Mr. X's work is its peculiar deadness', the reader accepts this as a simple difference opinion. If words like *black* and *white* were involved, instead of the jargon words *dead* and *living*, he would see at once that language was being used in an improper way. Many political words are similarly abused. The word *Fascism* has now no meaning except in so far as it signifies 'something not desirable'. The words *democracy, socialism, freedom, patriotic, realistic, justice* have each of them several different meanings which cannot be reconciled with one another. In the case of a word like *democracy*, not only is there no agreed definition, but the attempt to make one is resisted from all sides. It is almost universally felt that when we call a country democratic we are praising it: consequently the defenders of every kind of regime claim that it is a democracy, and fear that they might have to stop using that word if it were tied down to any one meaning. Words of this kind are often used in a consciously dishonest way. That is, the person who uses them has his own private definition, but allows his hearer to think he means something quite different. Statements like *Marshal Petain was a true patriot, The Soviet press is the freest in the world, The Catholic Church is opposed to persecution,* are almost always made with intent to deceive. Other words used in variable meanings, in most cases more or less dishonestly, are: *class, totalitarian, science, progressive, reactionary, bourgeois, equality.*

Now that I have made this catalogue of swindles and perversions, let me give another example of the kind of writing that they lead to. This time it must of its nature be an imaginary one. I am going to translate a passage of good English into modern English of the worst sort. Here is a well-known verse from *Ecclesiastes*:

I returned and saw under the sun, that the race is not to the swift, nor the battle to the strong, neither yet bread to the wise, nor yet riches to men of understanding, nor yet favour to men of skill; but time and chance happeneth to them all.

Here it is in modern English:

Objective considerations of contemporary phenomena compel the conclusion that success or failure in competitive activities exhibits no tendency to be commensurate with innate capacity, but that a considerable element of the unpredictable must invariably be taken into account.

This is a parody, but not a very gross one. Exhibit (3) above, for instance, contains several patches of the same kind of English. It will be seen that I have not made a full translation. The beginning and ending of the sentence follow the original meaning fairly closely, but in the middle the concrete illustrations—race, battle, bread—dissolve into the vague phrases 'success or failure in competitive activities'. This had to be so, because no modern writer of the kind I am discussing—no one capable of using phrases like 'objective considerations of contemporary phenomena'—would ever tabulate his thoughts in that precise and detailed way. The whole tendency of modern prose is away from concreteness. Now analyze these two sentences a little more closely. The first contains forty-nine words but only sixty syllables, and all its words are those of everyday life. The second contains thirty-eight words of ninety syllables: eighteen of those words are from Latin roots, and one from Greek. The first sentence contains six vivid images, and only one phrase ('time and chance') that could be called vague. The second contains not a single fresh, arresting phrase, and in spite of its ninety syllables it gives only a shortened version of the meaning contained in the first. Yet without a doubt it is the second kind of sentence that is gaining ground in modern English. I do not want to exaggerate. This kind of writing is not yet universal, and outcrops of simplicity will occur here and there in the worst-written page. Still, if you or I were told to write a few lines on the uncertainty of human fortunes, we should probably come much nearer to my imaginary sentence than to the one from *Ecclesiastes*.

As I have tried to show, modern writing at its worst does not consist in picking out words for the sake of their meaning and inventing images in order to make the meaning clearer. It consists in gumming together long strips of words which have already been set in order by someone else, and making the results presentable by sheer humbug. The attraction of this way of writing is that it is easy. It is easier—even quicker, once you have the habit—to say *In my opinion it is not an unjustifiable assumption that* than to say *I think*. If you use ready-made phrases, you not only don't have to hunt about for the words; you also don't have to bother with the rhythms of your sentences since these phrases are generally so arranged as to be more or less euphonious. When you are composing in a hurry—when you are dictating to a stenographer, for instance, or making a public speech—it is natural to fall into a pretentious, Latinized style. Tags like *a consideration which we should do well to bear in mind* or *a conclusion to which all of us would readily assent* will save many a sentence from coming down with a bump. By using stale metaphors, similes, and idioms, you save much mental effort, at the cost of leaving your meaning vague, not only for your reader but for yourself. This is the significance of mixed metaphors. The sole aim of a metaphor is to call up a visual image. When these images clash—as in *The Fascist octopus has sung its swan song, the jackboot is thrown into the melting pot*—it can be taken as certain that the writer is not seeing a mental image of the objects he is naming; in other words he is not really thinking. Look again at the examples I gave at the beginning of this essay. Professor Laski (1) uses five negatives in fifty three words. One of these is superfluous, making nonsense of the whole passage, and in addition there is the slip—*alien* for akin—making further nonsense, and several avoidable pieces of clumsiness which increase the general vagueness. Professor Hogben (2) plays ducks and drakes with a battery which is able to write prescriptions, and, while disapproving of the everyday phrase *put up with*, is unwilling to look *egregious* up in the dictionary and see what it means; (3), if one takes an uncharitable attitude towards it, is simply meaningless: probably one could work out its intended meaning by reading the whole of the article in which it occurs. In (4), the writer knows more or less what he wants to say, but an accumulation of stale phrases chokes him like tea leaves blocking a sink. In (5), words and meaning have almost parted company. People who write in this manner usually have a general emotional meaning—they dislike one thing and want to express solidarity with another—but they are not interested in the detail of what they are saying. A scrupulous writer, in every sentence that he writes, will ask himself at least four questions, thus: What am I trying to say? What words will express it? What image or idiom will make it clearer? Is this image fresh enough to have an effect? And he will probably ask himself two more: Could I put it more shortly? Have I said anything that is avoidably ugly? But you are not obliged to go to all this trouble. You can shirk it by simply throwing your mind open and letting the ready-made phrases come crowding in. The will construct your sentences for you—even think your thoughts for you, to a certain extent—and at need they will perform the important service of partially concealing your meaning even from yourself. It is at this point that the special connection between politics and the debasement of language becomes clear.

In our time it is broadly true that political writing is bad writing. Where it is not true, it will generally be found that the writer is some kind of rebel, expressing his private opinions and not a 'party line'. Orthodoxy, of whatever colour, seems to demand a lifeless, imitative style. The political dialects to be found in pamphlets, leading articles, manifestos, White papers and the speeches of undersecretaries do, of course, vary from party to party, but they are all alike in that one almost never finds in them a fresh, vivid, homemade turn of speech. When one watches some tired hack on the platform mechanically repeating the familiar phrases—*bestial, atrocities, iron heel, bloodstained tyranny, free peoples of the world, stand shoulder to shoulder*—one often has a curious feeling that one is not watching a live human being but some kind of dummy: a feeling which suddenly becomes stronger at moments when the light catches the speaker's spectacles and turns them into blank discs which seem to have no eyes behind them. And this is not altogether fanciful. A speaker who uses that kind of phraseology has gone some distance toward turning himself into a machine. The appropriate noises are coming out of his larynx, but his brain is not involved, as it would be if he were choosing his words for himself. If the speech he is making is one that he is accustomed to make over and over again, he may be almost unconscious of what he is saying, as one is when one utters the responses in church. And this reduced state of consciousness, if not indispensable, is at any rate favourable to political conformity.

In our time, political speech and writing are largely the defence of the indefensible. Things like the continuance of British rule in India, the Russian purges and deportations, the dropping of the atom bombs on Japan, can indeed be defended, but only by arguments which are too brutal for most people to face, and which do not square with the professed aims of the political parties. Thus political language has to consist largely of euphemism, question-begging and sheer cloudy vagueness. Defenceless villages are bombarded from the air, the inhabitants driven out into the countryside, the cattle machine-gunned, the huts set on fire with incendiary bullets: this is called *pacification*. Millions of peasants are robbed of their farms and sent trudging along the roads with no more than they can carry: this is called *transfer of population* or *rectification of frontiers*. People are imprisoned for years without trial, or shot in the back of the neck or sent to die of scurvy in Arctic lumber camps: this is called *elimination of unreliable elements*. Such phraseology is needed if one wants to name things without calling up mental pictures of them. Consider for instance some comfortable English professor defending Russian totalitarianism. He cannot say outright, 'I believe in killing off your opponents when you can get good results by doing so'. Probably, therefore, he will say something like this:

'While freely conceding that the Soviet regime exhibits certain features which the humanitarian may be inclined to deplore, we must, I think, agree that a certain curtailment of the right to political opposition is an unavoidable concomitant of transitional periods, and that the rigors which the Russian people have been called upon to undergo have been amply justified in the sphere of concrete achievement.'

The inflated style itself is a kind of euphemism. A mass of Latin words falls upon the facts like soft snow, blurring the outline and covering up all the details. The great enemy of clear language is insincerity. When there is a gap between one's real and one's declared aims, one turns as it were instinctively to long words and exhausted idioms, like a cuttlefish spurting out ink. In our age there is no such thing as 'keeping out of politics'. All issues are political issues, and politics itself is a mass of lies, evasions, folly, hatred, and schizophrenia. When the general atmosphere is bad, language must suffer. I should expect to find—this is a guess which I have not sufficient knowledge to verify—that the German, Russian and Italian languages have all deteriorated in the last ten or fifteen years, as a result of dictatorship.

But if thought corrupts language, language can also corrupt thought. A bad usage can spread by tradition and imitation even among people who should and do know better. The debased language that I have been discussing is in some ways very convenient. Phrases like *a not unjustifiable assumption, leaves much to be desired, would serve no good purpose, a consideration which we should do well to bear in mind,* are a continuous temptation, a packet of aspirins always at one's elbow. Look back through this essay, and for certain you will find that I have again and again committed the very faults I am protesting against. By this morning's post I have received a pamphlet dealing with conditions in Germany. The author tells me that he 'felt impelled' to write it. I open it at random, and here is almost the first sentence I see: '[The Allies] have an opportunity not only of achieving a radical transformation of Germany's social and political structure in such a way as to avoid a nationalistic reaction in Germany itself, but at the same time of laying the foundations of a co-operative and unified Europe.' You see, he 'feels impelled' to write—feels, presumably, that he has something new to say—and yet his words, like cavalry horses answering the bugle, group themselves automatically into the familiar dreary pattern. This invasion of one's mind by ready-made phrases (*lay the foundations, achieve a radical transformation*) can only be prevented if one is constantly on guard against them, and every such phrase anaesthetizes a portion of one's brain.

I said earlier that the decadence of our language is probably curable. Those who deny this would argue, if they produced an argument at all, that language merely reflects existing social conditions, and that we cannot influence its development by any direct tinkering with words and constructions. So far as the general tone or spirit of a language goes, this may be true, but it is not true in detail. Silly words and expressions have often disappeared, not through any evolutionary process but owing to the conscious action of a minority. Two recent examples were *explore every avenue* and *leave no stone unturned*, which were killed by the jeers of a few journalists. There is a long list of flyblown metaphors which could similarly be got rid of if enough people would interest themselves in the job; and it should also be possible to laugh the *not un-* formation out of existence (3), to reduce the amount of Latin and Greek in the average sentence, to drive out foreign phrases and strayed scientific words, and, in general, to make pretentiousness unfashionable. But all these are minor points. The defence of the English language implies more than this, and perhaps it is best to start by saying what it *does not* imply.

To begin with it has nothing to do with archaism, with the salvaging of obsolete words and turns of speech, or with the setting up of a 'standard English' which must never be departed from. On the contrary, it is especially concerned with the scrapping of every word or idiom which has outworn its usefulness. It has nothing to do with correct grammar and syntax, which are of no importance so long as one makes one's meaning clear, or with the avoidance of Americanisms, or with having what is called a 'good prose style'. On the other hand, it is not concerned with fake simplicity and the attempt to make written English colloquial. Nor does it even imply in every case preferring the Saxon word to the Latin one, though it does imply using the fewest and shortest words that will cover one's meaning. What is above all needed is to let the meaning choose the word, and not the other way around. In prose, the worst thing one can do with words is surrender to them. When you think of a concrete object, you think wordlessly, and then, if you want to describe the thing you have been visualising you probably hunt about until you find the exact words that seem to fit it. When you think of something abstract you are more inclined to use words from the start, and unless you make a conscious effort to prevent it, the existing dialect will come rushing in and do the job for you, at the expense of blurring or even changing your meaning. Probably it is better to put off using words as long as possible and get one's meaning as clear as one can through pictures and sensations. Afterward one can choose—not simply *accept*—the phrases that will best cover the meaning, and then switch round and decide what impressions one's words are likely to make on another person. This last effort of the mind cuts out all stale or mixed images, all prefabricated phrases, needless repetitions, and humbug and vagueness generally. But one can often be in doubt about the effect of a word or a phrase, and one needs rules that one can rely on when instinct fails. I think the following rules will cover most cases:

1. Never use a metaphor, simile, or other figure of speech which you are used to seeing in print.
2. Never use a long word where a short one will do.
3. If it is possible to cut a word out, always cut it out.
4. Never use the passive where you can use the active.
5. Never use a foreign phrase, a scientific word, or a jargon word if you can think of an everyday English equivalent.
6. Break any of these rules sooner than say anything outright barbarous.

These rules sound elementary, and so they are, but they demand a deep change of attitude in anyone who has grown used to writing in the style now fashionable. One could keep all of them and still write bad English, but one could not write the kind of stuff that I quoted in those five specimens at the beginning of this article.

I have not here been considering the literary use of language, but merely language as an instrument for expressing and not for concealing or preventing thought. Stuart Chase and others have come near to claiming that all abstract words are meaningless, and have used this as a pretext for advocating a kind of political quietism. Since you don't know what Fascism is, how can you struggle against Fascism? One need not swallow such absurdities as this, but one ought to recognise that the present political chaos is connected with the decay of language, and that one can probably bring about some improvement by starting at the verbal end. If you simplify your English, you are freed from the worst follies of orthodoxy. You cannot speak any of the necessary dialects, and when you make a stupid remark its stupidity will be obvious, even to yourself. Political language—and with variations this is true of all political parties, from Conservatives to Anarchists—is designed to make lies sound truthful and murder respectable, and to give an appearance of solidity to pure wind. One cannot change this all in a moment, but one can at least change one's own habits, and from time to time one can even, if one jeers loudly enough, send some worn-out and useless phrase— some *jackboot, Achilles' heel, hotbed, melting pot, acid test, veritable inferno,* or other lump of verbal refuse— into the dustbin where it belongs.

1946

# Questions for Comprehension

*Answer these questions as a comprehension reading quiz and/or for further clarification on the text:*

1. True/False. Orwell selects five sample passages in order to exemplify what he considers to be top-notch political writing.

2. Fill in the Blank. "A man may take to drink because he feels himself to be a failure, and then fail all the more completely because he _____."

3. Examine the first paragraph of the essay. What phrase or rhetorical device allows us to recognize that Orwell does not believe that "we cannot by conscious action do anything about [the decline of language]"?

4. Which are better to use in good writing, according to Orwell, concrete words or abstract words?

5. Use one of Orwell's elementary rules of good writing to improve the following vague sentence: *The populace was relocated using available routes.*

# The "N" Word

In 1993, comedian and political commentator Bill Maher named his long-running talk show *Politically Incorrect* with an understanding that virtually no one will step forward to defend the idea of "PC." The white comedian stirred outrage in 2017 for his use of the "n" word in a joke he made on his talk show *Real Time*, the successor to his show *Politically Incorrect*. Maher apologized for his insensitive, impromptu joke. (A guest on the show was lauding the merits of hard work in the field when Maher said he did not want to work in the field because he's a "house n****.") The outrage that followed furthered a discourse in which black artists and intellectuals defend their own re-appropriation of the "n" word while indicating that white artists may not do so. African American rap star and actor Ice Cube told Maher in an interview following the incident, "You can use [the "n" word] as a weapon, or you can use it as a tool. It's been used as a weapon against us by white people, and we [are] not going to let that happen again. . .. It's in the lexicon . . . but that's our word now, that's our word now, and you can't have it back." Ice Cube explained, "When I hear my homies say it, it don't feel like venom. When I hear white people say it, it feel like that knife stabbing, even if they don't mean it."

Other prominent black Americans have called for the elimination of the word even within African American communities, saying that artists who appropriate or co-opt the word display a lack of understanding of the word's hateful history. The origins of the word aren't completely understood or agreed upon. One explanation indicates that it comes from the Latinate verb "denigrate," which means literally "to blacken." A more straightforward etymology involves the Latin *niger*, meaning "black." There could also be connections to the great African river called the Niger. "Niger" itself may have developed initially in English as a descriptive term rather than a derogatory term.

African-American intellectual W.E.B. Du Bois foretold in his 1903 volume *The Souls of Black Folk* that "the problem of the Twentieth Century is the problem of the color line." He repeats his claim almost as a mantra throughout his text. Du Bois confronts the "n" word directly. The origin and history of the offensive word are inextricably entwined with the ugliness and brutality of American slavery, he tells us. The word, like the institution of slavery, sought to dehumanize an entire race and class of people who fueled America's 18th and 19th century economies. Du Bois recounts the history of free "people of color" who could not gain mainstream acceptance nor control of the language used to describe themselves. Leaders like Du Bois and Booker T. Washington strived to supplant the hateful "n" word with the more respectful term "Negro," which came into mainstream use through the 20th century Civil Rights Era. You will hear this word used in the works of Dr. Martin Luther King, Jr., for example. "Negro" is now an antiquated and even offensive term. Under "Further Inquiry & Research," you can find the citation for a 1967 *Ebony* magazine article that partakes in a heated public discourse over the terms "Negro," "Afro-American," and "Black." We know now that "African American" has come into mainstream use while "black" is also considered an acceptable, respectful term in most circumstances.

## Take Control of Your Curriculum

What can you find out regarding the history and controversy surrounding the hateful "n" word? Is it acceptable for rappers to co-opt the term and re-introduce it to the mainstream? (Is it acceptable for white rappers to co-opt the term?) Should the word be abolished completely? How has the word been used as a weapon of oppression? What is the effect on people resulting from the use of this word? What effects can language alone exact on the mind and the body?

If these are matters of interest or personal concern to you, propose a formal essay assignment to your instructor. Clarify the topic in writing and specify all parameters, including required source materials and length requirements. Present a formal proposal to your instructor and see if he or she is open to the topic. As you realize, there is a high level of sensitivity surrounding the use of socially unacceptable language in writing, in public discourse, and in the classroom, so this topic may strike some teachers and administrators as inappropriate. Be circumspect in your approach to this topic. As a teacher, I can imagine a variety of valid reasons why and how this topic could prove too problematic for an introductory composition course. In a single divisive word, we see a history of hate and oppression. Some black artists see in that word strength and resurgence. Public discourse on such a controversial topic must be undertaken with care and thoughtfulness.

# Jonathan Chait, "Not a Very P.C. Thing to Say: How the Language Police Are Perverting Liberalism" (2015)

Condemnation of "political correctness" is not new. In a 1991 article that appeared in *New York* magazine, contributing editor John Taylor expresses his skepticism. For Taylor, common sense has been left behind when it comes to PC. Since then, critics have questioned the accuracy of certain details that Taylor used to support his critique. Evidently, Taylor exaggerated (and likely fictionalized) a confrontation between a Harvard professor and PC-minded college students. (See the Hellerstein and Legum article "The Phony Debate About Political Correctness" listed under Unit Three "Further Inquiry & Research" for specifics.)

Nevertheless, critiques of the social movement persist. Taylor and others criticize PC's capacity to find political attitudes embedded in all aspects of language. Would George Orwell agree with the notion that "everything is political" or that "all language is political"? What does Orwell's "Politics and the English Language" have to say on the matter?

In his 2015 article "Not a Very P.C. Thing to Say," Jonathan Chait claims that "political correctness" has made an astounding resurgence in the 21st century. Citing numerous contemporary examples of incidents on social media and college campuses, Chait argues that "PC" is more than simple hyper-sensitivity to the use of language. He writes, "Political correctness is not a rigorous commitment to social equality so much as a system of left-wing ideological repression." In other words, politically correct censorship aims to stifle authentic political discourse as well as civic and political engagement. "Not only is it not a form of liberalism," he claims, "it is antithetical to liberalism." He even claims that "its most frequent victims turn out to be liberals themselves."

Chait's article went viral following its publication. The topic of "political correctness" seems to provide a distinct indicator of America's current dysfunctional political discourse. The irrational divisions that are so evident in social and mainstream media when it comes to our country's political dialogue can be seen in the discussions surrounding political correctness. In response to Chait's article, *Slate.com* published a critique entitled "What's Wrong (and Right) in Jonathan Chait's Anti-P.C. Screed." Readers who perceive the synthetic connections between these two articles can participate in political discourse relevant to our contemporary American experience. When setting down that participation in formal writing, we must recognize the public nature of the discourse. Presumably, if we participate in social media and online engagement on such topics, we also recognize the public nature of the discourse. It seems to me, though, that many people fail to acknowledge or understand the true public nature of social media. At the same time, we are also coming to understand the many ways in which social media itself can be utilized as a tool of manipulation.

Chait's obvious concerns regarding political repression in some ways mirror the concerns of George Orwell as expressed in the watershed novel *1984*. Orwell himself undoubtedly would have been alarmed at online and social media's capacity to manipulate the public in the 21st century. The internet provides mind-control tools that were unavailable to the fictitious authoritarian government of Big Brother represented in *1984* (which was composed in 1948 near the beginning of the Cold War). Big Brother has a Ministry of Truth which foists propaganda on its citizens. The internet has "deep fake" videos that manipulate and distort reality. When a person knows he or she is being propagandized, it is possible to build a mental defense. When one is unaware that he or she is being propagandized, it is almost impossible to build such a mental defense. Through this perspective, the subtle manipulations of the 21st century internet may be seen as more nefarious, and more effective, than the plodding manipulations of 20th century authoritarian governments.

To what extent do you find Chait's criticisms of PC persuasive? Do you believe that the people he criticizes have any legitimate basis for their PC mindset? Based on Chait's depiction of the social phenomenon called "political correctness," do you find that there is any validity to viewing society and language through the lens of "patriarchal" or "white male" oppression? Do you agree that the alarums of "social justice warriors" (which *dictionary.com* identifies as a "disparaging" noun) are ridiculous? When or where are they ridiculous, in your view? When or where are they not ridiculous? For example, is it unreasonable for advocates to insist on "someone who uses a wheelchair" rather than "someone confined to a wheelchair"? Do these subtleties of language make any real difference?

For you, where do the advocates for "political correctness" get it wrong and where do they get it right? When is a change in language justified? Is there a cause and effect relationship between language and social attitudes? Where do you place yourself in the ongoing "culture battle" between those who advocate sensitivity in the use of language and critics like Jonathan Chait who say that linguistic policing has gone too far?

## Questions to Consider

*Answer these questions as you read and annotate the text:*

- What are "microaggressions"?
- Chait writes that the online professional group Binders Full of Women Writers "soon found itself frequently distracted by bitter identity-politics recriminations, endlessly litigating the fraught requirements of p.c. discourse." What does Chait mean by "identity politics"? Start by looking up a definition of the term.
- To what extent are criticisms of sexism and racism in Western culture legitimate or illegitimate, in your view? Without denying the historical realities of sexism and racism, how would conservative critics defend American culture from the critique that the American system is at its very core racist and sexist?
- What distinctions does Chait make between "liberal" and "left wing" political alignments? The distinctions may be difficult to follow. What does Chait mean when he writes, "The modern left has borrowed the Marxist critique of liberalism"? If a Marxist critic views culture through an economic lens, through what sort of lens or perspective does the "modern left" view society, according to Chait?
- What is the "bedrock liberal ideal" that political correctness challenges, according to Chait? What makes "the p.c. left" philosophically threatening, according to the author's argument?
- What happened in the UC-Santa Barbara "free speech zone"? Why does the author include this incident in the article?
- What does Chait mean when he describes PC as a movement of "dour puritanism"?
- In his final paragraph, Chait claims that the "new political correctness" has silenced many of its own supporters. What does he mean?
- When it comes to convincing people of a political point of view, Chait says we must value what over coercion? Be sure to define "coercion" if you are not certain of the word's meaning.

## Jonathan Chait, Not a Very P.C. Thing to Say: How the Language Police Are Perverting Liberalism

Around 2 a.m. on December 12, four students approached the apartment of Omar Mahmood, a Muslim student at the University of Michigan, who had recently published a column in a school newspaper about his perspective as a minority on campus. The students, who were recorded on a building surveillance camera wearing baggy hooded sweatshirts to hide their identity, littered Mahmood's doorway with copies of his column, scrawled with messages like "You scum embarrass us," "Shut the fuck up," and "DO YOU EVEN GO HERE?! LEAVE!!" They posted a picture of a demon and splattered eggs.

This might appear to be the sort of episode that would stoke the moral conscience of students on a progressive campus like Ann Arbor, and it was quickly agreed that an act of biased intimidation had taken place. But Mahmood was widely seen as the perpetrator rather than the victim. His column, published in the school's conservative newspaper, had spoofed the culture of taking offense that pervades the campus. Mahmood satirically pretended to denounce "a white cis-gendered hetero upper-class man" who offered to help him up when he slipped, leading him to denounce "our barbaric attitude toward people of left-handydnyss." The gentle tone of his mockery was closer to Charlie Brown than to *Charlie Hebdo*.

*The Michigan Daily,* where Mahmood also worked as a columnist and film critic, objected to the placement of his column in the conservative paper but hardly wanted his satirical column in its own pages. Mahmood later said that he was told by the editor that his column had created a "hostile environment," in which at least one *Daily* staffer felt threatened, and that he must write a letter of apology to the staff. When he refused, the *Daily* fired him, and the subsequent vandalism of his apartment served to confirm his status as thought-criminal.

The episode would not have shocked anybody familiar with the campus scene from two decades earlier. In 1992, an episode along somewhat analogous lines took place, also in Ann Arbor. In this case, the offending party was the feminist videographer Carol Jacobsen, who had produced an exhibition documenting the lives of sex workers. The exhibition's subjects presented their profession as a form of self-empowerment, a position that ran headlong against the theories of Catharine MacKinnon, a law professor at the university who had gained national renown for her radical feminist critique of the First Amendment as a tool of male privilege. MacKinnon's beliefs nestled closely with an academic movement that was then being described, by its advocates as well as its critics, as "political correctness." Michigan had already responded to the demands of pro-p.c. activists by imposing a campuswide speech code purporting to restrict all manner of discriminatory speech, only for it to be struck down as a First Amendment violation in federal court.

In Ann Arbor, MacKinnon had attracted a loyal following of students, many of whom copied her method of argument. The pro-MacKinnon students, upset over the display of pornographic video clips, descended upon Jacobsen's exhibit and confiscated a videotape. There were speakers visiting campus for a conference on prostitution, and the video posed "a threat to their safety," the students insisted.

This was the same inversion of victim and victimizer at work last December. In both cases, the threat was deemed not the angry mobs out to crush opposing ideas, but the ideas themselves. The theory animating both attacks turns out to be a durable one, with deep roots in the political left.

The recent mass murder of the staff members of *Charlie Hebdo* in Paris was met with immediate and unreserved fury and grief across the full range of the American political system. But while outrage at the violent act briefly united our generally quarrelsome political culture, the quarreling quickly resumed over deeper fissures. Were the slain satirists martyrs at the hands of religious fanaticism, or bullying spokesmen of privilege? Can the offensiveness of an idea be determined objectively, or only by recourse to the identity of the person taking offense? On Twitter, "Je Suis Charlie," a slogan heralding free speech, was briefly one of the most popular news hashtags in history. But soon came the reactions ("Je Ne Suis Pas Charlie") from those on the left accusing the newspaper of racism and those on the right identifying the cartoons as hate speech. Many media companies, including the New York *Times,* have declined to publish the cartoons the terrorists deemed offensive, a stance that has attracted strident criticism from some readers. These sudden, dramatic expressions of anguish against insensitivity and oversensitivity come at a moment when large segments of American culture have convulsed into censoriousness.

After political correctness burst onto the academic scene in the late '80s and early '90s, it went into a long remission. Now it has returned. Some of its expressions have a familiar tint, like the protesting of even mildly controversial speakers on college campuses. You may remember when 6,000 people at the University of California–Berkeley signed a petition last year to stop a commencement address by Bill Maher, who has criticized Islam (along with nearly all the other major world religions). Or when protesters at Smith College demanded the cancellation of a commencement address by Christine Lagarde, managing director of the International Monetary Fund, blaming the organization for "imperialist and patriarchal systems that oppress and abuse women worldwide." Also last year, Rutgers protesters scared away Condoleezza Rice; others at Brandeis blocked Ayaan Hirsi Ali, a women's-rights champion who is also a staunch critic of Islam; and those at Haverford successfully protested former Berkeley chancellor Robert Birgeneau, who was disqualified by an episode in which the school's police used force against Occupy protesters.

At a growing number of campuses, professors now attach "trigger warnings" to texts that may upset students, and there is a campaign to eradicate "microaggressions," or small social slights that might cause searing trauma. These newly fashionable terms merely repackage a central tenet of the first p.c. movement: that people should be expected to treat even faintly unpleasant ideas or behaviors as full-scale offenses. Stanford recently canceled a performance of *Bloody Bloody Andrew Jackson* after protests by Native American students. UCLA students staged a sit-in to protest microaggressions such as when a professor corrected a student's decision to spell the word *indigenous* with an uppercase *I* — one example of many "perceived grammatical choices that in actuality reflect ideologies." A theater group at Mount Holyoke College recently announced it would no longer put on *The Vagina Monologues* in part because the material excludes women without vaginas. These sorts of episodes now hardly even qualify as exceptional.

Trigger warnings aren't much help in actually overcoming trauma—an analysis by the Institute of Medicine has found that the best approach is controlled exposure to it, and experts say avoidance can reinforce suffering. Indeed, one professor at a prestigious university told me that, just in the last few years, she has noticed a dramatic upsurge in her students' sensitivity toward even the mildest social or ideological slights; she and her fellow faculty members are terrified of facing accusations of triggering trauma—or, more consequentially, violating her school's new sexual-harassment policy—merely by carrying out the traditional academic work of intellectual exploration. "This is an environment of fear, believe it or not," she told me by way of explaining her request for anonymity. It reminds her of the previous outbreak of political correctness—"Every other day I say to my friends, 'How did we get back to 1991?' "

But it would be a mistake to categorize today's p.c. culture as only an academic phenomenon. Political correctness is a style of politics in which the more radical members of the left attempt to regulate political discourse by defining opposing views as bigoted and illegitimate. Two decades ago, the only communities where the left could exert such hegemonic control lay within academia, which gave it an influence on intellectual life far out of proportion to its numeric size. Today's political correctness flourishes most consequentially on social media, where it enjoys a frisson of cool and vast new cultural reach. And since social media is also now the milieu that hosts most political debate, the new p.c. has attained an influence over mainstream journalism and commentary beyond that of the old.

It also makes money. Every media company knows that stories about race and gender bias draw huge audiences, making identity politics a reliable profit center in a media industry beset by insecurity. A year ago, for instance, a photographer compiled images of Fordham students displaying signs recounting "an instance of racial microaggression they have faced." The stories ranged from uncomfortable ("No, where are you really from?") to relatively innocuous (" 'Can you read this?' He showed me a Japanese character on his phone"). BuzzFeed published part of her project, and it has since received more than 2 million views. This is not an anomaly.

In a short period of time, the p.c. movement has assumed a towering presence in the psychic space of politically active people in general and the left in particular. "All over social media, there dwell armies of unpaid but widely read commentators, ready to launch hashtag campaigns and circulate Change.org petitions in response to the slightest of identity-politics missteps," Rebecca Traister wrote recently in *The New Republic.*

Two and a half years ago, Hanna Rosin, a liberal journalist and longtime friend, wrote a book called *The End of Men,* which argued that a confluence of social and economic changes left women in a better position going forward than men, who were struggling to adapt to a new postindustrial order. Rosin, a self-identified feminist, has found herself unexpectedly assailed by feminist critics, who found her message of long-term female empowerment complacent and insufficiently concerned with the continuing reality of sexism. One Twitter hashtag, "#RIPpatriarchy," became a label for critics to lampoon her thesis. Every new continuing demonstration of gender discrimination—a survey showing Americans still prefer male bosses; a person noticing a man on the subway occupying a seat and a half—would be tweeted out along with a mocking #RIPpatriarchy.

Her response since then has been to avoid committing a provocation, especially on Twitter. "If you tweet something straightforwardly feminist, you immediately get a wave of love and favorites, but if you tweet something in a cranky feminist mode then the opposite happens," she told me. "The price is too high; you feel like there might be banishment waiting for you." Social media, where swarms of jeering critics can materialize in an instant, paradoxically creates this feeling of isolation. "You do immediately get the sense that it's one against millions, even though it's not." Subjects of these massed attacks often describe an impulse to withdraw.

Political correctness is a term whose meaning has been gradually diluted since it became a flashpoint 25 years ago. People use the phrase to describe politeness (perhaps to excess), or evasion of hard truths, or (as a term of abuse by conservatives) liberalism in general. The confusion has made it more attractive to liberals, who share the goal of combating race and gender bias.

But political correctness is not a rigorous commitment to social equality so much as a system of left-wing ideological repression. Not only is it not a form of liberalism; it is antithetical to liberalism. Indeed, its most frequent victims turn out to be liberals themselves.

I am white and male, a fact that is certainly worth bearing in mind. I was also a student at the University of Michigan during the Jacobsen incident, and was attacked for writing an article for the campus paper defending the exhibit. If you consider this background and demographic information the very essence of my point of view, then there's not much point in reading any further. But this pointlessness is exactly the point: Political correctness makes debate irrelevant and frequently impossible.

Under p.c. culture, the same idea can be expressed identically by two people but received differently depending on the race and sex of the individuals doing the expressing. This has led to elaborate norms and terminology within certain communities on the left. For instance, "mansplaining," a concept popularized in 2008 by Rebecca Solnit, who described the tendency of men to patronizingly hold forth to women on subjects the woman knows better—in Solnit's case, the man in question mansplained her own book to her. The fast popularization of the term speaks to how exasperating the phenomenon can be, and mansplaining has, at times, proved useful in identifying discrimination embedded in everyday rudeness. But it has now grown into an all-purpose term of abuse that can be used to discredit any argument by any man. (MSNBC host Melissa Harris-Perry once disdainfully called White House press secretary Jay Carney's defense of the relative pay of men and women in the administration "mansplaining," even though the question he responded to was posed by a male.) Mansplaining has since given rise to "whitesplaining" and "straightsplaining." The phrase "solidarity is for white women," used in a popular hashtag, broadly signifies any criticism of white feminists by nonwhite ones.

If a person who is accused of bias attempts to defend his intentions, he merely compounds his own guilt. (Here one might find oneself accused of man/white/straightsplaining.) It is likewise taboo to request that the accusation be rendered in a less hostile manner. This is called "tone policing." If you are accused of bias, or "called out," reflection and apology are the only acceptable response—to dispute a call-out only makes it worse. There is no allowance in p.c. culture for the possibility that the accusation may be erroneous. A white person or a man can achieve the status of "ally," however, if he follows the rules of p.c. dialogue. A community, virtual or real, that adheres to the rules is deemed "safe." The extensive terminology plays a crucial role, locking in shared ideological assumptions that make meaningful disagreement impossible.

Nearly every time I have mentioned the subject of p.c. to a female writer I know, she has told me about Binders Full of Women Writers, an invitation-only Facebook group started last year for women authors. The name came from Mitt Romney's awkwardly phrased debate boast that as Massachusetts governor he had solicited names of female candidates for high-level posts, and became a form of viral mockery. Binders was created to give women writers a "laid-back" and "no-pressure" environment for conversation and professional networking. It was an attempt to alleviate the systemic underrepresentation of women in just about every aspect of American journalism and literature, and many members initially greeted the group as a welcome and even exhilarating source of social comfort and professional opportunity. "Suddenly you had the most powerful women in journalism and media all on the same page," one former member, a liberal journalist in her 30s, recalls.

Binders, however, soon found itself frequently distracted by bitter identity-politics recriminations, endlessly litigating the fraught requirements of p.c. discourse. "This was the first time I had felt this new kind of militancy," says the same member, who requested anonymity for fear that her opinions would make her employer uncomfortable. Another sent me excerpts of the types of discussions that can make the group a kind of virtual mental prison.

On July 10, for instance, one member in Los Angeles started a conversation urging all participants to practice higher levels of racial awareness. "Without calling anyone out specifically, I'm going to note that if you're discussing a contentious thread, and shooting the breeze . . . take a look at the faces in the user icons in that discussion," she wrote. "Binders is pretty diverse, but if you're not seeing many WOC/non-binary POC in your discussion, it's quite possible that there are problematic assumptions being stated without being challenged." ("POC" stands for "people of color." "WOC" means "women of color." "Non-binary" describes people who are either transgender or identify as a gender other than traditionally male or female.)

Two members responded lightly, one suggesting that such "call-outs" be addressed in private conversation and another joking that she was a "gluten free Jewish WWC"—or Woman Without Color. This set off more jokes and a vicious backlash. "It seems appropriate to hijack my suggestion with jokes. I see," the Los Angeles member replied. "Apparently whatever WOC have to say is good for snark and jokes," wrote another. Others continued: "The level of belittling, derailing, crappy jokes, and all around insensitivity here is astounding and also makes me feel very unsafe in this Big Binder." "It is literally fucking insane. I am appalled and embarrassed."

The suggestion that a call-out be communicated privately met with even deeper rage. A poet in Texas: "I'm not about to private message folks who have problematic racist, transphobic, anti-immigrant, and/or sexist language." The L.A. member: "Because when POC speak on these conversations with snark and upset, we get Tone Argumented at, and I don't really want to deal with the potential harm to me and mine." Another writer: "You see people suggesting that PMs are a better way to handle racism? That's telling us we are too vocal and we should pipe down." A white Toronto member, sensing the group had dramatically underreacted, moved to rectify the situation: "JESUS FUCK, LIKE SERIOUSLY FUCK, I SEE MORE WHITE BINDERS POLICING WOC AND DEMANDING TO BE EDUCATED/UNEDUCATED AS IF IT'S A FUCKING NOBLE MISSION RATHER THAN I DUNNO SPEND TIME SHUTTING DOWN AND SHITTING ON RACIST DOUCHE CANOE BEHAVIOUR; WHAT ARE YOU GAINING BY THIS? WHAT ARE YOU DETRACTING? YOU NEED SCREENCAPS OF BURNING CROSSES TO BELIEVE RACIST SHIT IS HAPPENING? THIS THREAD IS PAINFUL. HUGS TO ALL THE WOC DURING THIS THREAD"

Every free society, facing the challenge of balancing freedom of expression against other values such as societal cohesion and tolerance, creates its own imperfect solution. France's is especially convoluted and difficult to parse: It allows for satire and even blasphemy (like cartoons that run in *Charlie Hebdo*) but not for speech that incites violence toward individuals (like provocative comments made by the comedian Dieudonné M'bala M'bala). This may appear to Americans as a distinction without a difference, but our distinctions are also confused, as is our way of talking about free speech as it overlaps with our politics.

The right wing in the United States is unusually strong compared with other industrialized democracies, and it has spent two generations turning *liberal* into a feared buzzword with radical connotations. This long propaganda campaign has implanted the misperception—not only among conservatives but even many liberals—that liberals and "the left" stand for the same things.

It is true that liberals and leftists both want to make society more economically and socially egalitarian. But liberals still hold to the classic Enlightenment political tradition that cherishes individuals rights, freedom of expression, and the protection of a kind of free political marketplace. (So, for that matter, do most conservatives.)

The Marxist left has always dismissed liberalism's commitment to protecting the rights of its political opponents—you know, the old line often misattributed to Voltaire, "I disapprove of what you have to say, but I'll defend to the death your right to say it"—as hopelessly naïve. If you maintain equal political rights for the oppressive capitalists and their proletarian victims, this will simply keep in place society's unequal power relations. Why respect the rights of the class whose power you're trying to smash? And so, according to Marxist thinking, your political rights depend entirely on what class you belong to.

The modern far left has borrowed the Marxist critique of liberalism and substituted race and gender identities for economic ones. "The liberal view," wrote MacKinnon 30 years ago, "is that abstract categories—like speech or equality—define systems. Every time you strengthen free speech in one place, you strengthen it everywhere. Strengthening the free speech of the Klan strengthens the free speech of Blacks." She deemed this nonsensical: "It equates substantive powerlessness with substantive power and calls treating these the same, 'equality.' "

Political correctness appeals to liberals because it claims to represent a more authentic and strident opposition to their shared enemy of race and gender bias. And of course liberals are correct not only to oppose racism and sexism but to grasp (in a way conservatives generally do not) that these biases cast a nefarious and continuing shadow over nearly every facet of American life. Since race and gender biases are embedded in our social and familial habits, our economic patterns, and even our subconscious minds, they need to be fought with some level of consciousness. The mere absence of overt discrimination will not do.

Liberals believe (or ought to believe) that social progress can continue while we maintain our traditional ideal of a free political marketplace where we can reason together as individuals. Political correctness challenges that bedrock liberal ideal. While *politically* less threatening than conservatism (the far right still commands far more power in American life), the p.c. left is actually more *philosophically* threatening. It is an undemocratic creed.

Bettina Aptheker, a professor of feminist studies at the University of California–Santa Cruz, recently wrote an essay commemorating the Berkeley Free Speech movement, in which she participated as a student in 1964. She now expressed a newfound skepticism in the merits of free speech. "Freedom of speech is a constitutional guarantee, but who gets to exercise it without the chilling restraints of censure depends very much on one's location in the political and social cartography," she wrote. "We [Free Speech movement] veterans . . . were too young and inexperienced in 1964 to know this, but we do now, and we speak with a new awareness, a new consciousness, and a new urgency that the wisdom of a true freedom is inexorably tied to who exercises power and for what ends."

These ideas have more than theoretical power. Last March at University of California–Santa Barbara, in, ironically, a "free-speech zone," a 16-year-old anti-abortion protester named Thrin Short and her 21-year-old sister Joan displayed a sign arrayed with graphic images of aborted fetuses. They caught the attention of Mireille Miller-Young, a professor of feminist studies. Miller-Young, angered by the sign, demanded that they take it down. When they refused, Miller-Young snatched the sign, took it back to her office to destroy it, and shoved one of the Short sisters on the way.

Speaking to police after the altercation, Miller-Young told them that the images of the fetuses had "triggered" her and violated her "personal right to go to work and not be in harm." A Facebook group called "UCSB Microaggressions" declared themselves "in solidarity" with Miller-Young and urged the campus "to provide as much support as possible."

By the prevailing standards of the American criminal-justice system, Miller-Young had engaged in vandalism, battery, and robbery. By the logic of the p.c. movement, she was the victim of a trigger and had acted in the righteous cause of social justice. Her colleagues across the country wrote letters to the sentencing judge pleading for leniency. Jennifer Morgan, an NYU professor, blamed the anti-abortion protesters for instigating the confrontation through their exercise of free speech. "Miller-Young's actions should be mitigated both by her history as an educator as well as by her conviction that the [anti-abortion] images were an assault on her students," Morgan wrote. Again, the mere expression of opposing ideas, in the form of a poster, is presented as a threatening act.

The website The Feminist Wire mounted an even more rousing defense of Miller-Young's behavior. The whole idea that the professor committed a crime by stealing a sign and shoving away its owner turns out to be an ideological construct. "The ease with which privileged white, and particularly young white gender and sexually normative appearing women, make claims to 'victimhood' and 'violation of property,' is not a neutral move," its authors argued. It concluded, "We issue a radical call for accountability to questions of history, representation, and the racialized gendering of tropes of 'culpability' and 'innocence' when considering Dr. Miller-Young's case."

These are extreme ideas, but they are neither isolated nor marginal. A widely cited column by a *Harvard Crimson* editorial writer last year demanded an end to academic freedom if freedom extended to objectionable ideas. "If our university community opposes racism, sexism, and heterosexism," asked the author, "why should we put up with research that counters our goals simply in the name of 'academic freedom'?" After the *Nation*'s Michelle Goldberg denounced a "growing left-wing tendency toward censoriousness and hair-trigger offense," Rutgers professor Brittney Cooper replied in Salon: "The demand to be reasonable is a disingenuous demand. Black folks have been reasoning with white people forever. Racism is unreasonable, and that means reason has limited currency in the fight against it."

The most probable cause of death of the first political-correctness movement was the 1992 presidential election. That event mobilized left-of-center politics around national issues like health care and the economy, and away from the introspective suppression of dissent within the academy. Bill Clinton's campaign frontally attacked left-wing racial politics, famously using inflammatory comments by Sister Souljah to distance him from Jesse Jackson. Barbara Jordan, the first black woman from a southern state elected to the House of Representatives, attacked political correctness in her keynote speech. ("We honor cultural identity. We always have; we always will. But separatism is not allowed. Separatism is not the American way. We must not allow ideas like political correctness to divide us and cause us to reverse hard-won achievements in human rights and civil rights.")

Yet it is possible to imagine that, as the next Clinton presidential campaign gets under way, p.c. culture may not dissolve so easily. The internet has shrunk the distance between p.c. culture and mainstream liberal politics, and the two are now hopelessly entangled. During the 2008 primary contest between Hillary Clinton and Barack Obama, the modern politics of grievance had already begun to play out, as each side's supporters patrolled the other for any comment that might indicate gender or racial bias. It dissipated in the general election, but that was partly because Obama's supporters worried about whether America really was ready to accept its first president who was not a white male. Clinton enters the 2016 race in a much stronger position than any other candidate, and her supporters may find it irresistible to amplify p.c. culture's habit of interrogating the hidden gender biases in every word and gesture against their side.

Or maybe not. The p.c. style of politics has one serious, possibly fatal drawback: It is exhausting. Claims of victimhood that are useful within the left-wing subculture may alienate much of

America. The movement's dour puritanism can move people to outrage, but it may prove ill suited to the hopeful mood required of mass politics. Nor does it bode well for the movement's longevity that many of its allies are worn out. "It seems to me now that the public face of social liberalism has ceased to seem positive, joyful, human, and freeing," confessed the progressive writer Freddie deBoer. "There are so many ways to step on a land mine now, so many terms that have become forbidden, so many attitudes that will get you cast out if you even *appear* to hold them. I'm far from alone in feeling that it's typically not worth it to engage, given the risks." Goldberg wrote recently about people "who feel emotionally savaged by their involvement in [online feminism]—not because of sexist trolls, but because of the slashing righteousness of other feminists." Former Feministing editor Samhita Mukhopadhyay told her, "Everyone is so scared to speak right now."

That the new political correctness has bludgeoned even many of its own supporters into despondent silence is a triumph, but one of limited use. Politics in a democracy is still based on getting people to agree with you, not making them afraid to disagree. The historical record of political movements that sought to expand freedom for the oppressed by eliminating it for their enemies is dismal. The historical record of American liberalism, which has extended social freedoms to blacks, Jews, gays, and women, is glorious. And that glory rests in its confidence in the ultimate power of reason, not coercion, to triumph.

## Questions for Comprehension

*Answer these questions as a comprehension reading quiz and/or for further clarification on the text:*

1. University of Michigan student Omar Mahmood was criticized (and eventually fired) for doing what?

2. True or False. Chait claims that "trigger warnings" attached to syllabi and texts are one reliable method for students to avoid and overcome trauma.

3. True or False. Chait claims that political correctness fails to foster a healthy climate of mutual respect in which public and political discourse can thrive.

4. True or False. According to Chait, the culture of political correctness recognizes that words have distinct, objective meanings that serve to clarify a person's intention when writing or speaking.

5. Chait claims that the "p.c. left" is philosophically threatening to our society. He claims, "It is an undemocratic creed." In as few words as possible, explain what he means that "PC" is an undemocratic creed.

# Assignments

## Paragraph Exercise #2

**Twenty points**

Fill in the blanks in this template in order to create a coherent body paragraph that analyzes and interprets a significant point in Jonathan Chait's "Not a Very P.C. Thing to Say." Pretend that the first sentence below is a topic sentence that would appear in a middle or "body" paragraph of a composition assignment that requires you to analyze Chait's text.

This exercise develops linguistic agility. You must write within the parameters outlined below. Make sure when you fill in the blanks that your sentences make grammatical sense and are free of usage errors. Reading your sentences aloud as you proofread can be an effective revision technique. Finally, make sure that your sentences relate to one another in a logical manner, one idea leading to the next. That's what instructors mean when they say to compose a "coherent" paragraph.

Note that you must quote directly from the text following the signal phrase "He observes." Place a comma after the signal phrase and use proper quotation marks just as it appears below.

Note that (xx) below stands for the textbook page number where your quotation selection appears. In accordance with proper MLA in-text citation format, you will need to fill in a page number but not the author's last name since you have already clearly mentioned it at a prior point in the paragraph.

Chait is probably most suspicious of the concept of "political correctness" because of
_____. He recounts an example of _____ when he discusses
_____. He observes, "_____" (xx). In making this observation,
Chait attempts to convince his readers that _____. Basically, his point is that
_____.

## Suggested Scoring Criteria

| | |
|---|---|
| The student completed and turned in the work on deadline. | 10 points |
| The student writes in grammatically sound sentences with proper syntax and punctuation. | 10 points |
| Bonus Criterion<br>*The student presents a coherent, well-organized paragraph that engages in focused text analysis.* | *up to +2 points* |

# An Exercise in Peer Critical Analysis

*Examine the following writing samples. Critique the views expressed in these compositions, and critique the form of the writing, including clarity of expression, effective use of language, ability to integrate meaningful quotations, and ability to attribute ideas to the proper authority or source material as well as to document sources in proper MLA format. You may find punctuation or usage errors. Where and how could these essays be improved? Where are they most effective and why? In other words, what are the strengths and what are the weaknesses of each composition? Do these compositions use sound reasoning? How effective are they in terms of engaging in civil public discourse? Finally, are they persuasive? Why or why not?*

## Sample Paper 1

In social environments, it is not acceptable to say racist words or use derogatory terms on people, many people would be startled by someone doing that because the people were taught that doing that is wrong. Political correctness is something that society has told us we all must have. It is the avoidance of certain words or phrases that would offend or oppress someone. Political correctness is something that I believe everyone should understand and try to possess at least slightly. I do not believe in censoring our language, but I do believe that some words should be avoided in specific situations, we should all have some sensitiveness.

In Alleen Pace Nilsen's essay "Sexism in English: A 1990s Update" she studies the English language and its underlying sexism. She discovers that many everyday words and phrases are inherently sexist and believes that the sexism in the English language needs to be in some way rivaled. Nilsen claims that "Language is like an X-ray in providing visible evidence of invisible thoughts" (57). The words that we each use reveal our true temperament. If we don't care to be sensitive to other people then we don't care about those other people or their problems, which is why it is important to choose the right words around people or in social environments.

On the other hand, author George Orwell believes that the type of censorship, which is political correctness, is making our language ugly. He thinks that we should stop using all these words and phrases that we have stored in our brains to later fit together like puzzle pieces where needed, and learn to think for ourselves. Since "(political arguments can be) too brutal for most people to face," Orwell insists that "political language has to consist largely of euphemism" (69). I agree with Orwell that political language has a lot of euphemism because it does, and I believe that it should be that way. Political correctness takes away the terms that have specific and oppressive meanings and forces use to find other way to express beliefs. Without political correctness, political language would be very limited in vocabulary because of these terms, so these terms would be used so often and would limit our language. The solution is finding better ways to express our feelings without offending others by thinking for ourselves and not sticking to the common phrases that have the very specific and oppressing connotations.

Political correctness is important and everyone needs it because insensitivity for one another divides us. Political correctness is not only avoiding offending or oppressing others, it is also being polite and caring for each other. It is not hard to refrain from saying something racist or derogatory to the people around you. We can all find ways around using the words with negative connotations and if we all tried the world would be a better place.

## Sample Paper 2

**Political Correctness: Friend or Foe?**

In his article "Politics and the English Language," George Orwell claims that language is something we can shape and use for our own purposes. Orwell suggests that language should be used "as an instrument for expressing and not for concealing or preventing thought" (72). This implies that language and word choice can be used to communicate ideas directly and with clear meaning. It also implies that language and word choice can be used to stop ideas from fully presenting themselves, or from presenting themselves at all. Political correctness focuses heavily on word choice; more specifically, what is and is not an "acceptable" word choice. What is the purpose behind political correctness? Does it express, conceal, or prevent thought? A man named John Taylor has something to say about this.

In his essay "Are You Politically Incorrect?" Taylor asserts that fundamentalists on the political left are using political correctness to advance their agendas and to silence their critics. These fundamentalists claim that they are fighting the inherent racism and sexism that exists in Western society. By replacing "offensive" terms and concepts with acceptable, politically correct ones, fundamentalists believe they will remove racism and sexism from society. According to Taylor, these fundamentalists declare that anyone who disagrees with them is unqualified to do so because he or she is a product of a racist and sexist environment. Taylor argues, "This circular reasoning enables the new fundamentalists to attack not just the opinions of their critics but the right of their critics to disagree. Alternate viewpoints are not allowed" (78). In other words, even though the fundamentalists' reasoning is not entirely correct, it sounds believable enough to discredit the people who disagree with them. These politically incorrect dissenters are a victim of their Western environment. As such, they do not know what they are talking about and have no right to have a different opinion from the fundamentalists. However, Taylor implies that the arguments of these fundamentalists make no sense because they are also products of the so-called "sexist, racist environment." So, what makes their point of view more valid than anyone else's? Ironically, in a supposed effort to rid society of offensive and alienating terms and concepts, the fundamentalists offensively alienate an entire group of people: anyone who disagrees with them. They refuse to listen to a point of view that is not their own.

Political correctness has embarked down a path of deciding that, not only certain words, but entire concepts are offensive and therefore have no right to be debated. It is used to seek control over what people say and think politically and morally. Why is it that the conservative right seems to be the only side with politically incorrect views? Why is it that when the political right wants to discuss a border wall, or illegal immigration, or the morality of homosexuality or abortion, they are not met with logical counter-arguments, but with emphatic cries from the politically correct left that they are racist, homophobic, women haters, or a host of other insulting names? Perhaps, these advocates of political correctness are not concerned with eradicating offensive language at all, because they do not hesitate to use it. Perhaps they are concerned with their beliefs dominating the political landscape at all costs, even if it means taking away the other side's right to express their thoughts. The practice of labeling people racists because they disagree with certain political ideas delegitimizes their right to explain their own point of view. It also creates a silencing fear within people who would dare disagree, lest they be unjustly labeled racist, homophobic, misogynist, etc. When this happens, only one political view is heard or considered. That is not freedom of speech or thought.

A couple of days ago in the news, it was reported that Twitter told a Tennessee candidate for senate that it would not allow her to promote her campaign ad on Twitter because it was "too inflammatory." In her ad, she said that she was "politically incorrect and proud of it" and that she helped stop Planned Parenthood from selling baby body parts. Due to political correctness, Twitter felt entitled to censor a congressional candidate's ad because of the political ideas and statements it contained. Thankfully, Twitter ended up reversing its decision. Still, whether you agree with what she said or not, political censorship is dangerous territory. If political correctness leads to political censorship, then it is indeed a dangerous foe.

## Sample Paper 3

### On the Topic of Political Correctness

Political correctness, or PC, is a method of speaking that promotes sensitivity to marginalized groups of people in order to avoid offending them. John Taylor argues that PC is an "epidemic" and is the source of much of the tension it is supposed to ease in his essay "Are You Politically Incorrect?" Furthering this idea, George Orwell in "Politics and the English Language" claims that the connection between politics and English is destroying the language as a whole. These two authors agree on one central point: there is something wrong with the English language.

In "Politically Incorrect," Taylor asserts that the ferocity of those in favor of political correctness is harmful to the way we view factual and historical events, quoting a college administrator responding to a young woman who wrote about the importance of an individual's rights: "[Individual] is a RED FLAG phrase, which many consider RACIST . . . Arguments that champion the individual over the group ultimately privilege the 'INDIVIDUALS' belonging to the largest or dominant group" (78). This view is part of what Taylor calls the 'new fundamentalism,' taking institutionalized political correctness to an extreme. Orwell takes a different route in "Politics," stating that politics and, by extension, political correctness are twisting and corrupting the English language itself. He suggests that "the decline of a language must ultimately have political and economic causes: it is not due simply to the bad influence of this or that individual writer" (61). Orwell's stance is that through the excessive ornamentation of speeches, politicians and those they speak for are making the English language one that is unexpressive and artificial.

I agree with both Taylor and Orwell that political correctness is a danger to the English language. However, I also believe that in order to be a social member of modern society one must observe some amount of PC. Offending people rarely has a positive outcome; in an argument, offending your opponent can easily cause them to stop listening to what you have to say. They believe they have been insulted in some way and therefore refuse to contribute to the conversation further. There is a fine line between being culturally sensitive and submitting to the authoritarian mindset clearly implied by the examples provided by John Taylor. I absolutely agree with Orwell's point of view that politicians have twisted English into a set of cookie-cutter phrases punctuated by brief twinkles of creativity that fade as quickly as they arrive.

# Unit Three Essay Topics

*See suggested assignment requirements, parameters, and scoring criteria below.*

*This composition assignment requires you to analyze source materials in order to participate in an important public discourse on the topic of "political correctness." You must incorporate multiple sources (at least two), and you must address an "outside audience" who has not read these source materials. Therefore, you must efficiently introduce texts to your readers so that they can understand the "discourse" or conversation that is taking place. In order to analyze the source materials, you must properly integrate, clarify, and/ or comment upon significant text quotations that you select. Before you begin, review effective methods of quotation integration.*

*The suggested word count is 500 to 750 words, about two to three pages.*
*Follow MLA format.*

### OPTION #1

Use two or more of our Unit Three *Engaging Discourse* texts as references. Connect the content of these texts with your own concepts and your own views on the general topic of "political correctness." Keep in mind an appropriate tone for an outside academic audience. Your paper must reference, contextualize, and quote from at least two of the following essays: George Orwell's "Politics and the English Language," Jonathan Chait's "Not a Very P.C. Thing to Say," and/or Alleen Pace Nilsen's "Sexism in the English Language: A 1990s Update." If necessary, define the concept of "political correctness" for your outside audience. You may reference a current event or events in order to clarify your points, but your focus must be on the readings and the concepts contained therein rather than on current events per se. This is not a "news of the day" article. Instead, through our analysis of the source materials, we are participating in an important public discourse. The three sample compositions included in this unit under "An Exercise in Peer Critical Analysis" were developed from this writing prompt (except that we had read an article entitled "Are You Politically Correct?" by John Taylor instead of the more recent Chait article).

### OPTION #2

Using Nilsen's article and one or more articles listed under Unit Three "Further Inquiry & Research," compose an essay in which you describe the origins of "political correctness" as a social movement that stems from the theories and concerns of academic (second wave) feminists.

### OPTION #3

Using Jonathan Chait's "Not a Very P.C. Thing to Say" and one or more articles listed under Unit Three "Further Inquiry & Research," compose an essay in which you analyze and comment upon the importance, or dangers, of maintaining "political correctness" in the classroom and/or in other situations where meaningful public discourse needs to take place.

### OPTION #4

In a *Slate.com* critique of the Chait text, J. Bryan Lowder assesses the validity of Chait's complaints regarding PC culture, agreeing with him on some points and disagreeing with him on others. (See the Unit

Three "Further Inquiry & Research" for a full citation of the Lowder source.) In a passage on "identity politics," Lowder writes the following:

> The problem with identity politics—in this particular manifestation, anyway—is that it assumes that just because a person claims a certain identity label, that person is necessarily empowered to be judge and jury on all issues pertaining to that category. The truth is, identity grants experience (and experience should be valued to a point); but it does not automatically grant wisdom, critical distance, or indeed, unassailable righteousness. To forget this is to turn individual people who possess a range of intelligences, backgrounds, self-interests, and flaws into two-dimensional avatars for the condition of humanity in which they happen to share. And, by corollary, to assert that it is impossible on some fundamental level for those who don't share that condition to ever relate or speak to that person as merely another human being with ideas and opinions.

What are "identity politics"? What problems do Chait and Lowder see with the PC manifestation of identity politics? When are so-called identity politics valid, at least in Lowder's view? What role do identity politics play in contemporary American politics? How have identity politics changed the country's political landscape in both positive and negative ways? Look for relevant passages in the Chait and Lowder articles to help you to assess the situation. In your view, when are identity politics valid? To what extent, if any, do you share the authors' concerns regarding the PC manifestation of identity politics? Focus on the Chait and Lowder texts as your primary source articles.

## OPTION #5

J. Bryan Lowder critiques the Chait text in a *Slate.com* article. (See the Unit Three "Further Inquiry & Research" for a full citation of the Lowder source.) To what extent do both authors agree that PC culture is "exhausting"? In what ways, according to one or both of these authors, does PC culture create "exhaustion"? When can such exhaustion be justified, according to Lowder? Explore the need for sensitivity in language versus the exhaustion created by such needs. Develop a viewpoint of your own regarding the need for the careful use of language in a free society and the need for people to be able to express themselves in authentic terms. To what extent is PC culture justified in its demand for mutual verbal respect? To what extent, if any, does PC culture overreach in its demands, causing censorship and hostility rather than discourse and understanding? Focus on the Chait and Lowder texts as your primary source articles.

## Suggested Scoring Criteria and Point Values

| | |
|---|---|
| Holistic Assessment<br>*The composition features thoughtful, relevant connection(s) made between multiple texts within the framework of the general topic.* | 40 points |
| Quotations<br>*The student demonstrates an ability to select, handle, integrate, and format relevant quotations from multiple texts.* | 20 points |
| Voice<br>*The student's grammar, usage, and syntax effectively communicate with the outside audience.* | 20 points |
| Deadline<br>*The student has met the instructor's deadline.* | 20 points |

Resources

## Further Inquiry & Research

Bennett, Lerone, Jr. "What's In a Name? Negro vs. Afro-American vs. Black." *Ebony* 23 (Nov. 1967): pp. 46–8, 50–2, 54. Found at *http://www.virginia.edu/woodson/courses/aas102%20(spring%2001)/articles/names/bennett.htm*.

Bump, Philip. "How 'Politically Correct' Moved From Commies to Culture and Back into Politics." *The Washington Post,* Dec. 17, 2015, *www.washingtonpost.com*.

Carmichael, Rodney. "Ice Cube Leaves Bill Maher Shaken And Stirred Over The N-Word." National Public Radio, *The Record: Music News from NPR,* June 12, 2017, *https://www.npr.org/sections/therecord/2017/06/12/532474238/ice-cube-leaves-bill-maher- shaken-and-stirred-over-the-n-word*.

DuBois, W.E.B. "The Name 'Negro.'" Letter to Roland A. Barton, Mar. 1928. *TeachingAmericanHistory.org, http://teachingamericanhistory.org/library/document/the-name- negro/*.

Florence, Joshua. "A Phrase in Flux: The History of Political Correctness." *Harvard Political Review,* Oct. 30, 2015, *http://harvardpolitics.com/united-states/phrase-flux-history- political-correctness/*.

Gibson, Caitlin. "How 'Politically Correct' Went from Compliment to Insult." *The Washington Post*, Jan. 13, 2016, *www.washingtonpost.com*.

Hellerstein, Erica and Judd Legum. "The Phony Debate About Political Correctness." *ThinkProgress*, Jan. 14, 2016, https://thinkprogress.org/the-phony-debate-about-political-correctness-f81da03b3bdb/.

Lowder, J. Bryan. "What's Wrong (and Right) in Jonathan Chait's Anti-P.C. Screed." *Slate.com*, Jan. 28, 2015, https://slate.com/human-interest/2015/01/jonathan-chait-s-anti-political-correctness-essay-unpacked.html.

Marin, Gary. "The Meaning and Origin of the Expression: Politically Correct." *The Phrase Finder,* 2018. *https://www.phrases.org.uk/meanings/287100.html*.

Sanneh, Kelefa and Zoe Chace. "Video Killed the Video Star," Act One of "Words You Can't Say." *This American Life*, vol. 637, Feb. 2, 2018, WBEZ Chicago, PRX Public Radio Exchange, *https://www.thisamericanlife.org/637/words-you-cant-say*.

Taylor, John. "Are You Politically Correct?" *Are You Politically Correct?: Debating America's Cultural Standards* (Prometheus, 1993), Eds. Francis Bethwick and Michael E. Bauman, https://openlibrary.org/books/OL8130922M/Are_You_Politically_Correct.

## Additional Source Materials by Topic

### Political Correctness and Millenials

Airaksinen, Toni. "STUDY: Politically-correct Millennials are Putting on an Act". *Campus Reform.* Aug 23, 2017, https://www.campusreform.org/?ID=9628

Bowman, Karlyn & O'Neil, Eleanor. "AEI Public Opinion Study: Polls on Political Correctness". *American Enterprise Institute.* June 28, 2017, http://www.aei.org/publication/polls-on-political-correctness/

French, David. "Blame Parents for Millennials' Laugable Fragility". *National Review.* May 14, 2016, https://www.nationalreview.com/2016/05/millennials-political-correctness-fragility-parenting/

Howe, Neil. "Why do Millennials Love Political Correctness? Generational Values". *Forbes.* Nov. 16, 2016, https://www.forbes.com/sites/neilhowe/2015/11/16/america-revisits-political-correctness/#a6c64c02de73

Jones, Matthew. "5 Things Millennials Want Everyone to Know about Political Correctness". *Inc.com.* July 18, 2017, https://www.inc.com/matthew-jones/5-things-all-millennials-want-gen-xers-to-know-abo.html

Ring, James. "Poll: 58% of Millennials Say Political Correctness has Gone too Far". *Red Alert Politics.* July 12, 2016, http://redalertpolitics.com/2016/07/12/poll-58-millennials-say-political-correctness-gone-far/

Schilling, Dave. "Has Politically Correct Culture Gone Too Far?". *The Guardian.* Dec. 14, 2015, https://www.theguardian.com/news/2015/dec/14/politically-correct-culture-millennials-generation

Smiley, Stephen. "Australia's Seniors Say the Political Correctness of Millennials is Ruining Society". *ABC News Australia.* Jul 26, 2017, http://www.abc.net.au/news/2017-07-26/political-correctness-is-ruining-society,-say-seniors/8744874

Watts, Nolan. "Political Correctness could be Making Millennials more Conservative than They Want to Be". *Rise: News.* July 31, 2017, https://risenews.net/2017/02/political-correctness-could-be-making-millennials-more-conservative-than-they-want-to-be/

## Social Media and Political Correctness

Adams, Joshua. "Time for Equal Media Treatment of 'Political Correctness'". *Columbia Journalism Review.* June 12, 2017, https://www.cjr.org/criticism/political-correctness-journalism.php

Demby, Gene. "What Research Says about the Consequences of PC Culture". *National Public Radio.* Jan. 30, 2015, https://www.npr.org/sections/codeswitch/2015/01/30/382475295/what-research-says-about-the-consequences-of-p-c-culture

Hess, Amanda. "How 'Political Correctness' Went from Punch Line to Panic". *The New York Times.* Jul. 19, 2016, https://www.nytimes.com/2016/07/24/magazine/how-political-correctness-went-from-punch-line-to-panic.html

Marius, Catalin. "Is Political Correctness in Media Going Too Far". *Quora.* Jun. 5, 2017, https://www.quora.com/Is-political-correctness-in-media-going-too-far

Schilling, Dave. "Has Politically Correct Culture Gone Too Far?". *The Guardian.* Dec. 14, 2015, https://www.theguardian.com/news/2015/dec/14/politically-correct-culture-millennials-generation

Sharpe, Matthew. "Words, Tweets, and Stones in the 'Political Correctness' Wars". *The Conversation.* Feb. 16, 2017, https://theconversation.com/words-tweets-and-stones-in-the-political-correctness-wars-73188

Sherwin, Kai. "Political Correctness: The Effects on Our Generation". *Huffington Post.* April 4, 2016, https://www.huffingtonpost.com/kai-sherwin/political-correctness-the_b_9600916.html

Singal, Jesse. "Social Media is Making Us Dumber. Here's Exhibit A". *The New York Times.* Jan. 11, 2018, https://www.nytimes.com/2018/01/11/opinion/social-media-dumber-steven-pinker.html

West, Ed. "Is Political Correctness Speeding Up?". *The Spectator.* Jan. 15, 2018, https://blogs.spectator.co.uk/2018/01/is-political-correctness-speeding-up/

Zurcher, Anthony. "A Political Correctness War that Never Really Ended". *BBC News.* Jan. 30, 2015, http://www.bbc.com/news/blogs-echochambers-31069779

# UNIT FOUR

# An Introduction to Research in the 21st Century

## Readings, Responsibilities, & Objectives for Unit Four: An Introduction to Research in the 21st Century

## Suggested Timeline: Two weeks

In this unit, we work on parallel tracks: 1) we want to think about the best ways to undertake information research in the 21st century, and 2) we will read a novel from the list below, unless your instructor has other plans—for example, to complete an annotated bibliography (a list of sources with notes on each source) on a research subject.

## Readings

Your instructor may choose to have you read one of these novels:

1. Mark Haddon, *The Curious Incident of the Dog in the Night-Time* (2003)
2. Alice Walker, *The Color Purple* (1982)
3. George Orwell, *1984* (1949)

## Responsibilities

This unit features a **Research Assignment** and a **Book Review Assignment** that are both associated with the selected novel. These assignments may be adapted to fit other projects, a research topic of your or your instructor's choosing, for example. Your instructor may choose to have you undertake an **Annotated Bibliography** in order to begin a research project. There is a **Character Diagnosis** essay assignment associated with the selected novel.

# Objectives

✓ This unit aims to provide students a basic understanding of the multi-faceted literacy skills needed for success in the 21st century.

✓ Students will become familiar with the complexities of information access in the 21st century.

✓ Students will begin to learn to assess information sources, including internet and other media sources. Students will assess a variety of information media, including print and electronic sources.

✓ Students will demonstrate the ability to produce clear, accurate, and correct academic discourse that reflects an acceptable level of critical thinking while employing the conventions of standard written English.

# Resources

Research in the 21st Century
    News You Cannot Use
    Data For Sale
    Curated and Non-Curated Information
    Wikipedia
    Facts or Ideas That Qualify as "Common Knowledge"
    Database vs. Search Engine
    Boolean Operators
    Internet and Institutional Resources
    Open Educational Resources (OER) and Open Movements
    Matching Your Research to Your Purpose and Audience
    Primary and Secondary Sources
A Few Key Definitions
The National Council of Teachers of English (NCTE) Definition of 21st Century Literacies
Major Research Question
    A Case Study in the Development of a "Major Research Question"
Further Inquiry & Research
Additional Source Material by Topic

# Assignments

# Book Review Assignment

There are different kinds of book reviews. Academic book reviews that appear in specialized journals take it for granted that readers have the work in question, and they aim to illuminate some aspect of the text. They are typically composed with a specialized academic audience in mind—an audience that may be familiar with highly specialized terms of literary criticism, for example. Book reviews that appear in popular general interest publications such as *Harper's Weekly* or *The New York Times* may be more careful about publishing "spoilers," that is, giving away a key plot twist or surprise. General interest readers may be perusing these publications in order to figure out whether they want to purchase the book in question or whether they would like to check out the book from the public library.

As always, *purpose* and *audience* are the most important factors that direct a composition's content.

For this assignment, we would like you to find an academic journal book review, a popular interest book review, and at least one other book review of your choosing. In addition, try to find at least one "contemporaneous" book review (that is, a book review that appeared at the time of the novel's publication) along with contemporary (that is, current) book reviews. It can be enlightening to read a book review that came out at the time of publication and to compare it to a book review (or literary essay) that appears twenty or fifty years after the novel's initial publication.

*Produce an* **MLA Works Cited List of Three Book Reviews** *on the assigned novel, either*

✓ *The Curious Incident of the Dog in the Night-Time* by Mark Haddon
✓ *The Color Purple* by Alice Walker, or
✓ *1984* by George Orwell

Purpose: Even if your instructor chooses not to read a novel this semester, he or she may require you to undertake this assignment. The purpose of this assignment is three-fold: 1) to familiarize you with your institution's library and database resources, 2) to broaden the scope of your knowledge regarding one of the novels listed above, and 3) to familiarize you with MLA Works Cited formatting (or another standard formatting style as specified by your instructor).

## Instructions:

- Retrieve three to five book reviews of the specified novel.
  - At least one of the book reviews should come from an academic journal.
  - At least *two* (2) of the book reviews should come from your institution's library databases, if at all possible. If your institution does not provide access to suitable electronic databases, discuss other research avenues with your instructor.
    - EBSCO, MagillOnLiterature Plus, Newspaper Source, and NewsBank are examples of databases that contain suitable book reviews.
  - At least one of the book reviews should come from an internet search engine search. As always, assess the source for its validity before including it in your Works Cited list.
- Document three to five relevant sources in proper MLA format.
  - Place the citations of these secondary sources in an alphabetized Works Cited list.
  - Find information on MLA citation and documentation style in a writer's handbook or online, via the Purdue Online Writing Lab <https://owl.english.purdue.edu/owl/> or another valid online resource.

## Suggested Scoring Criterion and Point Values

| | |
|---|---|
| The student provides a proper Works Cited list of three to five viable book review and/or academic essay sources in proper MLA format, turned in on deadline. | 25 points |

# Research Assignment Associated with the Novel

*Check with your instructor on whether you will undertake this assignment.*

Using your institution's library and electronic database resources, as well as legitimate internet resources, produce a brief annotated list of source materials that can help to provide you with a historical, social, and/or cultural "context" in which we can better understand the novelist's purpose or the historical, social, and cultural factors through which the novelist intends the reader to understand his or her protagonist.

✓ Identify the novel's publication date. What important historical or cultural events may have influenced the author in the year or years during which the novel was written?

✓ Identify the main dates and timelines associated with the novel's main plot and the major events in the life of the novel's protagonist. You may have to undertake "superficial" or encyclopedic research in order to determine these dates. These "superficial" or encyclopedic articles are not the goal of this bullet point. Once you have established the story dates, look into what important historical or cultural events may have touched or influenced the fictional life of the character.

✓ Identify the novel's setting. What cultural or historical information is important to know regarding the novel's historical setting?

✓ What records are there to indicate what the author him- or herself thought was important to know about the time and place in which the story was set?

✓ Produce three to five interesting sources that you can share with your classmates and instructor.

<u>Instructions:</u> Track down and **document the source materials** as described in the bullet points above. Produce an MLA style Works Cited bibliography listing these sources. Place **a brief note (a brief annotation)** of about thirty to forty words beneath each entry indicating why you selected the source and/or what relevant information the source provides. See "Sample MLA Annotation" on the Purdue Online Writing Lab at *<https://owl.english.purdue.edu/owl/resource/614/03/>* but note that our annotations (notes) for this assignment need to be very short and to the point. The notes for this assignment are not summary in nature.

## Suggested Scoring Criteria and Point Values

| | |
|---|---|
| The student provides a proper Works Cited list of at least three relevant sources in proper MLA format, turned in on deadline. | 20 points |
| The student provides a circa 30–40 word note beneath each entry clarifying why he or she selected the source and/or indicating what information the source provides relevant to the novel's social, political, historical, or cultural context. | 20 points |

# Library Assignment*

*Check with your instructor on whether you will conduct a* Library Assignment *in this course.*

Your search topic: _____

Track down _____ number of sources relevant to this search topic.

Track down an appropriate variety of source materials, including journals, magazines, e-books, and other types of sources *as specified by your instructor.*

## Objectives:

- To learn about your institution's library resources
- To learn a few effective search techniques
- To learn how to narrow results to peer-reviewed sources
- In some cases, to get started on researching a special topic or research paper

## Basic Database Search Techniques and Tips:

✓ Do not type a sentence in the search box. Break the search phrase into keywords.
  - *Not* this statement: *What are the issues of racial profiling in the United States?*
  - *Instead* this statement: *"Racial profiling" AND "United States"* (two phrases connected with the word AND).
✓ If your first search does not work, try other words or phrases.
  - Don't give up! Real research takes effort!
✓ Study your search results in order to find alternate keywords that will provide you different search results.
✓ Narrow your search by using several keywords or keyword phrases.
✓ Check out Rockwell Schrok's The Boolean Machine at http://rockwellschrock.com/rbs3k/boolean/index.htm to see how AND, OR, and NOT expand or limit search results.
✓ Work with your instructor, a librarian, or another information specialist in order to develop and revise search strategies.

## Useful Online Resources:

See "Research Methods" at http://libguides.tmcc.edu/researchmethods.

See "How to Write a Research Paper" at http://libguides.tmcc.edu/c.php?g=411640.

## Process:

✓ Understand your topic
  - Don't research until you are ready.
  - Develop a MSQ (Major Research Question) in order to guide your efforts.
  - See **Major Research Question** in this unit.
✓ Establish a context and background. Use a general database such as CQ Researcher or Opposing Viewpoints to find background information about your topic.
  - Start with a wide "horizontal" view.
  - As you learn more, narrow your focus to a specific "vertical" view.

---

*This resource has been adapted with permission from Truckee Meadows Community College (Reno, Nevada)

✓ General or background information sources may not be sufficient source materials for a college composition.
  • Always talk to your instructor regarding expectations, parameters, and rigor.
✓ When you think you have found a useful article, take note of:
  **a.** Author and title
  **b.** Date of publication
  **c.** Does the source contain statistics or "hard" data?
  **d.** In what publication and database does the article appear?
  **e.** How would this article help you write about your topic?

## Getting Deeper:

✓ Consider e-books such as appear in the EBSCO eBook Collection.
  • Make an effort to find at least one relevant book-length treatment of your subject matter.
✓ Consider reputable magazines and journals.
  • Which databases offer you the best options in this regard?
✓ Always note author, title, and other essential citation information.
  • Often you can email citation information to yourself.
✓ When searching for articles in databases such as EBSCO, it is helpful to use Boolean operators (AND, OR, NOT); for example:
  • Search for "climate change" AND "United States" AND policy
  • Instead of vague general searches such as *climate change*
✓ Depending on your needs, you can often narrow your parameters by date range or type of source (newspapers, peer-reviewed, etc.).
✓ In database searches, it is often possible to scan abstracts (summaries) or your results.
✓ Check for sources under "Scholarly Journals" or "Peer Reviewed" resources.
  • Remember to match your *purpose* and *audience* to your source materials.
  • Find sources that will help you to fulfill your specific purpose in addressing the particular audience to whom you are writing.

## Make Sure You Are In Control:

✓ Too many students settle on using the first few sources that they find.
  • Settling in research equates to settling for a less effective composition.
✓ Too many students get distracted too quickly.
  • They find a good source and think, "Maybe I'll write on this topic instead."
  • Find a topic that interests you and persist.
  • Remember to continue to develop, narrow, and hone your MRQ (Major Research Question).

# Annotated Bibliography Assignment

In general, an annotated bibliography is associated with a research paper. An annotated bibliography represents the final stage of your research process. It is a list of source citations with a descriptive note following each citation. Check with your instructor whether you will be writing a research paper in this course. If so, make sure that you are clear on your *purpose* (informative? argumentative?) and your *audience* (general readership? specialized readership?).

Of course, this assignment may function independently from a research paper. In other words, it is a great exercise to conduct the research in preparation for a term paper even if you don't actually compose the research assignment.

Your instructor may also choose to tweak the assignment below in accordance with his or her specific research assignment.

*Nota bene:* Each *Engaging Discourse* unit provides a foundation or starting point for research. Check the "Further Inquiry & Research" bibliography included at the end of each unit for possible research prompts.

## The Assignment

Offer an alphabetized MLA style list of valid source materials for possible in-text citation in a research article. Follow proper MLA citation format for each entry. See your writer's handbook and/or *<https://owl.english.purdue.edu/owl/resource/747/01/>*. *Suggested length*: two to four pages in MLA format. *Suggested volume:* I suggest listing a minimum of ten valid sources. *Title*: Feature an authentic title that lists a narrow topic of interest. Example: Annotated Bibliography on Neurochemical Reactions of the Fight-or-Flight Response.

*Pre-writing: understand what an annotated bibliography is. Study the following from the Purdue Online Writing Lab:* <http://owl.english.purdue.edu/owl/resource/614/01/>. *The purpose of your brief annotation (note) will be either to summarize, assess, or reflect upon the source material in question, depending on the source, your own judgment, your level of effort, and your overall purpose.*

List viable sources with the following *minimums*:

- One article from the *Engaging Discourse* textbook
- One article from one of the "Further Inquiry & Research" lists at the end of each unit
- Three to five authored articles with sound academic merit, preferably from curated databases (for example, articles from academic journals)
- Three to five authored article with sound journalistic merit from database or internet sources (for example, magazine and newspaper articles)
- One to three audio/visual programs of academic merit, such as a TED Talks or other lectures, podcasts, TV programs, documentaries, interviews, and so forth (from database resources or from legitimate internet sources)
- Two nonfiction books
  - In some cases, listing a book chapter is OK
- Do not list encyclopedia or Wikipedia articles. Such articles will not count toward the minimum requirements for this assignment.
- Listing superficial, unfocused or non-academic sources may detract from the overall evaluation of your bibliography assignment.
- Note that while you must include all of these sources in your annotated bibliography, you may, in fact, use fewer sources in your actual research paper. For example, a given research assignment may require only five to seven sources. Check with your instructor.

## Important Research Note:

Conduct focused research in order to produce your annotated bibliography. Avoid unfocused or "scattershot" bibliographies. Don't use the first source you come across. Compare and contrast possible source materials for the value they could bring to you and your composition. You may want to start with encyclopedic or Wikipedia articles, but do not stop there. Use these articles only as a starting point for further research. You might find good source materials linked in the footnotes/citations section of a high quality Wikipedia or other encyclopedic article.

Consult "Research in the 21st Century" in this unit for an introductory review of research methodologies.

## Suggested Evaluation Criteria and Point Values for the Annotated Bibliography Assignment

| | |
|---|---|
| Assignment turned in on deadline with appropriate title | 10 points |
| Appropriate Variety and Quality of Research Materials—moreover, sources appear to have a similar limited focus on a particular aspect of the stated topic<br>• *all required minimums and types of sources clearly listed (=60)*<br>• *minimum quantity or type not quite met, or unclear (=40-50)*<br>• *falls well short of minimum quantity or type (=30)* | 60 points |
| Evidence of Reading Completion and Comprehension<br>• *annotations consistently assess and reflect in clear prose (=20)*<br>• *annotations mainly summarize and/or contain distracting prose errors (=10)*<br>• *annotations convey little or no information or comprehension (=0-5)* | 20 points |
| MLA Format<br>• *student includes all required information in proper MLA format (=10)*<br>• *student doesn't appear to understand MLA or leaves out required info (=0-5)* | 10 points |

# Unit Four Essay Topics

*Check with your instructor before undertaking any essay topic.*

## Novel Reading Topics

**Character Study with Diagnosis**
> Length: four to five pages, 750–1250 words
> Source materials: the novel itself and one outside source

1. *The Curious Incident of the Dog in the Night-Time* by Mark Haddon (2003) – Identify the protagonist's symptoms and diagnose his condition. Although the word "autism" is never mentioned in the novel, it is clear that Christopher exhibits certain behaviors that are outside of the norm for a teenager. Connect his behavior with a valid outside source from the library, database, or internet that can help you to "diagnose" his condition.

2. *The Color Purple* by Alice Walker (1982) – Identify Celie's symptoms as a survivor of sexual and/or other forms of abuse. What are the most common effects resulting from sexual trauma and other forms of abuse? What behaviors does she display that stem from the trauma and abuse she has experienced? Connect her words and behavior in the novel with a valid outside source from the library, database, or internet that can help you to "diagnose" her condition.

3. *1984* by George Orwell (1949) – Analyze Winston's psychological conditioning and identify his state of mind at novel's end. In other words, explain why and how he can "love" Big Brother. Find a valid source from the library, database, or internet that can help you to define and clarify the sort of psychological conditioning which he undergoes.

## Alternate Essay Topic

Compose an essay which makes clear claims regarding the types of "literacies" and research capabilities that college students and adult citizens need to have in the 21st century. You can begin your research by reviewing "Research in the 21st Century" in this unit and with a review of source materials listed in this unit's "Further Inquiry & Research" page. Agree to length and other requirements and assignment parameters with your instructor before you begin your essay project.

## Suggested Evaluation Criteria and Point Values for the Unit Four Essay

| | |
|---|---|
| Holistic Evaluation<br>*The student presents an effective essay, writes clearly and knowledgeably, meets word count requirements, and turns in the assignment on deadline.* | 20 points |
| Thesis<br>*The student makes a major claim or offers a clear thesis that is responsive to the assignment guidelines.* | 10 points |
| Introduction of Texts<br>*The student engages in effective introductions of texts and source materials to an outside (or instructor-specified) audience.* | 10 points |
| Connection<br>*The student draws an effective, explicit connection between the novel and the outside source material.* | 10 points |
| Quotations and Text References<br>*The student quotes or specifically references at least three passages/scenes/episodes from the novel and appropriately quotes from or references outside source material. Quotations are properly integrated.* | 20 points |
| Voice<br>*The student demonstrates effective use of standard usage and syntax; the student demonstrates an adequate or effective prose style.* | 20 points |
| Format<br>*The student follows proper MLA (or other instructor-specified) format, including a proper header, in-text citation, Works Cited page, and other required format elements.* | 10 points |

# Resources

# Research in the 21st Century

Research is as simple as Googling a string of words, right?

The short answer is, Um, no.

Let me ask you this: Can you tell me what Google is and how it delivers information to you? Can you tell me how to distinguish "real" news from "fake" news? Do you have the capacity to assess the reliability of source materials?

Search engines like Google have made information access easier than at any point in human history. You, as a Millennial, or as a member of Generation Z, or however you want to identify yourself, have been born into an age that represents one of the fundamental shifts in the history of humankind. Scholars have likened the significance of the advent of the Internet Age to the prehistorical shift from a hunter-gatherer to an agriculture-based society. The fundamental importance of the internet has been compared to the development of the movable type printing press. The economic shift, we are told, is as significant as the impact of the Industrial Revolution. We now live in a "post-industrial" economy in which the flow of digital data is as important as the flow of goods and services.

When it comes to easy information access and data sharing, what many early observers of the internet failed to recognize was that "information" does not always mean "valid" or "reliable" information. We recognize now that there is plenty of "bad" or "unreliable" information out there on the internet. At times, unreliable and even malicious information seems to have as much impact on our public discourse as valid, reliable information has. Moreover, on the internet, information is often instantly "politicized" or distorted in a manner which, in my view, has a corrosive effect on our national discourse. When two people can't even agree on a common set of facts, how can they proceed with any kind of meaningful public discourse?

As teachers, we sometimes focus on these negatives for fear that our students will become prey to propaganda and manipulation. It is important to acknowledge as well that we live in an age of marvels and wonders. Not in my wildest boyhood imagination could I have come up with the realities that we take for granted in the 21st century. Were I to write this textbook in the 1980s (when I was much too young to write a textbook, by the way), I might spend an entire day at the library researching a few "free speech" court cases; nowadays, I can look up this information in a matter of minutes. I can instantly text, phone, or video link with my editor who lives a thousand miles away. And I can do it while I sip an Americano at Josef's, my favorite local café. I can play chess in real time with a friend who lives halfway around the world. (The 1980s version of this chess game took months or years and involved the actual composition of letters and the licking of stamps.) Via social media, I can engage in public discourse with likeminded citizens or with people who don't share my worldview.

This is the point when I tell my students (you've heard it before if you were paying attention), *You've got more computing power in your smartphone than NASA had on its Apollo 11 mission when it sent men to walk on the moon, and what do you do with all of this magnificent power? That's right. You play Candy Crush.*

Look, I like cat videos too.

Actually, I'm more of a dog person.

But you get the point.

So how does all this relate to research?

## News You Cannot Use

A 2018 study from the Massachusetts Institute of Technology (MIT) demonstrates that false news stories are 70 percent more likely to be shared on Twitter than actual news stories. To put it another way, "fake" news travels six times faster than "real" news. Computer science researchers who authored the study speculate that emotions of "surprise" and "disgust" when people encounter false news stories account for the drastically increased likelihood that fake news will be forwarded and shared. If fake news spreads like wildfire on Twitter, it is safe to assume, it appears to me, that fake news spreads in a similar fashion on other online and social media platforms.

After all, real news stories—which tend to take well-considered, moderate stances on the issues—are not nearly as exciting as internet posts that implicate U.S. presidential candidates in childhood slavery rings run out of pizza joints. Yes, that happened. In fact, an armed man fired off his AR-15 assault rifle in the pizzeria, convinced that employees were hiding kidnapped children in the restaurant. The controversial—and, I would add, unethical—web site *InfoWars.com* and its radio show host have had to apologize and pay fines on multiple occasions, including an apology for promoting the false story that inspired the gunman to terrorize this pizzeria. Yet the web site and its associated radio show plow forward, churning up dreck that some citizens mistake for actual news.

Keep in mind, my sources are always listed under "Further Inquiry & Research" at the end of each unit. I should also note that some commentators and journalists are not comfortable with the term "fake news" because "news," according to traditional denotations and connotations, is never "fake." Nevertheless, the term entered public discourse following the 2016 U.S. presidential campaign. When you encounter the term "fake news," consider: Who is using the term and why, and would the term "false information" serve as a better substitute?

Social scientists are alarmed. In an essay published in *Science*, a group of 16 political scientists and legal scholars call for research into ways that we can reduce the spread of false information within our "news ecosystem."

When encountering various forms of media, including print and electronic sources, are people, even reasonable people, capable of distinguishing *fact* and *opinion* and *real* from *fake*?

No prior generation has ever been challenged with an information/propaganda dilemma of such widespread, massive proportions.

If, like me, you value America's history of free speech protection, and if, like me, you appreciate the role of an educated populace in a functioning representational democracy like the United States, then, like me, you may recognize that we face a problem with no quick or easy solution.

## Data For Sale

As we go about our daily routines, we might forget that Google is a commercial entity peddling its for-profit service, funneling you toward advertisers who have paid top dollar to get your attention. The internet encourages skimming, encourages emotional responses to flickering and flashing stimuli. It does not encourage calm, well-reasoned cognition. It does not, generally speaking, encourage reflection or the meditative assessment of source materials. Even your teachers, if they are honest with you, will admit that they too have been on the losing end of distracting advertisements and "fake news" stories from time to time.

This is why your teachers worry.

And this is why research in the 21st century remains as complex as ever. Although it may only take me ten or fifteen minutes to look up those "free speech" court cases on the internet, the cognitive skills that are required to comprehend and assess the materials remain the same as in the 1980s when I needed an entire day to locate and review the materials. I could also, in that day of dedicated research, reflect upon my subject matter. I could ask the librarian a question or two. I could consult an information expert. I could learn the process.

The 21st century has cut out the middleman and called into question the authority of the expert. The utopian promise of the Internet Era involves the access of power—the power to go directly to an information source, for instance. And with great power comes . . . you guessed it . . . great responsibility.

## Curated and Non-Curated Information

Problems surrounding the reliability of information are not new. In the 1860s, Mark Twain produced a great deal of "fake news" and "alternate facts" as he entertained newspaper readers of Virginia City's *Territorial Enterprise*. Charlatanism goes back to the very origins of English language journalism with Richard Steele's *The Tatler* and its successor *The Spectator*, co-founded by Steele and Joseph Addison in 1711. Their friend and literary companion Jonathan Swift confused and outraged the public in 1729 when his anonymous essay "A Modest Proposal" suggested that England could solve the problem of dealing with so many poor Irish babies by cooking and eating them like calves and suckling swine. Swift's political satire is evident to the knowledgeable reader: bad English policies of governance are starving and consuming the poor of Ireland. Yet, in 1729, some readers missed the satire entirely and believed that a madman was actually proposing a scheme to harvest and consume babies. Each fall in American colleges and universities, a few naïve college freshman continue to fall prey to Swift's satirical charade.

One point is clear: when assessing information, you need to understand an author's "context." I use the word "context" here to represent the need for a holistic understanding of an author's purpose and intent, his or her social or political motives, if any, and the historical or publication context in which the author's text can be better understood. For example, when reading Judy Brady's "Why I Want A Wife," it is helpful to know that she published the article in *Ms.* magazine, a publication with a clear social and political agenda (a second wave feminist agenda). Knowing this information doesn't invalidate the article's content; it simply enhances our understanding of the article's content.

If an editor or publisher reviews and approves an article for publication, that article might be said to be a "curated" source of information. *To curate* typically means "to organize an art exhibit." In this case, however, *to curate* means "to put together and/or to select for presentation." Mainstream news sources such as CBS, CNN, NPR, *The Economist*, *National Review*, *The Nation*, *The Washington Post*, or *The Wall Street Journal* presumably present "curated" information, meaning that an editor or a fact-checker has reviewed the writer's work prior to publication or broadcast.

So, when researching, is it a good thing to seek "curated" sources of information?

Generally speaking, yes. Oftentimes, you can avoid being duped by a false information feed simply by ignoring non-curated sources of information. If an appalling news story makes its way to you from a web site that you have never heard of, then maybe you would be better off deleting the story and moving on with your life.

"Curated" information implies that the information source represents more than one person's opinion. It may represent a consensus view, or it may represent an analysis of a situation that multiple people have reviewed. In some cases, the source may represent a single person's view that an editor, board, or publication believes worthy of public consideration.

"Curated" information does not always mean "correct" information, however. Editors and editorial boards make mistakes. In the 1990s, several prestigious publications, including *The New Republic* and *Rolling Stone*, were taken in by the fabrications of writer Stephen Glass, who concocted from imagination what were supposed to be nonfiction news stories. He quoted people who didn't exist. His editors loved the vivid, telling details which he wove into his prose. No one bothered to check the facts. Later, it was determined that 27 of the 41 articles Glass wrote for *The New Republic* contained fabricated material.

I used to do this to my students: I would direct them into the password-protected confines of the college library's EBSCO database in order to find a story by Glass called "Hack Heaven." In the story, a teenaged hacker is rewarded for his crimes with an offer to become a security consultant for the company he hacked. The students and I would engage in a serious discussion of the issues. Was it OK for companies to hire teenaged criminals? Then, of course, I dropped the bomb: there was no hacker, there was no company. Glass had made it all up. Instead of being upset at Glass for his rotten journalistic ethics, the students, I got the feeling, were more upset at me. Of course, I was trying to prove a point: Even curated information can be false.

It's not often the case. I don't believe it is healthy or fair to engage in the kind of cynicism that says, You can't trust anything in this world! Instead, let's take on a healthy mantle of skepticism by admitting, We need to be careful about what sources of information we choose to trust.

If the dynamics surrounding the reliability of information were important to understand in a pre-internet world, then they seem critical to understand in the 21st century when data jumps at light speed from server to your computer. And don't forget that your phone too is a computer hooked up to those same servers and networks.

Clearly, if we must brandish skepticism with curated forms of information, then we must be even more careful with non-curated forms of information.

What non-curated forms of information do you see and hear every day?

How about Snapchat and Instagram? How about all manner of internet advertisement, including political advertisement? How about Twitter and Facebook? What else?

Recently, many of these companies have come under public pressure to moderate or "curate" the enormous streams of information that their platforms present, yet the very notion of "curation" runs counter to the early ideals of internet pioneers like John Perry Barlow, co-founder of the Electronic Freedom Foundation, who in his "A Declaration of the Independence of Cyberspace" (1996) wrote, "We are creating a world that all may enter without privilege or prejudice accorded by race, economic power, military force, or station of birth. . . . We are creating a world where anyone, anywhere may express his or her beliefs, no matter how singular, without fear of being coerced into silence or conformity."

If these internet companies wish to continue to abide by such foundational principles in the 21st century, how can they at the same time monitor and extinguish false information or "unacceptable" forms of speech, even hate speech?

Profound questions surrounding the distribution of non-curated forms of information are not entirely new in our country's history. State and federal governments have from time to time engaged in forms of censorship which were usually quickly overturned by the courts. More than any other nation on earth, America has offered legal protection to free speech, even to forms of speech that many citizens find offensive. In 1989 and 1990, for example, the U.S. Supreme Court upheld the First Amendment right of protestors to burn the U.S. flag. Most forms of speech and expression enjoy legal protection under U.S. law. Threats or speech deemed to cause imminent danger are examples of forms of expression that are not legally protected.

How will issues surrounding the distribution of non-curated forms of information on the internet intersect or clash with the American legacy of free speech protection?

Are there any forms of non-curated information that might prove useful when you are conducting research? What about a blog, for instance? What about an amateur podcast? How can you determine if the author/producer of such forms of non-curated information is an expert whose knowledge is worthy of your consideration or a charlatan whose work must be disregarded?

See the list of "A Few Key Definitions" in this unit. Why is it important to understand ".com" versus ".edu" versus ".org"? Will a "wiki" application tend to produce curated or non-curated information? And then there's this:

Doesn't everyone know you can't trust a "Wikipedia" article?

## Wikipedia

"Can you trust a Wikipedia article?" I ask my composition students this question every semester. They do not hesitate with their response: "No."

It's clear to me that the formula "Wikipedia BAD" has been drilled into their heads. So, naturally, I have to mess with their assumptions:

"Why not?"

Typically, a moment of silence follows. Then, "Because anyone can contribute to it."

That's right. Wikipedia is an online encyclopedia run by a "wiki" application, meaning that anyone can offer up an article or a detail for publication. Anyone, too, can flag a suspicious article or detail. Anyone can cite a presumed fact as needing citation. The best Wikipedia articles are filled with citations. In other words, the collective authors of these articles have taken the time to verify their sources of information.

Wikipedia is an electronic encyclopedia. As such, its articles are supposed to be informative, not argumentative. If you were to see a Wikipedia article in which the author is making unfounded claims or offering opinionated analysis, you would want to flag that article as needing citations or ignore it completely. Obviously, you wouldn't trust information in an article that is offering up unsubstantiated opinion. This is one reason that it is so important to be able to distinguish *fact* from *opinion*.

So how is Wikipedia, launched in 2001, different from other encyclopedias?

I would say there are two main things: 1) it is electronic, and 2) its articles are either semi-curated or non-curated.

A traditional print encyclopedia typically features more rigorous editorial curation than Wikipedia. Yet traditional encyclopedias can also contain falsehoods. My 1950 edition of *The Columbia Encyclopedia* identifies Pluto as a major planet discovered in 1930 which some scientists believe is bigger than Earth, while Wikipedia classifies it as a "dwarf planet" with five known moons, part of the Kuiper belt, the ring of more than a thousand "small bodies," which is a scientific designation distinct from the terms *planet*, *dwarf planet*, or *natural satellite*. All of the information is cited, and I can easily jump via hyperlinks from article to article to help broaden the horizon of my understanding.

So, at least in this single instance, Wikipedia is a far better source of information than my outdated print encyclopedia (which I love dearly and will not be trashing, thank you very much).

It is true that some "whacked" information has been published on the Wikipedia platform, especially in its early days. Teachers and professors hastened to warn off and even to forbid their students from reading Wikipedia articles. *Complex.com* offers a list of the "50 Craziest Lies in Wikipedia History," among them the slip-up (or intentional falsehood?) that Ernest Hemingway's *Death in the Afternoon*, a 1932 nonfiction book on bullfighting, concerns the "ceremony and traditions of Spanish whores." Could it have been an unfortunate typo, with the intended word being "mores," a noun from sociology meaning, according to Webster's, "folkways of central importance accepted without question and embodying the fundamental moral views of a group"? In any case, the Wikipedia entry now reads "Spanish bullfighting." The list of "lies" that *Complex.com* attributes to Wikipedia articles consists mostly of pranks ("Bin Laden was a top bloke and a chronic masturbator") and digital forms of "throwing shade" more than it involves serious attempts to manipulate information or to impugn someone's character. In 2005, an American public figure was alarmed to learn that the Wikipedia page under his name listed him as a suspect in the assassination of both President Kennedy and his brother, Bobby Kennedy. No perpetrator for the libelous entry was ever identified. As is unfortunately true in other internet venues, there exist politically motivated attacks as well, for example, identifying a politician as a vampire or an anti-Semite.

## Facts or Ideas That Qualify as "Common Knowledge"

So why would I put any faith in Wikipedia at all?

Answer: If I'm doing deep research, I do not use Wikipedia or any encyclopedia as source material. Encyclopedias, whether print or electronic, are starting points. They are never end points. However,

I will explore the citations listed at the bottom of a Wikipedia article. Why not? Often, I can find excellent source materials linked by way of Wikipedia citations, the same way that I can find solid citations in a high quality print encyclopedia.

Can I use Wikipedia to find "surface" information or to verify some item of "common knowledge"?

Answer: Absolutely. In the same way that I have to use a dictionary to remember how to spell a word from time to time, I can use Wikipedia to verify, for example, the capital of Missouri. (Jefferson City is the capital of Missouri. I just looked it up.) In this instance, I am not doing real research. I am verifying what is typically called "common knowledge." Even though I don't know the capital of Missouri, it is common knowledge that the capital of Missouri is Jefferson City. When a fact or idea qualifies as "common knowledge," then I don't have to cite my source of information on my bibliography.

What qualifies as "common knowledge"?

It's tricky. The idea is that information that most educated readers would know without having to look up qualifies as "common knowledge." You don't need to cite common knowledge information.

- If you quote data or statistics provided by an author or web site, it is not common knowledge and you must cite.
- If you paraphrase ideas that are new to you from a source with an author, it is not common knowledge and you must cite.
- If you don't know that the capital of Nevada is Carson City, you can look it up and assume that an average "educated reader" could know this fact, so you do not have to cite.
- There are certain scientific principles that a given audience might understand as common knowledge. For example, Pythagoras' theorem or Newton's first law of motion are common knowledge within a given community or audience. As such, these ideas require no citation.

## Database vs. Search Engine

As a college student or career professional, you must understand the difference between a "database" and a "search engine."

A database is a curated collection of information, typically free from ads and other peripheral distractions. You will likely encounter a number of databases in your school, college, university, or public library. As a college student, you very likely have access to a number of specialized databases. Databases such as *EBSCO* or *JSTOR* provide access to a broad range of publications in the liberal arts and social sciences. *CQ Researcher* provides overviews of social and political topics. *ERIC* houses education-related resources. *Medline Plus* contains a medical encyclopedia and dictionary, a drug and disease database, and surgery videos. There are dozens of databases aiming to help college students in their efforts to find reliable source materials. In the professional world, there are hundreds of specialized databases curated for the benefit of professionals such as accountants, lawyers, and entrepreneurs. These databases typically charge an access fee. In fact, as a college student, it is likely that you are paying a fee directly or indirectly connected with database usage . . . so you might as well get your money's worth, right?

A "search engine" is "free" only in the sense that the money doesn't come out of the end-consumer's pocket directly. Search engines run on an advertising model or fee structure, that is, payment for traffic generated. Hence, unless you are very careful, almost all of what you find over a search engine comes to you with an invisible price tag attached to it, often in the form of a software "cookie" which tracks your internet usage. Your habits and personal data have commercial value. Internet companies pay not only for the privilege to advertise to you; they pay to know what sites you visit, how long you spend there, whether a transaction is made, what hyperlinks you click on, and so forth.

Google, Bing, and Yahoo are examples of search engines.

Do I use these search engines? Yes, every day. I am also aware that I am constantly being sold something. This is the wearying price I pay for the use of a "free" search engine.

Is it possible to do deep research via a search engine?

The honest answer: it is difficult but not impossible.

## Boolean Operators

Google Scholar (*scholar.google.com*) represents a combination of database and search engine. The site touts itself as "a simple way to broadly search for scholarly literature" across many disciplines. Thousands of relevant article abstracts and book previews are available. Some full-text articles are available. However, based on my somewhat limited experience, the site seems to push you toward commercial products. Clearly, Google profits from such commercial traffic. For example, a search of "e-learning in the 21st century" offers me an e-book of the same title as a top pick. When I follow the link for this e-book, I am provided a preview of the book with a prominent "Get this book in print" link where I can slide over to Amazon.com or other retailers to purchase the product. Software will track my route from Google to the retailer, and Google would almost certainly receive a fractional payment if I were to purchase the book. This may be good information, but it's not free information. Nor am I arguing, necessarily, that all information should be free. As a writer, I value intellectual property and copyright protections, and I believe that writers and publishers who put in the hard work to produce a product deserve capital reward. I am only arguing for full awareness and full disclosure.

On the other hand, if I search Google Scholar for "e-learning in the 21st century," I find that the second source is a complete PDF file, an authored article with endnote citations in case I want to pursue deep study. This is good information, and it is free information.

Frequently, your first attempt at a keyword search in either a database or a search engine will not yield good results or will yield too many results. Via *google.com*, a search for "e-learning in the 21st century" yields 5.32 million results in .62 seconds. The top returns, of course, are commercial in nature, such as that same book for sale.

What are the chances that I will hunt through the first million results?

(Some rhetorical questions are so absurd that they deserve no response.)

"Boolean operators" can help us to control the information flow.

George Boole (1815–1864) was an English mathematician, educator, and philosopher who published several papers on the analysis of thought and logic. Today, his namesake "Boolean operators" are simple words—AND, OR, NOT, or AND NOT—used to combine or exclude keywords in a search engine or database search. Combining or excluding search terms can offer more focused and useful results.

In Google Scholar and many other web-based databases and search engines, you may have to look for an "Advanced Search" feature in order to take advantage of Boolean operators. Databases, on the other hand, will recognize Boolean operators, enhancing your capacity to more quickly find meaningful results.

- AND, OR, NOT, or AND NOT are Boolean operators used to combine or exclude terms in a database search
  - For example, weapons NOT guns
- Use quotation marks to create a "Boolean string" in order to search for a phrase instead of separate words
  - For example, "library resources" instead of *library resources* produces more focused results.
- Combine Boolean strings and Boolean operators to focus and enhance your results
  - For example, "nuclear weapon" AND submarine

## Internet and Institutional Resources

One of the great privileges of being a college student is that in most institutions you will have instant access to a wide variety of curated databases such as *EBSCO*, *CQ Researcher*, *JSTOR*, and numerous other databases. As mentioned, you almost certainly help to fund database access by way of student fees, so take advantage!

Check with your instructor and your institution on what library and database resources are available to you.

## Open Educational Resources (OER) and Open Movements

Increasingly, educational institutions are embracing what is known as OER, or Open Educational Resources. The web site *OER Commons* defines itself as a "public digital library of open educational resources." The site offers online building tools for teachers of all levels.

More generally, open educational resources are any resources that are available online at little or no cost for the purpose of teaching, learning, or research. The idea of "open" resources stems most directly from the computer revolution of the late 20th century in which some prominent digital pioneers emphasized the importance of "open source" software platforms built by a collective for the public good. Many educational institutions nationwide and globally have embraced the concept of developing free educational resource databases, including curated and peer-reviewed articles and full-text e-books. The hopeful idea of the internet as a vast, free public library may come closer to fruition with such efforts.

Skeptics like political scientist Langdon Winner, as you will read in Unit Six: The Web, rejected the utopian visions of early digital pioneers, and computer entrepreneurs like Microsoft co-founder Bill Gates built their fortunes on the outright rejection of the "open source software" or "shareware" mode of conducting business. Gates claimed patent and copyright protections for his software products and at various times in his career has been criticized for squelching competition and running monopolistic enterprises. To be clear, I am not endorsing or rejecting this view of Gates. I do think that the history of Microsoft embodies important developments in the history of the personal computer which should be understood by students today who probably take internet "openness" for granted.

An introduction to OER (Open Educational Resources) and a collection of open databases, advocacy organizations, and resources can be found under the "OER Resources" tab at *http://libguides.tmcc.edu/ OpenEducationalResources*.

The "openness" of the internet is something that we all take for granted, but as we see in the discussions above, the question of "openness" is a complicated one, made more complicated by issues of *copyright* and *public domain*. Define "copyright." Define "public domain." Look up exact definitions rather than muddling through with a vague, general ideas of what these terms mean.

One fun side note I like to add: I ask my students why Hollywood and London producers are so in love with Sherlock Holmes? Arthur Conan Doyle's fictional detective is a mythic figure who transcends time, right? Yet there may be a more prosaic answer for his popularity. Holmes—who first appeared in 1887—exists in the "public domain," meaning that stage, TV, and film producers don't have to pay the author's estate any licensing fees or royalties. "What about Philip Marlowe?" I ask my students. No one has heard of him. He is Raymond Chandler's famous detective who first appeared in the 1939 novel *The Big Sleep*. Under the U.S. Copyright Act of 1909, Chandler's detective Marlowe does not exist in the public domain, meaning that anyone who wants to produce a show starring this fictional detective will have to pay for the right to do so. It would be interesting to ask Raymond Chandler (1888–1959) which he would prefer—the monies he garnered as a result of copyright protections or the kind of universal renown that Arthur Conan Doyle and Sherlock Holmes have enjoyed.

Questions surrounding copyright protection are complicated. Think about musicians and songwriters of the 21st century. How do we expect these artists to continue to produce music if they don't have money to buy groceries? Yet Chance the Rapper tells *Vanity Fair* and other outlets, "I never wanted to sell my music, because I thought putting a price on it put a limit on it and inhibited me from making a connection."

Artists like Chance the Rapper, whose 2016 *Coloring Book* was the first streaming-only album to top a Billboard chart, adopted and expanded the "open source" concept of the computer pioneers who advocated for an internet filled with "shareware."

The book that you are holding in your hand is, I hope, a bit of a hybrid between OER "open source materials" and copyright-protected source materials. Due to the legal protections of copyright, I/we (the publisher) have to pay fees for the primary source materials. I can't apologize for that because some things are worth paying for, and, as many a wise elder will remind you, there is no such thing as a free lunch. At the same time, I/we have attempted to provide you at the end of each unit with a deep well of OER resources so that you can explore and research high quality, free materials. Unfortunately, a few of these "free" resources will come with blinking, distracting ads. These would be examples of the "no free lunch" principle. I truly dislike ads. And maybe I'm turning into a grouchy curmudgeon, but the situation seems to be worsening. Yet many of us can't afford to pay subscription fees to databases or web sites in order to avoid the ads. The dynamic between "open source materials" and ad-based content is one of the significant conundrums surrounding general interest research in the 21st century.

## Matching Your Research to Your Purpose and Audience

As noted in a prior unit, your understanding of *purpose* and *audience* are two key concepts to keep at the forefront of your mind when writing and researching. Often, you can make important decisions on where to research, how to research, and which sources to select if you remain aware of purpose and audience.

For example, if you are writing for a specialized audience, your research sources will tend to be more specialized. If you are writing a paper for an upper-division biology course, then you might favor peer-reviewed studies published in academic journals intended for biology professionals. "Peer-reviewed" publication means that an original study or article has been reviewed by other professionals in the field. Peer-reviewed articles may be found in specialized databases, or sometimes online if, for example, a professional organization has a web site that is open to the public. Peer-reviewed articles are clear examples of "curated" sources of information.

"Specialized" audiences have their own vocabulary. Your anthropology instructor may want you to utilize the specialized vocabulary of this particular academic discipline. If your purpose involves communicating directly to a specialized audience, then your research will gravitate toward specialized databases and possibly even peer-reviewed primary source material—that is, original accounts and studies authored by the scientists themselves.

In this course, as in many composition courses, assignments ask you to address a general "outside" audience. As always, check with your instructor. Most research assignments in a first year composition course call for the writer to address a general outside audience, but that is not always the case. For example, in a special topics composition course that I taught on "American Popular Music," I encouraged students to develop specialized vocabulary associated with music studies and with music criticism. Most of my composition courses, on the other hand, require students to address a wide, general readership.

## Primary and Secondary Sources

In different scholarly disciplines, "primary" and "secondary" source material can mean different things. In the field of history, a pioneer's 19th century diary entries can be considered "primary" source material, whereas a historian's overarching analytical account of such primary source materials can be called a "secondary" source. The scholar, in this case, summarizes the results of his or her analysis of historical documents.

In any given scientific field, a "primary" source could involve the published results of a scientist's experiment(s). Such a primary scientific source might feature jargon and mathematical symbols that would make it very difficult or even impossible for someone like me to follow. Although I am well educated, I simply don't have the background to be able to process a primary study in most scientific fields. In order to access this kind of information, I must rely on "secondary" source material. For example, a science writer may publish a journalistic account that summarizes the findings of an original study. I would find this secondary source much more useful. And, if I wanted to write an essay for publication on a scientific topic, I would have to track down and rely upon secondary sources.

In the humanities and in literary studies, there may be some confusion even among instructors regarding what constitutes a "primary" or a "secondary" source. Always check with your instructors. In a world literature class, a "primary" source is the author's original text, whereas an article that offers a contemporary reassessment of the author's literature may be called a "secondary" source. However, some instructors may call this latter article a primary source as well. It doesn't really matter (to me) if we call the scholarly article a primary or a secondary source, as long as we are all thinking in clear terms regarding our source materials.

Note that there is no *better* or *worse* when it comes to "primary" and "secondary" source material. What I mean is, primary sources are not necessarily "better" than secondary sources. If the true primary source material in a world literature class was written in ancient Greek, for example, then we must rely on a secondary source, the English language interpretation of the original material, in order to access the information. Scholars who operate within a discipline on a very high level tend to deal with primary source material. These scholars generate secondary source materials that enable the rest of us to be able to engage in the pertinent discourse.

All of the assignments in this textbook ask you to address a general audience. (Again, always check with your instructor. He or she may want you to take on a particular topic by addressing a particular audience.)

When you address a general audience, your sources will tend to be more general in nature. You will probably want to avoid primary source materials that are aimed at a specialized audience and which utilize field-specific jargon. Here's a note for consideration: If you can't understand the field-specific jargon in an article, should you be listing that article on your Works Cited page or trying to quote from the article?

Well-researched analytical secondary source materials that appear in general interest publications will likely prove to be more useful for you and for your audience. For example, if I am writing an article on human efforts to manipulate genetics in the animal kingdom, am I better off using a cover story from *National Geographic* which offers a summary-analysis of recent developments, or am I better off using an original peer-reviewed study from the *Journal of Genetic Engineering and Biotechnology*?

The answer to this question, I believe, depends on two things: *purpose* and *audience*. If you are a graduate student studying genetic engineering, you must seek out specialized information for a specialized audience. If you are a first year college student who wishes to participate in an important public discourse on ethical responsibilities when it comes to genetic manipulation, you are clearly better off integrating important quotations from a well-respected general interest magazine.

## A Few Key Definitions

How can we claim to be 21st-century literate unless we can actually *define* the basic elements imbuing our everyday lives? Define the words and terms below, not with inexact phraseology (*it's sort like a thing that . . .*) but with an exact definition that an outside reader could comprehend. Write down these definitions. Your instructor may choose to turn this task into a formal exercise.

- What is a "search engine"? What is a "browser"?
- What is a "database"?
- What is the "internet"?
- What is a "server"?
- What is a "domain"?
- What is the "cloud"?
- Define "cybersecurity" and "wireless."
- Can you distinguish between email, videoconferencing, blogs, chats, messaging, tweets, alerts, and podcasts? Describe each.
- What is a "wiki"? What is "UGC, or user-generated content"?
- What is a "user interface"?
- What is an "avatar"?
- What is an "IP address"?
- What is a "URL address"? What is "DOI"?
- What is "Google"?
- What is "http" and "https"?
- What do ".com," ".org," and ".edu" mean?
- What is "Wikipedia"?
- What is "shareware"?
- What is "crowdsourcing"?
- What is a "course management system"?
- What is "concept mapping"?
- What is an "app"?
- What are "tags"? What is "metadata"?
- Define "AI" and "deep learning."
- What is "GIS"?

What other definitions of terms do you think are necessary to know in the 21st century? (What about a "cookie"? Hint: you can't eat it.)

## The National Council of Teachers of English (NCTE) Definition of 21st Century Literacies

*Updated February, 2013, Adopted by the NCTE Executive Committee, February 15, 2008*

Literacy has always been a collection of cultural and communicative practices shared among members of particular groups. As society and technology change, so does literacy. Because technology has increased the intensity and complexity of literate environments, the 21st century demands that a literate person possess a wide range of abilities and competencies, many literacies. These literacies are multiple, dynamic, and malleable. As in the past, they are inextricably linked with particular histories, life possibilities, and social trajectories of individuals and groups. Active, successful participants in this 21st century global society must be able to

- Develop proficiency and fluency with the tools of technology;
- Build intentional cross-cultural connections and relationships with others so [as] to pose and solve problems collaboratively and strengthen independent thought;
- Design and share information for global communities to meet a variety of purposes;
- Manage, analyze, and synthesize multiple streams of simultaneous information;
- Create, critique, analyze, and evaluate multimedia texts;
- Attend to the ethical responsibilities required by these complex environments.

*This position statement may be printed, copied, and disseminated without permission from NCTE. From* http://www2.ncte.org/statement/21stcentdefinition/.

# Major Research Question

One of the first steps in writing a research paper involves developing a "major research question." The idea is for you to develop a central question that will guide your research efforts.

✓ A central major research question is usually an open-ended "How" or "Why" question. It is not a binary Yes/No question. "How" and "Why" provide for avenues of inquiry, whereas "yes" or "no" provides no path forward for further inquiry.
  - "Why is it important to understand social context when assessing peer interactions that take place over social media?" *This is a big question that can propel us toward further insights and knowledge. We will almost always need to pare down our original draft question later on in order to provide ourselves with a sharper focus on content and audience.*
  - "Is it important to understand social context when assessing peer interactions that take place over social media?" *Immediately we can say "Yes" or "No." In either case, we have given ourselves a barrier to further inquiry.*

You will also want to identify your prospective *audience*. Is it a specialized audience who expects to read specialized analysis, or is it a general audience who will appreciate more generalized information? Does your general audience want a list of information on a given topic, or do they want the writer to analyze the information in order to provide an insightful analysis of the topic?

## A Case Study in the Development of a "Major Research Question"

Let's take a hypothetical situation and pursue a major research question.
  *The Assigned Topic*: Global Warming and Geoengineering: Science or Fiction?
  First, ask yourself: What do I know about this topic? Answer: Not much. As a first year college student, you don't know a great deal about a great deal. You are learning. So . . . forget what you think you know and take on the attitude of "I don't know; therefore, I can learn." Some of the smartest, wisest people in the world begin their own inquiries with a conceit of "Let's say I know nothing. . . . Where would I start?"

"What is global warming?" "How does global warming affect the climate?" "What is geoengineering?" "Are there any proven instances of geoengineering solving an environmental problem?" Are these good major research questions? No, not yet. Remember that a major research question, in order to be effective, cannot be structured as a Yes/No inquiry.

Whether any given question is a serviceable major research question may depend on the *purpose* of your research paper. Does your instructor want you to write an *informational* research paper? If so, then, in your composition, you might be able to describe and define "global warming" as a scientific phenomenon. Chances are better, however, that your instructor will want you to write an *analytical* or *argumentative* research paper. In this case, defining "global warming" or "geoengineering" won't be enough to satisfy the paper requirements.

- You may need to resort to superficial, encyclopedic research in order to produce a good major research question. Call this phase "preliminary research." It will involve such tasks as nailing down good definitions of terms such as "global warming" and "geoengineering."
- When developing a paper topic and a major research question, try to do two impossible things: 1) take the politics (or "partisanship") out of the topic, and 2) forget whatever it is you think you know about the topic.

In the case of global warming, long before this issue was politicized or made a partisan issue, environmental and other scientists suspected that the globe was warming. Since the last Ice Age, global warming, in fact, appears to represent a natural cycle. The question since the late 20th century hasn't been whether global warming is real, the question is whether human activity has caused or accelerated the phenomenon. There really is no longer credible disagreement about the fact that the globe is warming. Some scientists cannot conclude that global warming is *caused by* human activity. Most scientists do conclude that global warming is being accelerated by human activity. So the crux of the matter isn't what "climate skeptics" or "environmental radicals" have to say on the issue. When it comes to environment, I put more faith in the scientific community than I put into political pundits on either extreme of the spectrum who often seem to have agendas that do not involve facts. And once we do a bit of research and understand the scope of the issue, we should also, in my view, be wary of commentators who either deny a phenomenon exists or who offer easy solutions to extremely complex problems.

Now you can propose some questions that you might answer. Call this stage "intermediate research." At this point, we have moved beyond the preliminary definitions of terms and we have to uncover some questions that will help us understand the topic on a broad basis. "What scientific evidence exists that global warming is caused by human activity?" "What scientific evidence exists that global warming is not caused by human activity?" Avoid asking, "Is there scientific evidence to prove that global warming exists?" since this is a Yes/No question which will consequently limit your inquiry. "What credible instances of geoengineering exist in order to address issues of global warming and climate change?"

In the course of answering these "intermediate research" questions, we come across a general readership article on the NASA web site (with cited scientific references) that provides a list of the gases that contribute to the "greenhouse effect" of global warming: water vapor, nitrous oxide, methane, and carbon dioxide appear to be the main culprits. By checking the citations on the NASA web page, we find several apparently valid sources verifying the likelihood that human activity is a factor in global warming. A group of 1,300 scientists conclude that there's a "more than 95 percent probability that activities over the past 50 years have warmed our planet."[1]

---

[1] "A Blanket Around the Earth." *NASA Global Climate Change: Vital Signs of the Planet*, "Facts," "Causes," *https://climate.nasa.gov/causes/*, Site updated Mar. 19, 2018, Accessed Mar. 19, 2018.

After our intermediate research, questions like "What scientific evidence exists that global warming is caused by human activity?" can be sharpened to focus on particular aspects of the phenomenon. Focusing on one of the greenhouse gases is a clear possibility.

Finally, after a bit of preliminary and intermediate research, you can begin to draft a major research question. In this case, we will want to incorporate the terms from each aspect of the proposed topic "Global Warming and Geoengineering: Science or Fiction?" Can we find a question that involves the terms "global warming" and "geoengineering"? Can we find a question that has a narrow enough focus so that we can provide our audience meaningful information and/or analysis within the assignment parameters?

In our hypothetical scenario, you, as the writer, take a more keen interest in "methane" than the other greenhouse gases due to the fact that methane is associated with livestock and agriculture and you have an interest in the food chain. Maybe you are a "foodie" who likes the idea of locally sourced products, so you put it all together:

✓ What viable solutions can geoengineering offer small-scale agricultural operations to address problems associated with methane production in agricultural industries?

The nice thing about a sharp major research question is that it can make the actual research and drafting of your composition much easier than it would be otherwise. Rather than scrambling through volumes of sources attempting to narrow your focus on a broad topic, you have already narrowed your focus through the "major research question" production process.

The production of a good major research question is similar to the production of a useful keyword search in a search engine or database. If your keywords are too broad, you are presented with a million (search engine) or ten thousand (database) possibilities to follow. If you find the right words and the correct Boolean operators, you can hone your search and make it much more productive.

Better yet, let's say the production of a good major research question is like finding the perfect pair of shoes on that massive web site on which, I admit, I have shopped. If I shop for "black shoes," I might spend days finding the right kicks. First, I tag "Men's Shoes" (because I'm not interested in "Women's Shoes" at the moment). Then, I put in my size and color preference. I need to pick a particular style of shoe in order to get it down to a reasonable number. Then I can mark whether I want laces or a zipper, leather or synthetic. I insert the price I'm willing to pay. When I get it down to a reasonable number of entries, I scan the page. Yes, I'm picky. More to the point, I value my time. Although I try to keep my dollars local, in this case I don't have time to spend hours or a whole day hunting for the shoes I want. I can select what I want in a short period of time so that I can go do other things. For you, with the major research question and with the research paper in general, there are very likely other things that you need to do along with your work in this course. So be wise. Develop a solid, narrowly focused major research question up front . . . and then you'll have time to enjoy shopping for those shoes later.

## Further Inquiry & Research

Coiro, Julie. "Predicting Reading Comprehension on the Internet: Contributions of Offline Reading Skills, Online Reading Skills, and Prior Knowledge." *Journal of Literary Research*, Vol. 43, No. 4 (2011), *doi: 10.1177/1086296X11421979.*

Coiro, Julie. "Talking About Reading as Thinking: Modeling the Hidden Complexities of Online Reading Comprehension." *Theory Into Practice*, Vol. 50, No. 2 (2011), pp. 107–115, *doi: 10.1080/00405841.2011.558435.*

Coiro, Julie and David W. Moore. "New Literacies and Adolescent Learners: An Interview With Julie Coiro." *Journal of Adolescent & Adult Literacy*, Vol. 55, No. 6 (Mar. 2012), pp. 551–553, *http://www.jstor.org/stable/41827858.*

Darnton, Robert. "The Research Library in the Digital Age." Harvard University Library, 2008, *http://hul.harvard.edu/publications/Darnton_ResearchLibraryDigitalAge.pdf.*

Davlashyan, Naira, and Irina Titova. Associated Press (AP). "Ex-Workers at Russian Troll Factory Say Mueller Indictments Are True." *Time.com,* Feb. 19, 2018, *http://time.com/5165805/russian-troll-factory-mueller-indictments/.*

Kang, Cecilia, and Adam Goldman. "In Washington Pizzeria Attack, Fake News Brought Real Guns." *The New York Times, nytimes.com, Dec. 5, 2016, https://www.nytimes.com/2016/12/05/business/media/comet-ping-pong-pizza-shooting-fake- news-consequences.html.*

Kleinman, Zoe. "Cambridge Analytica: The Story So Far." *BBC News,* Technology, Mar. 20, 2018. *http://www.bbc.com/news/technology-43465968.*

Knobel, Michele and Colin Lankshear. "Studying New Literacies." *Journal of Adolescent & Adult Literacy,* Vol. 58, No. 2 (Oct. 2014), pp. 97–101, *http://www.jstor.org/stable/24034699.*

Leu, Donald J. et al. "The New Literacies of Online Research and Comprehension: Rethinking the Reading Achievement Gap." *Reading Research Quarterly*, Vol. 50, No. 1 (Jan.-Mar. 2015), pp. 37–59, *doi: 10.1002/rrq.85.*

McCarthy, Tom. "Sherlock Holmes is public property . . . But Steer Clear of Watson's Second Wife." *The Guardian,* Dec. 27, 2013, *https://www.theguardian.com/world/2013/dec/27/sherlock-holmes-copyright-ruling-public- domain.*

Meyer, Robinson. "The Grim Conclusions of the Largest-Ever Study of Fake News." *The Atlantic, theatlantic.com,* Mar. 8, 2018, *https://www.theatlantic.com/technology/archive/2018/03/largest-study-ever-fake-news-mit- twitter/555104/.*

Robinson, Lisa. "Why Chance the Rapper Makes Music for Free (and How He Actually Makes Money)." *Vanity Fair,* Feb. 9, 2017, *https://www.vanityfair.com/hollywood/2017/02/why-chance-the-rapper-music-is-free-and-how- he-makes-money.*

Rosenberg, Eli. "Alex Jones Apologizes for Promoting 'Pizzagate' Hoax." *The New York Times, nytimes.com,* Mar. 25, 2017, *https://www.nytimes.com/2017/03/25/business/alex-jones- pizzagate-apology-comet-ping-pong.html.*

Schultz, Colin. "'Sherlock Holmes' Is Now Officially Off Copyright and Open for Business." *Smithsonian.com,* June 19, 2014, *https://www.smithsonianmag.com/smart-news/sherlock-holmes-now-officially-copyright-and- open-business-180951794/.*

"To Our Readers." *New Republic,* vol. 218, no. 22, June 1, 1998, pp. 8–9. EBSCO*host.*

"What Is Common Knowledge?" *Academic Integrity at MIT: A Handbook for Students.* Massachusetts Institute of Technology, *integrity.mit.edu, https://integrity.mit.edu/handbook/citing-your-sources/what-common-knowledge.*

## Additional Source Materials by Topic

### The Curious Incident of the Dog in the Night-Time

Berger, James. "Alterity and Autism: Mark Haddon's Curious Incident in the Neurological Spectrum". *The Society for Critical Exchange.* Oct. 28, 2005, http://case.edu/affil/sce/Texts_2005/Autism%20and%20Representation%20Berger.htm

Carter, Bucky. "Imagetext in The Curious Incident of the Dog in the Night-time." *ImageTexT: Interdisciplinary Comics Studies.* 3.3 (2007). Dept of English, University of Florida. 28 Sep 2018, http://www.english.ufl.edu/imagetext/archives/v3_3/carter/

Draaisma, Douwe. "Stereotypes of Autism." *Philosophical Transactions of the Royal Society B, Biological Sciences,* Apr. 13, 2009, doi: 10.1098/rstb.2008.0324, http://rstb.royalsocietypublishing.org/content/364/1522/1475.short

Effron, Malcah. *The Millennial Detective: Essays on Trends in Crime Fiction, Film and Television, 1990–2010.* McFarland, Oct. 6, 2011, *books.google.com*

Osteen, Mark. *Autism and Representation.* Routledge, 2010, *books.google.com*

Rapezzi et al. "White Coats and Fingerprints: Diagnostic Reasoning in Medicine and Investigative Methods of Fictional Detectives." *BMJ* 2005, 331:1491, Dec. 22, 2005, doi: https://doi.org/10.1136/bmj.331.7531.149

Rose, Irene. "What Can We Do with 'The Curious Incident of the Dog in the Night-Time?' Popular Fiction and Representations of Disability." *Popular Narrative Media*, Vol. 1, No. 1 (Apr. 2008): pp. 43+, *Gale Academic One-File,* via *scholar.google.com*

## The Color Purple

Abbandonato, Linda. "A View from 'Elsewhere': Subversive Sexuality and the Rewriting of the Heroine's Story in *The Color Purple. PMLA, vol. 106, No. 5 (Oct., 1991), pp. 1106–1115,* via jstor.org

Babb, Valerie. "*The Color Purple*: Writing to Undo What Writing has Done". *Phylon (1960-),* Vol. 47, No. 2 (2nd Qtr., 1986), pp. 107–116. Published by *Clark Atlanta University,* via jstor.org, http://www.jstor.org

Bloom, Harold. *The Color Purple: New Edition*. Infobase Publishing, 2008, *books.google.com*

Bobo, Jacqueline. "Sifting Through the Controversy: Reading *The Color Purple*". *Callaloo, No. 39, (Spring, 1989), pp. 332–342.* Published by *The Johns Hopkins University Press.* Via jstor.org

Cheung, King-Kok. "'Don't Tell': Imposed Silences in *The Color Purple* and *The Woman Warrior*". *PMLA, Vol. 103, No. 2 (Mar.,1988), pp. 162–174,* http://www.jstor.org

Cutter, Martha. "Philomela Speaks: Alice Walker's Revisioning of Rape Archetypes in *The Color Purple*". *MELUS,* vol. 25, No. ¾, Revising Traditions Double Issue (Autumn – Winter, 2000), pp. 161–180. Published by *Oxford University Press* on behalf of *Society for the Study of the Multi-Ethnic Literature of the United States.* Via jstor.org

Harris, Trudier. "On *The Color Purple*, Stereotypes, and Silence". *Black American Literature Forum, vol. 18, No. 4 (Winter, 1984), pp. 155–161,* via jstor.org

Hite, Molly. "Romance, Marginality, Matrilineage: Alice Walker's 'The Color Purple' and Zora Neale Hurston's 'Their Eyes were Watching God'". *Novel: A Forum on Fiction*, Vol. 22, No. 3, (Spring, 1989), pp. 257–273. Published by *Duke University Press,* via jstor.org

Marvin, Thomas F. "'Preachin' the Blues': Bessie Smith's Secular Religion and Alice Walker's *The Color Purple*". *African American Review,* Vol. 28, No. 3 (Autumn, 1994), pp. 411–421. Published by *Indiana State University,* via jstor.org

Selzer, Linda. "Race and Domesticity in *The Color Purple*". *African American Review,* vol. 29, No. 1, (Spring, 1995), pp. 67–82. Published by *Indiana State University,* via jstor.org

Storey, John. *Cultural Theory and Popular Culture*. University of Georgia Press, 1997, *books.google.com*

Tucker, Lindsey. "Alice Walker's *The Color Purple*: Emergent Woman, Emergent Text". *Black American Literature Forum,* vol. 22, No. 1, Black Women Writers Issue (Spring, 1998), pp. 81–95. Published by: *African American Review, (St Louis University),* via jstor.org

## 1984

Harris, Harold J. "Orwell's Essays and 1984". *Twentieth Century Literature*, Vol. 4, No. 4 (Jan., 1959), pp. 154–161. Published by *Duke University Press,* accessed via jstor.org

Kateb, George. "The Road to 1984". *Political Science Quarterly,* Vol. 81, No. 4 (Dec., 1966), pp. 564-580. Published by *The Academy of Political Science* via jstor.org

Kellner, Douglas. "From *1984* to One-Dimensional Man: Critical Reflections on Orwell and Marcuse". *Graduate School of Education & Information Studies, University of California – Los Angeles.* 1990, https://pages.gseis.ucla .edu/faculty/kellner/essays/from1984toonedimensional.pdf

Orwell, George. *Nineteen Eighty-Four*. Knopf Doubleday Publishing Group, Jan. 14, 2019, *books.google.com*

## Plagiarism in the Internet Era

Ercegovac, Zorana and John V. Richardson. "Academic Dishonesty, Plagiarism Included, in the Digital Age: A Literature Review." *College & Research Libraries*, Vol. 65, No. 4 (2004), doi: *https://doi.org/10.5860/crl.65.4.301*

Gabriel, Trip. "Plagiarism Lines Blur for Students in Digital Age." *The New York Times,* Education, Aug. 1, 2010, *www.nytimes.com, https://www.nytimes.com/2010/08/02/education/02cheat.html?_r=2*

### Millennials and Research

Bland, Helen W., et al. "Stress tolerance: new challenges for millennial college students." *College Student Journal,* vol. 46, no. 2, 2012, p. 362+. Academic OneFile

Head, Alison and Eisenberg, Michael. "How College Students Use the Web to Conduct Everyday Life Research". (April 4, 2011). *First Monday,* Vol. 16, No. 4, April 4, 2011. Available at SSRN, https://papers.ssrn.com/sol3/papers.cfm?abstract_id=2281533

Jodie Eckleberry-Hunt, Jennifer Tucciarone, (2011) The Challenges and Opportunities of Teaching "Generation Y". *Journal of Graduate Medical Education*: December 2011, Vol. 3, No. 4, pp. 458–461. http://www.jgme.org/doi/full/10.4300/JGME-03-04-15

McGlynn, Angela Provltera. "Teaching Millennials, Our Newest Cultural Cohort". *The Hispanic Outlook in Higher Education,* 16 (Oct. 10, 2005) 19–20, via *scienceearth.com*

Ng, E., Lyons, S., & Scheritizer, L. "Managing the New Workforce: International Perspectives on the Millennial Generation". *Edward Elgar Publishing,* Jan. 1, 2012, *books.google.com*

Sweeney, Richard T. "Reinventing Library Buildings and Services for the Millennial Generation". *American Library Association,* Vol. 19, No. 4 (2005), https://journals.tdl.org/llm/index.php/llm/article/viewFile/1544/824

# UNIT FIVE

# Social Psychology

## Readings, Responsibilities, & Objectives for Unit Five: Social Psychology

## Suggested Timeline: Two to Three Weeks

Stanley Milgram's infamous experiments on obedience continue to stir controversy more than fifty years after they were first conducted. What was his experiment? How was it set up and who participated? Was it ethical? Why or why not? What was his purpose? Was there a scientific purpose, in your view? Is it a "scientific" experiment? Why or why not?

In 1963, Milgram published an article entitled "Behavioral Studies of Obedience" in *The Journal of Abnormal and Social Psychology*. The article was written for a specialized peer audience of psychologists and social psychologists. In the article, he sums up his findings regarding a series of controversial experiments he conducted at Yale University. Milgram's article "The Perils of Obedience," published in *Harper's Magazine* in 1973, serves the same purpose: to summarize for a curious world what, in his final analysis, Milgram believes his experiments demonstrate. This latter article, however, which appears in our *Engaging Discourse* textbook, is clearly aimed at a non-specialized or general readership audience.

Do some quick internet research on Milgram and his experiments. Be aware of your sources of information! It's possible in this cyber age of wonder to track down Milgram's original film(s) that he put together in order to explain his experiment and its results to the world. It's also possible to find a lot of more contemporary material that claims to replicate or update Milgram's experiment. Be wary of taking any of these sources of information at face value.

Part of your challenge and your responsibility in this unit will be to sift fact from opinion and historical truth from historical misunderstanding.

We must engage in this cognitive exercise not only in regard to Milgram's experiments, but also in regard to the killing of Catherine (Kitty) Genovese, whose murder became one of the most famous homicide cases in American history and whose death came to symbolize, according to various observers, some key facets of the human condition.

Were these observers, however, working from a common set of facts? To what extent did misinformation influence the interpretations surrounding her murder? To what extent do the sorrowful facts of the case substantiate these interpretations?

Stanley Milgram and Paul Hollander, in an article first published in *The Nation* in 1964, take it for granted that their audience knows something about the details of the famous Genovese murder. So many decades later, however, we don't. So verify the facts before you undertake any of the writing assignments.

Your task in Essay Four is to identify, explain, and critique a common or similar concern expressed by social psychologists in these two articles, which are written on completely different topics. Despite the disparate subject matter—an obedience experiment and a young woman's murder—there are connections: one's sense of responsibility or moral obligation to our fellow humans, the diffusion of responsibility, the effect of groups on a person's mentality and behavior. From the aspect of social psychology, in fact, there are numerous vital connections. Narrowing your focus is one of your biggest challenges. In approaching this composition, you must be especially wary of misstating the facts and of other forms of inaccuracy, in particular, making inaccurate interpretations of the arguments contained in these source essays. Make sure that you and your classmates understand the facts and the authors' interpretations of those facts. It's easy to get sidetracked and to neglect to focus on one particular issue or subtopic. Your goal is to develop a major claim (also called a *thesis*) in response to these texts. Obviously, you must present your major claim so that it's persuasive to your audience.

## Readings

1. Stanley Milgram and Paul Hollander, "Paralyzed Witnesses: The Murder They Heard" (1964)
2. Stanley Milgram, "The Perils of Obedience" (1973)

## Responsibilities

**Reader Response #5** and **Reader Response #6** anticipate **Essay Four**.

## Objectives

✓ Students will annotate texts, engage in group discussions, and produce critical, creative connections in discussion and in formal compositions between the texts themselves and between the texts and the student's life experience.

✓ This unit aims to reinforce the development of sound critical and analytical thinking through the detailed evaluation of source materials.

✓ This unit challenges students to turn sound critical and analytical thinking on complex topics into clear prose.

✓ Students must produce writing with clear organization, appropriate logic, detailed text analysis, and solid support for their own views, with appropriately cited source information.

✓ Students will develop critical thinking, reading, and writing strategies in order to produce notes, drafts, and a final essay that exhibits synthetic connections between source materials.

✓ Students will demonstrate the ability to produce clear, accurate, and correct academic discourse that reflects an acceptable level of critical thinking while employing the conventions of standard written English.

# Resources

A Worksheet on Stanley Milgram and Paul Hollander's "Paralyzed Witnesses: The Murder They Heard"

Integrating a Minor Source

The Rhetorical Situation

A Worksheet on Stanley Milgram's "The Perils of Obedience"

Comparing Quotations

Offering a Contrary Viewpoint as an Effective Rhetorical Strategy

Readability Score

Readings

On March 27, 1964, a *New York Times* news report appeared with the heading, "37 Who Saw Murder Didn't Call the Police." The article begins, "For more than half an hour 38 respectable, law-abiding citizens in Queens watched a killer stalk and stab a woman in three separate attacks in Kew Gardens." A police inspector is quoted in the article saying that Kitty Genovese "might not be dead now" if anyone had called the police when the murderer first attacked Genovese. According to sources quoted in the article, the assailant "returned twice to complete the job" over a period of 35 minutes.

The *Times* article caused public shock and outrage. Writing in *The Nation* in 1964, social psychologist Stanley Milgram and sociologists Paul Hollander assume that readers are familiar with the case. Near the beginning of their article, they note that a U.S. Senator from Georgia has taken the unusual step of reading *The New York Times* article into the *Congressional Record*, which is the official daily record of the proceedings of the U.S. Congress. Senator Russell's outrage at the seeming indifference of the witnesses of Catherine Genovese's murder reflects a general public outrage. Critics used this episode to comment on the indifference and lack of humanity that exists in modern America, especially in urban environments.

Social psychologists took a very different lesson from the murder of Catherine (Kitty) Genovese. Social psychologists like Milgram and Hollander focused on the prevailing social dynamics that took place on the night of the murder. Social psychologists described a human behavioral effect that they called "the bystander effect" or "Genovese syndrome." It is important to note that nowhere in the following article do the authors use the terms "bystander effect" or "Genovese syndrome." Clearly, though, the observations and claims contained in "Paralyzed Witnesses" are synonymous with the ideas underlying these other terms. Milgram and Hollander write that a "collective paralysis may have developed" among the witnesses. As you read, assess whether you find their arguments persuasive. They seem to ask us, as readers, to step back in order to view the entire "context" of the situation. Place yourself there on the night of the murder. What would you have done?

Our task, in reading this article, is complicated. First, we must understand the authors' basic arguments. Why do they choose to focus on the situation rather than on individual behavior? Second, we must understand the historical context of this article. Without understanding the significance of a senator reading the *Times* article into the *Congressional Record*, for example, we would fail to understand the major national impact that this murder had on American public discourse at the time. Third, and perhaps most difficult of all, we are obligated to look at the facts of the case in order to determine whether Milgram and Hollander, as well as other commentators, have arrived at sound conclusions.

*The New York Times* reviewed its 1964 article in 2004 and found some inconsistencies and inaccuracies in the original reporting. Nevertheless, Kitty Genovese remains, for sad and unfortunate reasons, a powerful figure in American history and in the American imagination. The circumstances surrounding her murder have become staple subject matter for sociology, psychology, and other academic textbooks.

## Questions to Consider

*Answer these questions as you read and annotate the text:*

- The authors write that it is noteworthy that public anger is not directed toward the criminal, but toward those who failed to prevent the crime. They then draw an analogy with "recent trends in moralizing about the Nazi era." Explain what they mean here.

- The authors argue that we cannot determine people's moral or ethical values from "the actual behavior of people in concrete situations." Explain this key point of their argument. What language would you quote in order to explain this point of argument to someone outside the classroom?
- What specific explanations do Milgram and Hollander provide in order to clarify or explain the inaction of the residents of Kew Gardens?
- The authors observe that "modern societies are so organized as to discourage even the most beneficial, spontaneous group action." Explain this idea. What do they mean? What aspects of social organization do you think they have in mind?
- What factors may have generated a "collective paralysis" among the residents?
- The authors assert, "Awareness of an ideal response often paralyzes a move toward the less than ideal alternative." In this specific situation, what does that mean? What was an "ideal response" and what was a "less than ideal" response? Do you find their assertion persuasive? Why or why not? Do you have any experience(s) that might influence whether you understand or accept this particular assertion?
- Why do the authors invoke the escaped criminal Willie Sutton? Do you find that this is an effective rhetorical strategy? Why or why not?
- What, according to the authors, is the purpose of their essay?
- Do any recent news events seem relevant to you in regard to this article and the authors' arguments? Clarify what connections you perceive.

## Stanley Milgram and Paul Hollander, Paralyzed Witnesses: The Murder They Heard

Catherine Genovese, coming home from a night job in the early hours of a March morning, was stabbed repeatedly and over an extended period of time. Thirty-eight residents of a respectable New York City neighborhood admit to having witnessed at least a part of the attack, but not one of them went to her aid or even so much as called the police until after she was dead.

We are all certain that we would have done better. Our indignation toward the residents of Kew Gardens swells to a sense of outrage. The crime, or more precisely, the lack of civic response to it, was so vile that Senator (Richard B.) Russell of Georgia read *The New York Times* account of it into the *Congressional Record*. The fact that it *was* Senator Russell is an indication of the complex social reactions touched off by this neighborhood tragedy.

It is noteworthy, first, that anger is directed not toward the crime or the criminal, but toward those who failed to halt the criminal's actions. It is a curious shift, reminiscent of recent trends in moralizing about the Nazi era. Writers once focused on the sins of the Nazis; it is now more fashionable to discuss the complicity of their victims. The event is significant, also, for the way it is being exploited. Senator Russell is but one case in point. In his home state, several brutal murders of Negroes have taken place before large crowds of unprotesting white onlookers, but the Senator has never felt called upon to insert reports of *these* brutalities into the *Record*. The crime against Miss Genovese no longer exists in and of itself. It is rapidly being assimilated to the uses and ideologies of the day.

For example, the Kew Gardens incident has become the occasion for a general attack on the city. It is portrayed as callous, cruel, indifferent to the needs of the people, and wholly inferior to the small town in the quality of its personal relationships. The abrasiveness of urban life cannot be argued; it is not sure, however, that personal relationships are necessarily inferior in the city. They are merely organized on a different principle. Urban friendships and associations are not primarily formed on the basis of physical proximity. A person with numerous close friends in different parts of the city may not know the occupant of an adjacent apartment. Some hold this to be an advantage of the city: men and women can conduct lives unmonitored by the constant scrutiny of neighbors. This does not mean that a city dweller has fewer friends than does a villager or knows fewer persons who will come to his aid; however, it does mean that his allies are not constantly at hand. Miss Genovese required immediate aid from those physically present; her predicament was desperate and not typical of the occasions when we look for the support of friends. There is no evidence that the city had deprived Miss Genovese of human associations, but the friends who might have rushed to her side were miles from the scene of her tragedy.

A truly extraordinary aspect of the case is the general readiness to forget the man who committed a very foul crime. This is typical of social reactions in present-day America. It begins to seem that everyone, having absorbed a smattering of sociology, looks at once beyond the concrete case in an eager quest for high-sounding generalizations that imply an enlightened social vista. What gets lost in many of these discussions—and what needs at least partial restoration—is the notion that people may occasionally be responsible for what they do, even if their acts are criminal. In our righteous denunciation of the thirty-eight witnesses, we should not forget that they did not commit the murder; they merely failed to prevent it. It is no more than clear thinking to bear in mind the moral difference.

A related and equally confusing error is to infer ethical values from the actual behavior of people in concrete situations. For example, in the case of Miss Genovese we must ask: did the witnesses remain passive because they thought it was the right thing to do, or did they refrain from action *despite* what they thought or felt they should do? We cannot take it for granted that people always do what they consider right. It would be more fruitful to inquire why, in general and in this particular case, there is so marked a discrepancy between values and behavior. What makes people choose a course of action that probably shames them in retrospect? How do they become reduced to resignation, acquiescence, and helplessness?

Those who vilify the residents of Kew Gardens measure them against the standard of their own ability to formulate high-minded moral prescriptions. But that is hardly a fair standard. It is entirely likely that many of the witnesses, at the level of stated opinion, feel quite as strongly as any of us about the moral requirement of aiding a helpless victim. They too, in general terms, know what *ought* to be done, and can state their values when the occasion arises. This has little if anything, to do with actual behavior under the press of circumstances.

Furthermore, we must distinguish between the facts of the murder as finally known and reported in the press and the events of the evening as they were experienced by the Kew Gardens residents. We can now say that if the police had been called after the first attack, the woman's life might have been saved, and we tend to judge the inaction of the Kew Gardens residents in the light of this lost possibility. This is natural, perhaps, but it is unrealistic. If those men and women had had as clear a grasp of the situation as we have now, the chances are that many of them would have acted to save Miss Genovese's life. What they had, instead, were fragments of an ambiguous, confusing, and doubtless frightening episode—one, moreover, that seemed totally incongruous in a respectable neighborhood. The very lack of correspondence between the violence of the crime and the character of the neighborhood must have created a sense of unreality which inhibited rational action. A lesser crime, one more in character with the locale—say, after-hours rowdiness from a group of college students—might have led more readily to a call for the police.

The incongruity, the sheer improbability of the event predisposed many to reject the most extreme interpretation: that a young woman was in fact being murdered outside the window. How much more probable, not to say more consoling, was the interpretation that a drunken party was sounding off, that two lovers were quarreling, or that youths were playing a nasty prank. Bruno Bettelheim, in *The Informed Heart* (1960), describes how resistant many German Jews were to the signs around them of impending disaster. Given any possibility for fitting events into an acceptable order of things, men are quick to seize it. It takes courage to perceive clearly and without distortion. We cannot justly condemn all the Kew Gardens residents in the light of a horrible outcome which only the most perspicacious could have foreseen.

Why didn't the group of onlookers band together, run out into the street, and subdue the assailant? Aside from the fact that such organization takes time, and that the onlookers were not in communication (who in such a community knows his neighbors phone number?), there is another factor that would render such action almost impossible. Despite our current fears about the contagion of violence in the mass media, the fact remains that the middle-class person is totally unequipped to deal with its actual occurrence. More especially, he is unable to use personal violence, either singly or collectively, even when it is required for productive and socially valued ends.

More generally, modern societies are so organized as to discourage even the most beneficial, spontaneous group action. This applies with particular sharpness to the law-abiding, respectable segments of the population—such as the people of Kew Gardens—who have most thoroughly accepted the admonition: "Do not take the law into your own hands." In a highly specialized society, such people take it for granted that certain functions and activities—from garbage collection to fire protection, from meat certification to the control of criminals—are taken care of by specially trained people. The puzzle in the case under consideration is the reluctance to supply to the police even the barest information which it was essential they have if they were to fulfill their acknowledged functions.

Many facts of the case have not been made public, such as the quality of the relationship between Miss Genovese and the community, the extent to which she was recognized that night, and the number of persons who knew her. It is known that her cries for help were not directed to a specific person: they were general. But only individuals can act, and as the cries were not specifically directed, no particular person felt a special responsibility. The crime and the failure of the community response seem absurd to us. At the time, it may well have seemed equally absurd to the Kew Gardens residents that not one of the neighbors would have called the police. A collective paralysis may have developed from the belief of each of the witnesses that someone else must surely have taken that obvious step.

If we ask why they did not call the police, we should also ask what were the alternatives. To be sure, phoning from within an apartment was the most prudent course of action, one involving the minimum of both physical inconvenience and personal involvement with a violent criminal. And yet, one has to assume that in the minds of many there lurked the alternative of going down to the street and defending the helpless woman. This indeed might have been felt as the ideal response. By comparison, a mere phone call from the safety of home  may have seemed a cowardly compromise with what should be done. As often happens, the ideal solution was difficult, probably dangerous;

but, as also happens, the practical, safe alternative may have seemed distasteful in the light of the ideal. Awareness of an ideal response often paralyzes a move toward the less than ideal alternative. Rather than accept the belittling second-best, the person so beset prefers to blot out the whole issue. Therefore, he pretends that there is nothing to get upset about. Probably it was only a drunken brawl.

The symbolic significance of "the street" for the middle-class mentality may have some relevance to the case. Although it cannot explain in full the failure to grab the telephone and call the police, it may account in part for the inertia and indifference. For the middle class resident of a big city, the street and what happens on the street are often symbolic of all that is vulgar and perilous in life. The street is the antithesis of privacy, security, and the support one derives from contemplating and living amidst prized personal possessions. The street represents the world of pushing and shoving crowds, potentially hostile strangers, sweat, dust, and noise. Those who spend much time on the street have nothing better to do and nowhere better to go; the poor, the footloose, the drifters, juvenile delinquents. Therefore, the middle-class person seeks almost automatically to disengage himself from the life of the street; he is on it only from necessity, rarely for pleasure. Such considerations help explain the genesis of attitudes that prevented the witnesses from making the crucial phone call. The tragic drama was taking place on the street, hence hardly relevant to their lives; in fact, in some ways radically opposed to their oudook and concerns.

In an effort to make the strongest possible case against the Kew Gardens citizens, the press ignored actual dangers of involvement, even at the level of calling the police. They have treated the "fears" of the residents as foolish rationalizations, utterly without basis. In doing so they, have conveniently forgotten instances in which such involvement did not turn out well for the hero. One spectacular case in the early fifties, amply publicized by the press, concerned the misfortune of Arnold Schuster. While riding in the subway, this young Brooklyn man spotted Willie Sutton, an escaped, criminal. He reported this information to the police, and it led to Sutton's arrest. Schuster was proclaimed a hero, but before a month was up Schuster was dead—murdered in reprisal for his part in Sutton's recapture. Schuster had done nothing more than phone the police.

The fact is that there *are* risks even in minimal forms of involvement, and it is dishonest to ignore them. One becomes involved with the police, with the general agents of publicity that swarm to such events, and possibly with the criminal. If the criminal is not caught immediately, there is the chance that he will learn who called the police (which apartment did they enter first, whose pictures are in the papers, etc.) and may fear that the caller can identify him. The caller, then, is of special concern to the criminal. If a trial is held, the person who telephoned is likely to be a witness. Even if he is jailed, the criminal may have underworld friends who will act to avenge him. One is a responsible citizen and a worthy human being not because of the absence of risk but because one acts in the face of it.

In seeking explanations for their inaction, we have not intended to defend, certainly not to excuse, Kew Gardens' passive witnesses. We have sought, rather, to put ourselves in their place, to try to understand their response. The causes we have suggested are in no way sufficient reason for inaction. Perhaps we should have started with a more fundamental question: Why should anyone have gone to the aid of the victim? Why should anyone have taken the trouble to call the police? The answer must be that it is a matter of common decency to help those who are in distress. It is a humane and compassionate requirement in the relations between people. Yet how generally is it observed?

In New York City it is not at all unusual to see a man, sick with alcohol, lying in a doorway; he does not command the least attention or interest from those who pass by. The trouble here, as in Kew Gardens, is that the individual does not perceive that his interests are identified with others or with the community at large. And is such a perception possible? What evidence is there in the American community that collective interests have priority over personal advantage?

There are, of course, practical limitations to the Samaritan impulse in a major city. If a citizen attended to every needy person, if he were sensitive to and acted on every altruistic impulse that was evoked in the city, he could scarcely keep his own affairs in order. A calculated and strategic indifference is an unavoidable part of life in our cities, and it must be faced without sentimentality or rage. At most, each of us can resolve to extend the range of his responsibilities in some perceptible degree, to rise a little more adequately to moral obligations. City life is harsh; still, we owe it to ourselves and to our fellows to resolve that it be no more harsh than is inevitable.

## Questions for Comprehension

*Answer these questions as a comprehension reading quiz and/or for further clarification on the text:*

1. True/False. According to Milgram and Hollander, it is not possible to determine the moral and ethical values of people based on the way they behave in concrete situations.

2. List at least three reasons that a Kew Garden resident may have hesitated from picking up the phone or going down into the street, according to these authors.

Would you harm another human being for the sake of an experiment, just because a man in a white lab coat told you to do so? Not many of us raise our hands to say, "Yes, I would do that." In fact, almost no one wants to think that he or she would harm another human being for the sake of an experiment. Yet Stanley Milgram claims that more than six out of ten of us "normal" people would harm another person if an authority figure orders us to do so.

Milgram's controversial obedience experiments had a revolutionary impact in the fields of psychology, social psychology, sociology, and human studies in general. Milgram was not interested in asking people how they would behave in theoretical situations; instead, he wanted to place people in those situations and record their responses. Whether these experiments are, in fact, scientific in nature is one question that you must consider as you read and annotate the text.

It is important to understand something about the scientific method and to consider whether experiments involving humans can follow the scientific method. The basic scientific method involves asking a question, developing a hypothesis, testing by experiment, and analyzing the results in order to draw a conclusion. In some fields, the actual goal of the experimenter is to attempt to *disprove* his or her own hypothesis. Following this stringent method, a researcher can definitively prove a hypothesis only by failing to disprove it. In this way, researchers hope to avoid potential bias. The basic concept is that if an experimenter aims to prove a certain hypothesis, bias will creep into the process, and the researcher will develop an experiment that leans toward certain results. It's also important in the scientific method that the experiment itself can be recreated and conducted by others and that it will generate the same or similar results.

In the scientific method in general, and in Milgram's experiments in particular, it's important to distinguish between *results* and *conclusions*. The results here are the numerical data Milgram presents. His interpretations of that data constitute his conclusions. It is possible to accept the results of an experiment and to reject the researcher's conclusions. Be clear on Milgram's results and conclusions.

It is important to note that Milgram conducted many variations of his main experiment.

The experiments that he describes in the following article were later deemed unethical by various professional organizations. The stress put on the unknowing subject or "Teacher" was harmful, according to Milgram's peers. ABC News filmed a recreation of Milgram's basic experiment in 2006. The experiment was carried out at Santa Clara University and vetted by the American Psychological Association. The "Teachers," in this recreation, were screened for psychological stability and told that they could pull out of the experiment at any time. Instead of proceeding the whole way to the top (450 volts) of the supposed shock generator, the modified experiment cut off the experiment at 150 volts. This modification was intended to ease ethical concerns regarding stress experienced by the test subject. The recreated experiment found the same results as Milgram's original main experiment, and the university researcher Jerry M. Burger, who oversaw the experiment, drew the same conclusions as Milgram had. Additionally, he found similar levels of obedience among both male and female subjects. Psychology professor Alex Haslam, on the other hand, accepts Milgram's results yet disagrees with Milgram's conclusions. (See sources in "Further Inquiry & Research" at the end of the unit.)

Social psychologists like Milgram draw a distinction between actual human behavior and what people call "character." Most of us assume that a person's good character determines how he or she will act in a given situation. The work of Milgram and other social psychologists calls this fundamental assumption into doubt. Actual behavior, they claim, has little or nothing to do with a person's character. Milgram and others designed experiments to demonstrate this principle. The infamous Stanford Prison Experiment stands out as an example of this principle.

In the field of social psychology, the concept of people placing undue emphasis on their own character or intention rather than on external factors such as environment or situation (what I like to call "context") is called the fundamental attribution error (FAE). This error, in the view of social psychologists, involves the persistent belief that how people behave is a direct reflection of their character, and that a person's character determines how he or she actually behaves in any given situation. Social psychologists argue that a person's character has very little to do with how the person will behave within a given "context" or situation.

As you examine the following article, you might draw connections between the ideas that Milgram argues in this article and the ideas that Milgram and Hollander argue in "Paralyzed Witnesses." What common principles of social psychology do the authors point out in both articles?

In "The Perils of Obedience," published in *Harper's Magazine*, Milgram revises work published in a prior academic journal article. He revises his language and condenses and rearranges his content in order to address a wide general interest readership.

## Questions to Consider

*Answer these questions as you read and annotate the text:*

- Milgram very clearly identifies his thesis at the end of a traditional introductory paragraph. What is his thesis?
- With whom do you most closely identify, Gretchen Brandt or Fred Prozi? Why?
- What are the most important variations of the experiment in your view? Why?
- What prompted Milgram to develop these experiments?
- Who is "Eichmann"? Note that Milgram assumes that his audience is familiar with this person.
- Be sure to complete the Worksheet on Stanley Milgram's "The Perils of Obedience." Check with your instructor on whether to complete this worksheet as a group or individually.

### Stanley Milgram, The Perils of Obedience

Obedience is as basic an element in the structure of social life as one can point to. Some system of authority is a requirement of all communal living, and it is only the person dwelling in isolation who is not forced to respond, with defiance or submission, to the commands of others. For many people, obedience is a deeply ingrained behavior tendency, indeed a potent impulse overriding training in ethics, sympathy, and moral conduct.

The dilemma inherent in submission to authority is ancient, as old as the story of Abraham, and the question of whether one should obey when commands conflict with conscience has been argued by Plato, dramatized in *Antigone,* and treated to philosophic analysis in almost every historical epoch. Conservative philosophers argue that the very fabric of society is threatened by disobedience, while humanists stress the primacy of the individual conscience.

The legal and philosophic aspects of obedience are of enormous import, but they say very little about how most people behave in concrete situations. I set up a simple experiment at Yale University to test how much pain an ordinary citizen would inflict on another person simply because he was ordered to by an experimental scientist. Stark authority was pitted against the subjects' strongest moral imperatives against hurting others, and, with the subjects' ears ringing with the screams of the victims, authority won more often than not. The extreme willingness of adults to go to almost any lengths on the command of an authority constitutes the chief finding of the study and the fact most urgently demanding explanation.

In the basic experimental design, two people come to a psychology laboratory to take part in a study of memory and learning. One of them is designated as a "teacher" and the other a "learner." The experimenter explains that the study is concerned with the effects of punishment on learning. The learner is conducted into a room, seated in a kind of miniature electric chair; his arms are strapped to prevent excessive movement, and an electrode is attached to his wrist. He is told that he will be read lists of simple word pairs, and that he will then be tested on his ability to remember the second word of a pair when he hears the first one again. Whenever he makes an error, he will receive electric shocks of increasing intensity.

The real focus of the experiment is the teacher. After watching the learner being strapped into place, he is seated before an impressive shock generator. The instrument panel consists of thirty lever switches set in a horizontal line. Each switch is clearly labeled with a voltage designation ranging from 15 to 450 volts. The following designations are clearly indicated for groups of four switches, going from left to right: Slight Shock, Moderate Shock, Strong Shock, Very Strong Shock, Intense Shock, Extreme Intensity Shock, Danger: Severe Shock. (Two switches after this last designation are simply marked XXX.)

When a switch is depressed, a pilot light corresponding to each switch is illuminated in bright red; an electric buzzing is heard; a blue light, labeled "voltage energizer," flashes; the dial on the voltage meter swings to the right; and various relay clicks sound off.

The upper left-hand corner of the generator is labeled SHOCK GENERATOR, TYPE ZLB, DYSON INSTRUMENT COMPANY, WALTHAM, MASS. OUTPUT 15 VOLTS-450 VOLTS.

Each subject is given a sample 45-volt shock from the generator before his run as teacher, and the jolt strengthens his belief in the authenticity of the machine.

The teacher is a genuinely naive subject who has come to the laboratory for the experiment. The learner, or victim, is actually an actor who receives no shock at all. The point of the experiment is to see how far a person will proceed in a concrete and measurable situation in which he is ordered to inflict increasing pain on a protesting victim.

Conflict arises when the man receiving the shock begins to show that he is experiencing discomfort. At 75 volts, he grunts; at 120 volts, he complains loudly; at 150, he demands to be released from the experiment. As the voltage increases, his protests become more vehement and emotional. At 285 volts, his response can be described only as an agonized scream. Soon thereafter, he makes no sound at all.

For the teacher, the situation quickly becomes one of gripping tension. It is not a game for him; conflict is intense and obvious. The manifest suffering of the learner presses him to quit; but each time he hesitates to administer a shock, the experimenter orders him to continue. To extricate himself from this plight, the subject must make a clear break with authority.[*]

The subject, gretchen brandt,[**] is an attractive thirty-one-year-old medical technician who works at the Yale Medical School. She had emigrated from Germany five years before.

On several occasions when the learner complains, she turns to the experimenter coolly and inquires, "Shall I continue?" She promptly returns to her task when the experimenter asks her to do so. At the administration of 210 volts, she turns to the experimenter, remarking firmly, "Well, I'm sorry, I don't think we should continue."

---

[*] The ethical problems of carrying out an experiment of this sort are too complex to be dealt with here, but they receive extended treatment in the book from which this article is adapted.
[**] Names of subjects described in this piece have been changed.

EXPERIMENTER: The experiment requires that you go on until he has learned all the word pairs correctly.

BRANDT: He has a heart condition, I'm sorry. He told you that before.

EXPERIMENTER: The shocks may be painful but they are not dangerous.

BRANDT: Well, I'm sorry, I think when shocks continue like this, they *are* dangerous. You ask him if he wants to get out. It's his free will.

EXPERIMENTER: It is absolutely essential that we continue. . . .

BRANDT: I'd like you to ask him. We came here of our free will. If he wants to continue I'll go ahead. He told you he had a heart condition. I'm sorry. I don't want to be responsible for anything happening to him. I wouldn't like it for me either.

EXPERIMENTER: You have no other choice.

BRANDT: I think we are here on our own free will. I don't want to be responsible if anything happens to him. Please understand that.

She refuses to go further and the experiment is terminated.

The woman is firm and resolute throughout. She indicates in the interview that she was in no way tense or nervous, and this corresponds to her controlled appearance during the experiment. She feels that the last shock she administered to the learner was extremely painful and reiterates that she "did not want to be responsible for any harm to him."

The woman's straightforward, courteous behavior in the experiment, lack of tension, and total control of her own action seem to make disobedience a simple and rational deed. Her behavior is the very embodiment of what I envisioned would be true for almost all subjects.

## An Unexpected Outcome

Before the experiments, I sought predictions about the outcome from various kinds of people—psychiatrists, college sophomores, middle-class adults, graduate students and faculty in the behavioral sciences. With remarkable similarity, they predicted that virtually all subjects would refuse to obey the experimenter. The psychiatrists, specifically, predicted that most subjects would not go beyond 150 volts, when the victim makes his first explicit demand to be freed. They expected that only 4 percent would reach 300 volts, and that only a pathological fringe of about one in a thousand would administer the highest shock on the board.

These predictions were unequivocally wrong. Of the forty subjects in the first experiment, twenty-five obeyed the orders of the experimenter to the end, punishing the victim until they reached the most potent shock available on the generator. After 450 volts were administered three times, the experimenter called a halt to the session. Many obedient subjects then heaved sighs of relief, mopped their brows, rubbed their fingers over their eyes, or nervously fumbled cigarettes. Others displayed only minimal signs of tension from beginning to end.

When the very first experiments were carried out, Yale undergraduates were used as subjects, and about 60 percent of them were fully obedient. A Colleague of mine immediately dismissed these findings as having no relevance to "ordinary" people, asserting that Yale undergraduates are a highly aggressive, competitive bunch who step on each other's necks on the slightest provocation. He assured me that when "ordinary" people were tested, the results would be quite different. As we moved from the pilot studies to the regular experimental series, people drawn from every stratum of New Haven life came to be employed in the experiment: professionals, white-collar workers, unemployed persons, and industrial workers. *The experimental outcome was the same as we had observed among the students.*

Moreover, when the experiments were repeated in Princeton, Munich, Rome, South Africa, and Australia, the level of obedience was invariably somewhat *higher* than found in the investigation reported in this article. Thus one scientist in Munich found 85 percent of his subjects obedient.

Fred prozi's reactions, if more dramatic than most, illuminate the conflicts experienced by others in less visible form. About fifty years old and unemployed at the time of the experiment, he has a good-natured, if slightly dissolute, appearance, and he strikes people as a rather ordinary fellow. He begins the session calmly but becomes tense as it proceeds. After delivering the 180-volt shock, he pivots around in his chair and, shaking his head, addresses the experimenter in agitated tones:

PROZI: I can't stand it. I'm not going to kill that man in there. You hear him hollering?

EXPERIMENTER: As I told you before, the shocks may be painful, but . . .

PROZI: But he's hollering. He can't stand it. What's going to happen to him?

EXPERIMENTER (his voice is patient, matter-of-fact): The experiment requires that you continue, Teacher.

PROZI: Aaah, but, unh, I'm not going to get that man sick in there—know what I mean?

EXPERIMENTER: Whether the learner likes it or not, we must go on, through all the word pairs.

PROZI: I refuse to take the responsibility. He's in there hollering!

EXPERIMENTER: It's absolutely essential that you continue, Prozi.

PROZI (indicating the unused questions): There's too many left here, I mean, Jeez, if he gets them wrong, there's too many of them left. I mean, who's going to take the responsibility if anything happens to that gentleman?

EXPERIMENTER: I'm responsible for anything that happens to him. Continue, please.

PROZI: All right. (Consults list of words.) The next one's "Slow—walk, truck, dance, music." Answer, please. (A buzzing sound indicates the learner has signaled his answer.) Wrong. A hundred and ninety-five volts. "Dance." (Zzumph!)

LEARNER (yelling): Let me out of here! My heart's bothering me! (Teacher looks at experimenter.)

EXPERIMENTER: Continue, please.

LEARNER (screaming): Let me out of here! You have no right to keep me here! Let me out of here, my heart's bothering me, let me out!

PROZI (shakes head, pats the table nervously): You see, he's hollering. Hear that? Gee, I don't know.

EXPERIMENTER: The experiment requires . . .

PROZI (interrupting): I know it does, sir, but I mean—hunh! He don't know what he's getting in for. He's up to 195 volts! (Experiment continues, through 210 volts, 225 volts, 240 volts, 255 volts, 270 volts, at which point Prozi, with evident relief, runs out of word-pair questions.)

EXPERIMENTER: You'll have to go back to the beginning of that page and go through them again until he's learned them all correctly.

PROZI: Aw, no. I'm not going to kill that man. You mean I've got to keep going up with the scale? No sir. He's hollering in there. I'm not going to give him 450 volts.

EXPERIMENTER: The experiment requires that you go on.

LEARNER: Ohhh. I absolutely refuse to answer anymore. (Shouting urgently now.) Let me out of here! You can't hold me here! Get me out. Get-me-out-of-here!

EXPERIMENTER: Continue. The next word is "Green," please.

PROZI: "Green—grass, hat, ink, apple." (Nothing happens. No answering buzz. Just gloomy silence.)

PROZI: I don't think he is going to answer.

EXPERIMENTER: If the learner doesn't answer in a reasonable time, about four or five seconds, consider the answer wrong. And follow the same procedures you have been doing for wrong answers. Say, "Wrong," tell him the number of volts, give him the punishment, read him the correct answer. Continue, please.

PROZI: "Green—grass, hat, ink, apple." Answer, please. (More silence. Subject just sits there.)

EXPERIMENTER: Go on with the procedure, please.

PROZI: Three hundred and fifteen volts. The answer is "ink." (Zzumph!)

LEARNER: Ohh. Ooohh.

PROZI (relieved to hear response): Next one . . .

LEARNER: I absolutely refuse to answer.

PROZI: You got to. You get a shock if you don't answer. (Experiment continues with learner refusing to answer, and, finally, failing even to grunt or groan. At 375 volts, the subject stands up.)

PROZI: I think something's happened to that fellow in there. I don't get no answer. He was hollering at less voltage. Can't you check in and see if he's all right, please?

EXPERIMENTER (with same detached calm): Not once we've started. Please continue, Teacher.

PROZI (sits down, sighs deeply): "Cool—day, shade, water, paint." Answer, please. Are you all right in there? Are you all right?

EXPERIMENTER: Please continue, Teacher. Continue, please. (Subject pushes lever. Zzumph!)

PROZI (swiveling around in his chair): Something's happened to that man in there. (Swiveling back.) Next one. "Low—dollar, necklace, moon, paint." (Turning around again.) Something's happened to that man in there. You better check in on him, sir. He won't answer or nothing.

EXPERIMENTER: Continue. Go on, please.

PROZI: You accept all responsibility?

EXPERIMENTER: The responsibility is mine. Correct. Please go on. (Subject returns to his list, starts running through words as rapidly as he can read them, works through to 450 volts.)

PROZI : That's that.

EXPERIMENTER: Continue using the 450 switch for each wrong answer. Continue, please.

PROZI: But I don't get anything!

EXPERIMENTER: Please continue. The next word is "white."

PROZI: Don't you think you should look in on him, please?

EXPERIMENTER: Not once we've started the experiment.

PROZI: What if he's dead in there? (Gestures toward the room with the electric chair.) I mean, he told me he can't stand the shock, sir. I don't mean to be rude, but I think you should look in on him. All you have to do is look in on him. All you have to do is look in the door. I don't get no answer, no noise. Something might have happened to the gentleman in there, sir.

EXPERIMENTER: We must continue. Go on, please.

PROZI: You mean keep giving him what? Four-hundred-fifty volts, what he's got now?

EXPERIMENTER: That's correct. Continue. The next word is "white."

PROZI (now at a furious pace): "White—cloud, horse, rock, house." Answer, please. The answer is "horse." Four hundred and fifty volts. (Zzumph!) Next word, "Bag—paint, music, clown, girl." The answer is "paint." Four hundred and fifty volts. (Zzumph!) Next word is "Short—sentence, movie . . ."

EXPERIMENTER: Excuse me, Teacher. We'll have to discontinue the experiment.

## Peculiar Reactions

Morris braverman, another subject, is a thirty-nine-year-old social worker. He looks older than his years because of his bald head and serious demeanor. His brow is furrowed, as if all the world's burdens were carried on his face. He appears intelligent and concerned.

When the learner refuses to answer and the experimenter instructs Braverman to treat the absence of an answer as equivalent to a wrong answer, he takes his instruction to heart. Before administering 300 volts he asserts officiously to the victim, "Mr. Wallace, your silence has to be considered as a wrong answer." Then he administers the shock. He offers halfheartedly to change places with the learner, then asks the experimenter, "Do I have to follow these instructions literally?" He is satisfied with the experimenter's answer that he does. His very refined and authoritative manner of speaking is increasingly broken up by wheezing laughter.

The experimenter's notes on Mr. Braverman at the last few shocks are:

*Almost breaking up now each time gives shock. Rubbing face to hide laughter.*
*Squinting, trying to hide face with hand, still laughing.*
*Cannot control his laughter at this point no matter what he does.*
*Clenching fist, pushing it onto table.*

In an interview after the session, Mr. Braverman summarizes the experiment with impressive fluency and intelligence. He feels the experiment may have been designed also to "test the effects on the teacher of being in an essentially sadistic role, as well as the reactions of a student to a learning situation that was authoritative and punitive."

When asked how painful the last few shocks administered to the learner were, he indicates that the most extreme category on the scale is not adequate (it read EXTREMELY PAINFUL) and places his mark at the edge of the scale with an arrow carrying it beyond the scale.

It is almost impossible to convey the greatly relaxed, sedate quality of his conversation in the interview. In the most relaxed terms, he speaks about his severe inner tension.

EXPERIMENTER: At what point were you most tense or nervous?

MR. BRAVERMAN: Well, when he first began to cry out in pain, and I realized this was hurting him. This got worse when he just blocked and refused to answer. There was I. I'm a nice person, I think, hurting somebody, and caught up in what seemed a mad situation . . . and in the interest of science, one goes through with it.

When the interviewer pursues the general question of tension, Mr. Braverman spontaneously mentions his laughter.

"My reactions were awfully peculiar. I don't know if you were watching me, but my reactions were giggly, and trying to stifle laughter. This isn't the way I usually am. This was a sheer reaction to a totally impossible situation. And my reaction was to the situation of having to hurt somebody. And being totally helpless and caught up in a set of circumstances where I just couldn't deviate and I couldn't try to help. This is what got me."

Mr. Braverman, like all subjects, was told the actual nature and purpose of the experiment, and a year later he affirmed in a questionnaire that he had learned something of personal importance: "What appalled me was that I could possess this capacity for obedience and compliance to a central idea, i.e., the value of a memory experiment, even after it became clear that continued adherence to this value was at the expense of violation of another value, i.e., don't hurt someone who is helpless and not hurting you. As my wife said, 'You can call yourself Eichmann.' I hope I deal more effectively with any future conflicts of values I encounter."

## The Etiquette of Submission

One theoretical interpretation of this behavior holds that all people harbor deeply aggressive instincts continually pressing for expression, and that the experiment provides institutional justification for the release of these impulses. According to this view, if a person is placed in a situation in which he has complete power over another individual, whom he may punish as much as he likes, all that is sadistic and bestial in man comes to the fore. The impulse to shock the victim is seen to flow from the potent aggressive tendencies, which are part of the motivational life of the individual, and the experiment, because it provides social legitimacy, simply opens the door to their expression.

It becomes vital, therefore, to compare the subject's performance when he is under orders and when he is allowed to choose the shock level.

The procedure was identical to our standard experiment, except that the teacher was told that he was free to select any shock level on any of the trials. (The experimenter took pains to point out that the teacher could use the highest levels on the generator, the lowest, any in between, or any combination of levels.) Each subject proceeded for thirty critical trials. The learner's protests were coordinated to standard shock levels, his first grunt coming at 75 volts, his first vehement protest at 150 volts.

The average shock used during the thirty critical trials was less than 60 volts—lower than the point at which the victim showed the first signs of discomfort. Three of the forty subjects did not go beyond the very lowest level on the board, twenty-eight went no higher than 75 volts, and thirty-eight did not go beyond the first loud protest at 150 volts. Two subjects provided the exception, administering up to 325 and 450 volts, but the overall result was that the great majority of people delivered very low, usually painless, shocks when the choice was explicitly up to them.

This condition of the experiment undermines another commonly offered explanation of the subjects' behavior—that those who shocked the victim at the most severe levels came only from the sadistic fringe of society. If one considers that almost two-thirds of the participants fall into the category of "obedient" subjects, and that they represented ordinary people drawn from working, managerial, and professional classes, the argument becomes very shaky. Indeed, it is highly reminiscent of the issue that arose in connection with Hannah Arendt's 1963 book, *Eichmann in Jerusalem*. Arendt contended that the prosecution's effort to depict Eichmann as a sadistic monster was fundamentally wrong, that he came closer to being an uninspired bureaucrat who simply sat at his desk and did his job. For asserting her views, Arendt became the object of considerable scorn, even calumny. Somehow, it was felt that the monstrous deeds carried out by Eichmann required a brutal, twisted personality, evil incarnate. After witnessing hundreds of ordinary persons submit to the authority in our own experiments, I must conclude that Arendt's conception of the banality of evil comes closer to the truth than one might dare imagine. The ordinary person who shocked the victim did so out of a sense of obligation—an impression of his duties as a subject—and not from any peculiarly aggressive tendencies.

This is, perhaps, the most fundamental lesson of our study: ordinary people, simply doing their jobs, and without any particular hostility on their part, can become agents in a terrible destructive process. Moreover, even when the destructive effects of their work become patently clear, and they are asked to carry out actions incompatible with fundamental standards of morality, relatively few people have the resources needed to resist authority.

Many of the people were in some sense against what they did to the learner, and many protested even while they obeyed. Some were totally convinced of the wrongness of their actions but could not bring themselves to make an open break with authority. They often derived satisfaction from their thoughts and felt that—within themselves, at least—they had been on the side of the angels. They tried to reduce strain by obeying the experimenter but "only slightly," encouraging the learner, touching the generator switches gingerly. When interviewed, such a subject would stress that he had "asserted my humanity" by administering the briefest shock possible. Handling the conflict in this manner was easier than defiance.

The situation is constructed so that there is no way the subject can stop shocking the learner without violating the experimenter's definitions of his own competence. The subject fears that he will appear arrogant, untoward, and rude if he breaks off. Although these inhibiting emotions appear small in scope alongside the violence being done to the learner, they suffuse the mind and feelings of the subject, who is miserable at the prospect of having to repudiate the authority to his face. (When the experiment was altered so that the experimenter gave his instructions by telephone instead of in person, only a third as many people were fully obedient through 450 volts.) It is a curious thing that a measure of compassion on the part of the subject—an unwillingness to "hurt" the experimenter's feelings—is part of those binding forces inhibiting his disobedience. The withdrawal of such deference may be as painful to the subject as to the authority he defies.

## Duty without Conflict

The subjects do not derive satisfaction from inflicting pain, but they often like the feeling they get from pleasing the experimenter. They are proud of doing a good job, obeying the experimenter under difficult circumstances. While the subjects administered only mild shocks on their own initiative, one experimental variation showed that, under orders, 30 percent of them were willing to deliver 450 volts even when they had to forcibly push the learner's hand down on the electrode.

Bruno Batta is a thirty-seven-year-old welder who took part in the variation requiring the use of force. He was born in New Haven, his parents in Italy. He has a rough-hewn face that conveys a conspicuous lack of alertness. He has some difficulty in mastering the experimental procedure and needs to be corrected by the experimenter several times. He shows appreciation for the help and willingness to do what is required. After the 150-volt level, Batta has to force the learner's hand down on the shock plate, since the learner himself refuses to touch it.

When the learner first complains, Mr. Batta pays no attention to him. His face remains impassive, as if to dissociate himself from the learner's disruptive behavior. When the experimenter instructs him to force the learner's hand down, he adopts a rigid, mechanical procedure. He tests the generator switch. When it fails to function, he immediately forces the learner's hand onto the shock plate. All the while he maintains the same rigid mask. The learner, seated alongside him, begs him to stop, but with robotic impassivity he continues the procedure.

What is extraordinary is his apparent total indifference to the learner; he hardly takes cognizance of him as a human being. Meanwhile, he relates to the experimenter in a submissive and courteous fashion.

At the 330-volt level, the learner refuses not only to touch the shock plate but also to provide any answers. Annoyed, Batta turns to him, and chastises him: "You better answer and get it over with. We can't stay here all night." These are the only words he directs to the learner in the course of an hour. Never again does he speak to him. The scene is brutal and depressing, his hard, impassive face showing total indifference as he subdues the screaming learner and gives him shocks. He seems to derive no pleasure from the act itself, only quiet satisfaction at doing his job properly.

When he administers 450 volts, he turns to the experimenter and asks, "Where do we go from here, Professor?" His tone is deferential and expresses his willingness to be a cooperative subject, in contrast to the learner's obstinacy.

At the end of the session he tells the experimenter how honored he has been to help him, and in a moment of contrition, remarks, "Sir, sorry it couldn't have been a full experiment."

He has done his honest best. It is only the deficient behavior of the learner that has denied the experimenter full satisfaction.

The essence of obedience is that a person comes to view himself as the instrument for carrying out another person's wishes, and he therefore no longer regards himself as responsible for his actions. Once this critical shift of viewpoint has occurred, all of the essential features of obedience follow. The most far-reaching consequence is that the person feels responsible *to* the authority directing him but feels no responsibility *for* the content of the actions that the authority prescribes. Morality does not disappear—it acquires a radically different focus: the subordinate person feels shame or pride depending on how adequately he has performed the actions called for by authority.

Language provides numerous terms to pinpoint this type of morality: *loyalty, duty, discipline* all are terms heavily saturated with moral meaning and refer to the degree to which a person fulfills his obligations to authority. They refer not to the "goodness" of the person per se but to the adequacy with which a subordinate fulfills his socially defined role. The most frequent defense of the individual who has performed a heinous act under command of authority is that he has simply done his duty. In asserting this defense, the individual is not introducing an alibi concocted for the moment but is reporting honestly on the psychological attitude induced by submission to authority.

For a person to feel responsible for his actions, he must sense that the behavior has flowed from "the self." In the situation we have studied, subjects have precisely the opposite view of their actions—namely, they see them as originating in the motives of some other person. Subjects in the experiment frequently said, "If it were up to me, I would not have administered shocks to the learner."

Once authority has been isolated as the cause of the subject's behavior, it is legitimate to inquire into the necessary elements of authority and how it must be perceived in order to gain his compliance. We conducted some investigations into the kinds of changes that would cause the experimenter to lose his power and to be disobeyed by the subject. Some of the variations revealed that:

- *The experimenter's physical presence has a marked impact on his authority.* As cited earlier, obedience dropped off sharply when orders were given by telephone. The experimenter could often induce a disobedient subject to go on by returning to the laboratory.
- *Conflicting authority severely paralyzes action.* When two experimenters of equal status, both seated at the command desk, gave incompatible orders, no shocks were delivered past the point of their disagreement.
- *The rebellious action of others severely undermines authority.* In one variation, three teachers (two actors and a real subject) administered a test and shocks. When the two actors disobeyed the experimenter and refused to go beyond a certain shock level, thirty-six of forty subjects joined their disobedient peers and refused as well.

Although the experimenter's authority was fragile in some respects, it is also true that he had almost none of the tools used in ordinary command structures. For example, the experimenter did not threaten the subjects with punishment—such as loss of income, community ostracism, or jail—for failure to obey. Neither could he offer incentives. Indeed, we should expect the experimenter's authority to be much less than that of someone like a general, since the experimenter has no power to enforce his imperatives, and since participation in a psychological experiment scarcely evokes the sense of urgency and dedication found in warfare. Despite these limitations, he still managed to command a dismaying degree of obedience.

I will cite one final variation of the experiment that depicts a dilemma that is more common in everyday life. The subject was not ordered to pull the lever that shocked the victim, but merely to perform a subsidiary task (administering the word-pair test) while another person administered the shock. In this situation, thirty-seven of forty adults continued to the highest level on the shock generator. Predictably, they excused their behavior by saying that the responsibility belonged to the man who actually pulled the switch. This may illustrate a dangerously typical arrangement in a complex society: it is easy to ignore responsibility when one is only an intermediate link in a chain of action.

The problem of obedience is not wholly psychological. The form and shape of society and the way it is developing have much to do with it. There was a time, perhaps, when people were able to give a fully human response to any situation because they were fully absorbed in it as human beings. But as soon as there was a division of labor things changed. Beyond a certain point, the breaking up of society into people carrying out narrow and very special jobs takes away from the human quality of work and life. A person does not get to see the whole situation but only a small part of it, and is thus unable to act without some kind of overall direction. He yields to authority but in doing so is alienated from his own actions.

Even Eichmann was sickened when he toured the concentration camps, but he had only to sit at a desk and shuffle papers. At the same time the man in the camp who actually dropped Cyclon-b into the gas chambers was able to justify *his* behavior on the ground that he was only following orders from above. Thus there is a fragmentation of the total human act; no one is confronted with the consequences of his decision to carry out the evil act. The person who assumes responsibility has evaporated. Perhaps this is the most common characteristic of socially organized evil in modern society.

## Questions for Comprehension

*Answer these questions as a comprehension reading quiz and/or for further clarification on the text:*

1.  True or False: Milgram argues that a person's personal sense of ethics and integrity will usually override the person's desire to obey authority.

2.  The three main players in the Milgram's experiment are called:

3.  Of the three players, the subject of Milgram's experiment is the . . .

4.  In the article, Milgram describes a woman named Gretchen Brandt. According to Milgram, she does something praiseworthy. What? Answer in a few words.

5.  True or False: Milgram's experiment was conducted at various places all over the world.

# Assignments

## Reader Response #5

Two pages in MLA format (about 500 words)
Focus on the article "Paralyzed Witnesses" by Stanley Milgram and Paul Hollander.

### Writing Prompt

The central question at the core of this article is, "Why didn't anyone act?" The answer to this question could represent the authors' thesis. What are the reasons people fail to act in a given circumstance where their help is needed, according to these authors? Do these people lack sympathy or empathy? What factors, according to the authors, contribute to behavior that seems to run contrary to common ethical or moral standards? Offer a clear statement of their thesis and your response to it. Include quotations and/ or paraphrases as necessary.

### Suggested Evaluation Criteria and Point Values

| | |
|---|---|
| Accurate representation of authors' thesis. Turned in on deadline. | 10 points |
| Ability to handle quotations and paraphrases: language selection, integration, and appropriate commentary or explanation | 10 points |

## Reader Response #6

Two pages in MLA format (about 500 words)
Focus on Stanley Milgram's essay "The Perils of Obedience."

## Writing prompt:

Briefly describe the main experiment and one or two of the most important variations. What were the results? Based on these results, what did Milgram conclude? What is Milgram's thesis? What are your own conclusions or opinions which may or may not coincide with Milgram's? What factors prompt you to draw your conclusions?

## Suggested Evaluation Criteria and Point Values

| | |
|---|---|
| Accurate representation of author's thesis and results. Turned in on deadline. | 10 points |
| Ability to handle quotations and paraphrases: language selection, proper integration, and appropriate commentary or explanation | 10 points |

*Consider the following for your own understanding and looking ahead to the next essay. You do not have to address these concerns in Reader Response #6. Address these matters below only if the answers arise organically from your response to the writing prompt above, and only if they fit within the assignment's limited word count.*

What prompted Milgram to do this experiment? Who is Adolph Eichmann and what does he have to do with Milgram's motives? Are the teachers "bad" people, according to Milgram? Do they do the right or wrong thing because they are "good" or "bad" people? Is their behavior related to their morality and values? If not, why do they obey? Does their obedience have anything to do with what we call "human nature" or is it a result of their situation and social environment?

# Unit Five Essay Topics

Length: 1000 to 1500 words (about five to seven pages) in MLA format *or another acceptable standard format as indicated by the instructor.*
Required sources: "The Perils of Obedience" and "Paralyzed Witnesses"

### OPTION #1.

Compose an essay in which you identify a general concept of social psychology that appears in both articles. How does this general concept, which is relevant to the field of social psychology, present itself in each source article? What evidence is there to support the validity of the concept?

### OPTION #2.

Define "diffusion of responsibility" and "fundamental attribution error" within the context of these two articles. How do these concepts relate to each article and what evidence do the authors present in order to clarify or validate these concepts?

### OPTION #3. *I can write the most with this topic and I have more experience writing these essays*

Compose an essay in which you make a considered evaluation of the moral or ethical values of the subjects/people involved in these distinct situations. What evidence or claims do the authors present regarding the character and values of the subjects and people involved?

The best composition will have a controlling voice and direction, that is, the essay will purposefully convey a main point or thesis in direct response to the source material. The main point (or "thesis" or "claim" or "substantiated opinion") will stem from the supporting evidence presented from the source material. Check with your instructor on assignment parameters. Suggested assignment parameters and suggested evaluation criteria appear below.

One of the suggested default requirements on this assignment involves your ability to articulate a valid counter-argument or alternate point of view that stands in opposition or contrast to your main point. In other words, usually in a separate paragraph, articulate a contrary viewpoint that expresses doubt as to your major claim or presents contradictory evidence. By incorporating this rhetorical technique, you demonstrate to your audience that you have constructed a thoughtful, well-considered composition. See "Offering a Contrary Viewpoint as a Rhetorical Strategy."

Follow best practices: As you introduce each text to your outside audience, be sure to, either directly or indirectly, assess the text's "rhetorical situation." See **Rhetorical Situation** in this unit.

As always, check with your instructor on final assignment parameters and requirements.

### Suggested Requirements

✓ You must present a thesis or major claim.
✓ You must clarify the thesis or major claim of each source article.
✓ As always, you must properly select and integrate an acceptable number of quotations from each source article.
✓ You must identify a valid counter-argument or alternate viewpoint which tends to dispute your own thesis or some aspect of it.
✓ Your essay must present evidence from the texts to support your major claim.
✓ Include adequate quotation. (See the evaluation criteria for details.)

*Summary Notes:* Introduce and analyze each text for the benefit of an outside audience. Communicate the thesis, methods, evidence, and/or conclusions of each text as appropriate to your purpose. Decide which points to paraphrase and which points to detail. Demonstrate reading comprehension through an accurate depiction of the authors' views. You must also establish your own views. Support your points with evidence from the texts. Your essay must include paraphrase, significant quotation, sound paragraph development, sound transitions, and overall clear organization. After drafting, you may want to revise your essay by placing your own main point (your thesis statement) within your introductory paragraph.

## Suggested Evaluation Criteria and Point Values

| | |
|---|---|
| **Holistic Assessment**<br>*The essay addresses the given topic in a thoughtful manner, and is: well-organized and purposeful in its presentation of ideas and supporting evidence, clear and accurate in its representations of the source materials, meets length requirement, turned in on deadline.* | 10 points |
| **Controlling Idea**<br>*The student articulates a thesis statement/major claim/main point which is consistently pursued and supported.* | 10 points |
| **Accuracy**<br>*The essay accurately and concisely communicates the thesis, methods, and/or conclusions of each source essay and/or the authors' relevant main points.* | 10 points |
| **Rhetorical Consideration**<br>*The essay identifies a valid counter-argument or alternate perspective on the subject matter, major claim, and/or the student's own conclusion(s).* | 10 points |
| **Text Introductions**<br>*Effective introduction of texts/source materials presented to an outside audience; clear connections within the source materials presented in a manner that outside audience can follow.* | 20 points |
| **Quotations and Text References**<br>*Effective use of text references from both source articles; effective quotation selection and integration with a minimum of (3) quotations or short quoted phrases from each source.* | 20 points |
| **Controlling Voice**<br>*The student uses appropriate, effective grammar, usage, and syntax.* | 10 points |
| **Proper MLA Format (or another standard format as indicated by the instructor)**<br>*Includes proper header, Works Cited, in-text citation, and general formatting.* | 10 points |

Fundamental Attribution Error (FAE)
Normal Premise: Morals/values dictate behavior
This is an error.
Circumstances actually dictate behavior.

Grading based on
Outside Audience
Text Intros
Quotation Integrations
Citation (in- and end-of-paper)
Syntax

# Resources

*Come up with best responses in groups or write out your individual responses in a notebook. Check with your instructor.*

The authors note that a senator from Georgia has read the original *New York Times* article into the *Congressional Record*, the official record of Congress. They write, "The crime against Miss Genovese no longer exists in and of itself. It is rapidly being assimilated to the uses and ideologies of the day." What do you think they mean here?

The authors claim, "We cannot take it for granted that people always do what they consider right." Why not? Explain what they mean, especially as it relates to the situation on the night of the murder.

The article seeks to explain why "there is so marked a discrepancy between values and behavior." How do "values" and "behavior" differ in this situation?

What do the authors mean when they write that what the Kew Garden residents had "were fragments of an ambiguous, confusing and doubtless frightening episode"?

What is your response to the idea that the "incongruity, the sheer improbability of the event predisposed many to reject the most extreme interpretation: that a young woman was in fact being murdered outside the window"?

What do you think the authors mean when they write that "modern societies are so organized as to discourage even the most beneficial, spontaneous group action"?

The authors note that a "collective paralysis may have developed from the belief of each of the witnesses that someone else must surely have taken that obvious step." Social psychologists have also termed this "collective paralysis" the "bystander effect." Define "collective paralysis" or the "bystander effect."

How does the "bystander effect" relate to the idea of the "fundamental attribution error," which is another concept that stems from the field of social psychology?

Why do the authors invoke the anecdote involving Arnold Schuster and Willie Sutton, an escaped criminal? Do you find this anecdote to be a convincing piece of evidence when you consider the authors' overall argument?

What is your interpretation of the final paragraph? What's the most important single idea that you pull from this paragraph?

Stepping back from the article and assessing it on a global level, do you find the authors' argument convincing? What is their argument? Define their claim. Then state whether you find it convincing. Explain why or why not.

# Integrating a Minor Source

Major sources of information should always be introduced formally and as completely as possible, offering your reader a "context" for understanding the source material. Frequently, the writer uses a full paragraph to introduce important texts or source materials. See the "Introducing Texts" resource sheet in Unit One.

Minor sources do not require full, formal introductions. If you are in doubt, favor formal text introduction. If the source material in question provides several quotations that you use in your composition, it qualifies as a major source, not a minor one. However, if you are referencing a source only one time, and it does not play a major role in your analysis or argument, then you can usually integrate the minor source with a simple signal. Typically, you can integrate a minor source with the following useful device:

*According to X,* _____.

*For example:*

According to the National Institute of Neurological Disorders and Stroke, one of the symptoms of autism spectrum disorder involves "insistence of sameness of activities and surroundings, and repetitive patterns of behavior [that] affect the daily functioning of the individual" ("Autism Fact Sheet").

*In this example, I have identified "X" as the source of information. In this case, there is no author, only an article title. I must cite the article title parenthetically, unless I choose to follow this method:*

According to the "Autism Fact Sheet" from the National Institute of Neurological Disorders and Stroke, one of the symptoms of autism spectrum disorder involves "insistence of sameness of activities and surroundings, and repetitive patterns of behavior [that] affect the daily functioning of the individual."

*In the example above, I have named the article title within my sentence, so I do not need to cite it parenthetically at the end of the sentence. In MLA format, source materials are organized by author (last name, first). If there is no author, as is the case here, then I organize the entry by title. The final period appears inside the end quotation mark. Note that I have chosen for clarity's sake to add the word "that" to the quotation. I indicate that I have done so with brackets around the word "that."*

*Note that I can also move my "According to X" device to the* middle *or* end *of the sentence:*

One of the symptoms of autism spectrum disorder, according to the National Institute of Neurological Disorders and Stroke, involves "insistence of sameness of activities and surroundings, and repetitive patterns of behavior [that] affect the daily functioning of the individual" ("Autism Fact Sheet").

*The device appears in the middle of the example above. Or:*

One of the symptoms of autism spectrum disorder involves "insistence of sameness of activities and surroundings, and repetitive patterns of behavior [that] affect the daily functioning of the individual," according to the "Autism Fact Sheet" of the National Institute of Neurological Disorders and Stroke.

*The device appears at the end of the example above.*

All of the examples above use MLA citation format. In MLA format, in-text references work in coordination with the end-of-text bibliographic entry on the "Works Cited" page in order to provide the reader a complete and transparent record of information sources.

The "Works Cited" page bibliographic entry for the source used in the examples above appears as follows:

## Works Cited

"Autism Fact Sheet." National Institute of Neurological Disorders and Stroke, *www.ninds.nih.gov,* 6 Dec. 2017, *https://www.ninds.nih.gov/Disorders/Patient-Caregiver-Education/Fact-Sheets/Autism-Spectrum-Disorder-Fact-Sheet.* Accessed 20 Mar. 2018.

# The Rhetorical Situation

When we compose essays and when we analyze literary texts (and other forms of texts), it is important to remain aware of the "rhetorical situation." If our task is to analyze a text, we want to integrate commentary on the rhetorical situation, or at least remain aware of the rhetorical situation so that this awareness informs our text analysis. An abundance of valuable resource materials regarding rhetorical situation are available online.

First, let's define "text." A text can mean any form of human communication, including, but not limited to, a literary text. Various forms of texts may include: a music video, a song, a novel, a film, a photograph, a blog, or a post. And, of course, any article that appears in *Engaging Discourse* qualifies as a "text." My editorial commentaries, too, are a type of text.

The rhetorical situation of a given "text" consists of:

✓ The **text** itself which communicates in words, in images, in sounds, or in a combination of ways
✓ An **author** or set of authors
✓ An **audience**, that is, the recipient(s) of the communication
✓ The **purpose**, that is, the reason(s) for the communication
✓ A **context**, the time/setting/place/situation/environment which encompasses the text/instance of communication

Remember that the purpose of analyzing the rhetorical situation depends upon whether you are the *author* of a text/composition or a member of the *audience* of the text/composition.

If you are the author of a text, you need to assess the rhetorical situation so that your text communicates effectively. For example:

You are on your way to the grocery store, and you write yourself out a list. This list is a text. (Remember that any form of communication qualifies as a text.) Who is your audience? Yourself. What is your purpose? To get food to feed yourself. The context in this case is pretty nondescript. The list exists within the here-and-now of the daily grind. Once you establish a basic analysis of the rhetorical situation, you can decide how to compose: Is it OK to use emoticons and indecipherable symbols that only you can understand? Sure. It's your list. You are the audience. As long as you understand, it works. You achieve your goal, and I hope it involves some fresh fruits and vegetables too.

You wish to contribute to a *Star Trek* fan blog. Who is your audience? Fans of the long-running TV and movie series who obsess over every detail of the various productions. There might even be sub-groups who specialize in "new" Trekkie lore or "old" Trekkie lore. These folks get bored if posts aren't hyper-focused on tiny details or if posts fail to utilize special terminology. An awareness of the various audiences who might appreciate your blog post determines how you will compose. Your purpose could be to entertain or to bring a new insight or a new idea. Your purpose may simply be to share your enthusiasm for the subject matter. This community will have an easy time understanding your enthusiasm, whereas a different audience might not so readily understand your enthusiasm. The context of this rhetorical situation is pretty clear, especially if you find a particular sub-group that shares your special interests in Vulcan culture.

If you were to write an article in an academic journal, the situation would be much the same, minus the interest in Vulcan culture. Sociologists and psychologists have their own specialized terminology, as do other academicians and scholars. An understanding of audience and the rhetorical situation must guide your writing efforts.

If you write for a general interest audience—let's say an essay that requires interviews and research for a popular magazine—your editor will be pleased when you write in clear prose with standard usage that is widely accepted by a broad, educated audience. I encourage my students to write in this general mode—using clear, simple prose to explain complicated ideas in straightforward, comprehensible language. I find that cultivating a capacity to communicate to a wide audience provides the practice and habit of linguistic flexibility that can serve students well in a variety of career and academic situations.

Not all writing instructors share this philosophy of practicing to write for a general audience. And, in fact, there is clear merit in developing the ability to communicate with a specialized audience.

Initiate a discussion with your instructor regarding rhetorical situation and the intended audience with whom he or she expects you to communicate.

We can also think of rhetorical situation from the perspective of an audience member. Oftentimes, that is exactly what we do when we are asked to analyze an article or piece of literature. We approach it first as an audience member. Then we can step back to consider the author, the author's purpose, and the author's "context," which may involve the author's historical situation. As I have pointed out elsewhere, it is much easier to analyze Judy Brady's purpose in her brief essay "Why I Want A Wife" if we recognize her rhetorical situation. Likewise, if you process Russell Baker's article "School vs. Education" as a somber academic reflection on the state of American education, you are likely to miss some of his main points. We must recognize the entire "context" of Baker's article, or we will miss a great deal of important information as he alludes to school bussing, desegregation, teacher strikes, and other news events of the day. We must recognize that the article was published in an urban newspaper in the mid-1970s, or we could really get lost as we try to make sense of his text.

**Take control of your curriculum:** Write a 300–400 word post to an imaginary online fanzine that specializes in the study of (or obsession with) your favorite book series, Netflix show, film, video game, or whatever. Now "translate" that post for a general interest audience. Write a separate 300–400 word article that expresses your same subject matter in language that would appeal to a broad general readership. Present these compositions side by side to your instructor in order to demonstrate your comprehension of *audience* and *rhetorical situation*.

# A Worksheet on Stanley Milgram's "The Perils of Obedience"

*Come up with best responses in groups or write out your individual responses in a notebook. Check with your instructor.*

Obedience is [necessary/unnecessary] for a society to subsist, according to Milgram.

Milgram writes that the conflict between obedience and disobedience represents an ancient dilemma. Explain:

Name the three participants in Milgram's basic experiment:

- _____
- _____
- _____

Who is the "subject" of the experiment? Why is this person considered the subject?



What does "Gretchen Brandt" choose to exert? Why does Milgram emphasize her role and her attitude?



List three significant biographical details on Gretchen Brandt:

- _____
- _____
- _____

Milgram uses someone as a "foil" (a contrast) to Gretchen Brandt. Name this person:
List two significant biographical details on this person:

- _____
- _____

Another person named "Mr. Braverman" has a peculiar reaction to the experiment. What is it?



What are the numerical results of Milgram's basic experiment?

Identify one variation on Milgram's main experiment and indicate how the results of this variation tend to reinforce Milgram's basic thesis and/or conclusions:

Who is Adolph Eichmann and why does Milgram bring him into the essay?

Why does Milgram reject the interpretation that the subjects harbor deeply aggressive instincts and that this phenomenon accounts for the results?

What do you make of the behavior of "Bruno Batta"? What conclusions does Milgram seem to draw from this man's behavior?

To whom does the subject feel responsible, according to Milgram?

What is the final variation that Milgram mentions in his third to last paragraph and how does his interpretation of the results of this variation reinforce his fundamental conclusions regarding the meaning of the experiments?

Why, in your view, did the Experimenter seem to hold so much authority in this scenario?

What is the most important element, according to Milgram and other social psychologists, in determining an individual's behavior or how he/she will act?

Based on your interpretation of Milgram's article, what elements are required for an individual to resist authority?

# Comparing Quotations

When you are asked to compare or to develop a "synthetic connection" between two sources, you want to understand both texts on a *global* level. However, in order to demonstrate an actual connection, you must operate on the *local* level by offering your audience a close reading and examination of the actual language involved in each text.

Unit Five requires you to draw a synthetic connection between the texts "Paralyzed Witnesses" and "The Perils of Obedience." Look for common *words or ideas* in each text. The following exercise will help you to establish synthetic connections between these sources.

*Identify five significant quotations from each source.* Quote main ideas and important points. Don't worry whether the quotations relate to one another. Write them out in the boxes below or in a notebook. Simply draw a line down the middle of a page and write out the ten quotations, five on each side of the middle line.

| Column 1. "Paralyzed Witnesses" | Column 2. "The Perils of Obedience" |
|---|---|
| Q1. | Q1. |
| Q2. | Q2. |
| Q3. | Q3. |
| Q4. | Q4. |
| Q5. | Q5. |

### Find common nouns:

Circle any common or similar nouns in each quotation and in each column. Draw lines to connect the circled words.

### Label each quote:

Characterize the concept or idea of each of the ten quotations that you have selected. In other words, identify the gist of each quotation with a single word or a few words. Can you find common groups within each source and between the columns? What similar ideas appear within the quotations and in opposite columns?

### Label contradictory concepts:

Don't shy away from identifying contradictory words or ideas. Identifying oppositions or contradictions between the columns may also develop into synthetic connections.

Finding commonalities between quotations from the separate texts is one of the most immediate methods of identifying and developing a synthetic connection between sources.

## Offering a Contrary Viewpoint as an Effective Rhetorical Strategy

Allow your critics to have a say. Allowing space for a contradictory viewpoint in your composition validates your own viewpoint. Think about it. Wouldn't you yourself instinctively trust source material that implies, *Let's take a spectrum of views into consideration* rather than, *There is only one viewpoint worth considering on this matter?*

Acknowledging an alternate perspective can be accomplished in a single paragraph that begins with a topic sentence such as

- Some people may doubt my interpretation of the situation by objecting that _____ _____.
- Other experts find this interpretation unconvincing. They contend that _____ _____.
- _____ may wish to point out that _____.
  Example: Ethicists may wish to point out that a person's behavior is the final measure of character.
- Critics of Milgram take the contrary view that _____.

It is important that you represent such alternate, skeptical views with fairness and respect. The whole idea here (from the standpoint of rhetorical strategy) is to gain the trust of the audience and thereby become more persuasive in your analysis. If you appear to disrespect or dismiss an alternate viewpoint or naysayer, then you harm your own cause.

Why not simply leave out all dissent? Why not present only one viewpoint? First of all, presenting only one viewpoint may appear to your audience as a flaw on your part, a failure of imagination. It is entirely possible that your audience is already thinking about the very same doubt that you express. By acknowledging that doubt, you validate your audience and yourself. In Aristotelian terms, you have increased your *ethos*, the audience's sense that you are a trustworthy source of analysis. Including a skeptical view is also a sound method of *logos* or logical argument when you clarify the reasons why you do not embrace this other viewpoint.

Related: Look up "Rogerian Argument" online. On top of simply being an effective means of composition, argument, and persuasion, there are emotional and psychological reasons to employ the strategy of offering a contrary viewpoint in a fair, respectful manner.

It's embarrassing. This online text analysis service says that my writing isn't very good. The algorithm indicates that my sentences are too long and that my words are too complicated. Pasting text into *https://readable.io/text/* can be a worthy exercise.[i]

I do not endorse any commercial service. Readability.io offers a free text analysis service, and it also encourages you to upgrade to a premium service that is not free. With internet businesses, it's hard to know when "free" services will be yanked, so get there while you don't have to pay!

The site claims that you have seven seconds to catch someone's attention with clear writing. Obviously, the site's focus involves improving online text or online writing. The idea is to make your writing as clear and simple as possible. Along with many editors, I too value clear prose with simple, straightforward syntax (sentence structures).

Readability.io claims to analyze your text by a number of measures, including the Flesch Reading Ease scale (developed in 1948) and the Flesch-Kincaid Grade Level scale (developed in 1975). Essentially, the idea is for you as a writer to move *down* the grade level scale, so that your prose is simpler and easier for a wide audience to understand. *The New York Times*, according to the site, is written at about a 10th grade Flesch-Kincaid Grade Level. This textbook ranges from 7th to 15th. At times, the textbook's reading level spikes when dealing with complicated subject matter. To what extent is it the writer's job to keep that reading level down? For example, the site's analytical tool doesn't like it when I use multisyllabic words such as "bibliography." The computer recommends that I use shorter words. It would prefer if I substitute "list of sources" for "bibliography." Readability.io tells us to "Aim for grade 8 or below to ensure your content is readable by 80% or more of Americans." Visit the hyperlinked pages from the Score Text page (*https://readable.io/text/*) or go directly to *https://readable.io/content/the-flesch-reading-ease-and-flesch-kincaid-grade-level/* for more information.

I am of two minds here. While I value clarity of usage and intent along with simplicity of syntax, I also realize that academic study and web site marketing are two different things. Sometimes we must use complicated, multisyllabic words. However, as George Orwell recommends, it's wise to follow the dictum, "Never use a long word where a short one will do."

Copy a paragraph from one of your latest Reader Response assignments. Paste the text into the online machine at <https://readable.io/text/> and see what the algorithm tells you about the readability of your prose.

## Further Inquiry & Research

"ABC Channel's Milgram Experiment Remake." *YouTube.com, https://www.youtube.com/watch?v=JnYUl6wlBF4.*

Gansberg, Martin. "37 Who Saw Murder Didn't Call the Police." *The New York Times,* Archives, *www.nytimes.com,* Mar. 27, 1964, *https://www.nytimes.com/1964/03/27/37-who-saw-murder-didnt-call-the-police.html.*

Grayson, Audrey and ABC News Medical Unit. "Researcher Revives 'Shocking' Human Experiment." ABC News, *ABCNews.go.com,* Dec. 19, 2008, *http://abcnews.go.com/Health/MindMoodNews/story?id=6496911&page=1.*

Haslem, Alex. "The Psychology of Tyranny: Did Milgram Get It Wrong?" TEDx Talks, Sept. 2, 2016, *https://www.youtube.com/watch?v=HxXMKg8-7o0.*

Merry, Stephanie. "Kitty Genovese Murder: The Real Story of the Woman Killed 'In Front of 38 Witnesses' in Queens in 1964." *Independent, www.independent.co.uk,* 4 July 2016, *https://www.independent.co.uk/news/world/*

---

[i] Actually, the opening paragraph above is OK, according to the site. It gets an "A" with a Flesch-Kincaid Grade Level score of 7.3. My prose that opens this unit, however, bombs. Those complicated paragraphs earned me an "F" with a 15 grade level score.

americas/kitty-genovese-murder-the-real-story-of-the-woman-killed-in-front-of-38-witnesses-in-queens-in-1964-a7118876.html.

Rasenberger, Jim. "Kitty, 40 Years Later." *The New York Times, www.nytimes.com, Feb. 8, 2004, http://www.nytimes.com/2004/02/08/nyregion/kitty-40-years-later.html.*

## Additional Source Materials by Topic

### The Murder of Kitty Genovese

"A New Look at the Killing of Kitty Genovese: The Science of False Confessions". *Association for Psychological Science.* June 30, 2017, https://www.psychologicalscience.org/publications/observer/obsonline/a-new-look-at-the-killing-of-kitty-genovese-the-science-of-false-confessions.html

Fuchs, Erin. "How the Murder of 28-year-old Kitty Genovese Became America's Most Misunderstood Crime". *Business Insider.* Mar. 12, 2014, http://www.businessinsider.com/how-the-murder-of-kitty-genovese-is-misunderstood-2014-3

Gansberg, Martin. "Thirty-Eight Who Saw Murder Didn't Call the Police". *New York Times.* Mar. 27, 1964, http://www2.southeastern.edu/Academics/Faculty/scraig/gansberg.html

Haberman, Clyde. "What the Kitty Genovese Killing can Teach Today's Digital Bystanders". *New York Times.* June 4, 2017,  https://www.nytimes.com/2017/06/04/us/retro-report-bystander-effect.html

JimBobJenkins. "Game Theory 101: The Murder of Kitty Genovese (Volunteer's Dilemma)". *YouTube.* Dec. 28, 2011, https://www.youtube.com/watch?v=FJf5Iw9dDzk

Merry, Stephanie. "Her Shocking Murder Became the Stuff of Legend. But Everyone Got the Story Wrong." *Washington Post.* June 29, 2016, https://www.washingtonpost.com/lifestyle/style/her-shocking-murder-became-the-stuff-of-legend-but-everyone-got-the-story-wrong/2016/06/29/544916d8-3952-11e6-9ccd-d6005beac8b3_story.html

Powers, John. "The Witness' Exposes the Myths, Misconcepts of Kitty Genovese's Murder". *National Public Radio.* June 16, 2016, https://www.npr.org/2016/06/16/482313144/the-witness-exposes-the-myths-misconceptions-of-kitty-genoveses-murder

Signal, Jesse. "How the False Story of Kitty Genovese's Murder Went Viral". *The Cut.* Apr. 5, 2016, https://www.the-cut.com/2016/04/how-the-false-story-of-kitty-genovese-s-murder-went-viral.html

Taylor, Ella. "The Witness' Looks Back at Those Accused of Ignoring Murder". *National Public Radio.* June 2, 2016, https://www.npr.org/2016/06/02/480442769/the-witness-looks-back-at-those-accused-of-ignoring-a-murder

### Human Behavior and Context and Character

"9 General Characteristics of Human Behavior". *Psychology Discussion.* Mar. 11, 2017, http://www.psychologydiscussion.net/behaviour/human-behaviour/9-general-characteristics-of-human-behaviour-psychology/2817

"Difference between Character and Behavior". *Difference Between.* Aug. 14, 2015, http://www.differencebetween.info/difference-between-character-and-behavior

Lickerman, Alex. "Personality vs Character". *Psychology Today.* April 3, 2011, https://www.psychologytoday.com/us/blog/happiness-in-world/201104/personality-vs-character

Maestripieri, Dario. "Are There Universals in Human Behavior? Yes". *Psychology Today.* Nov. 7, 2012, https://www.psychologytoday.com/us/blog/games-primates-play/201211/are-there-universals-in-human-behavior-yes

Reis, Harry, Collins, Willard, & Berscheid, Ellen. "The Relationship Context of Human Behavior and Development". *Psychological Bulletin.* Dec. 2000, https://www.researchgate.net/publication/12219997_The_Relationship_Context_of_Human_Behavior_and_Development

Sayed, Abu. "What is Human Behavior? Classification, characteristics and causation of human behavior". *Textile Apex.* Aug. 2014, https://textileapex.blogspot.com/2014/08/human-behavior.html

Sidman, Murray. "The Analysis of Human Behavior in Context". *National Center for Biotechnology Information.* June 12, 2017, https://www.ncbi.nlm.nih.gov/pmc/articles/PMC2755400/pdf/behavan00004-0059.pdf

## Stanley Milgram

Encina, Gregorio. "Milgram's Experiment on Obedience to Authority". *University of California.* Nov. 15, 2004, https://nature.berkeley.edu/ucce50/ag-labor/7article/article35.htm

Helm, Charles & Morelli, Mario. "Stanley Milgram and the Obedience Experiment: Authority, Legitmacy, and Human Action". *Sage Productions, Inc., Vol. 7, No. 3, pp. 321–345, 1979,* https://www.jstor.org/stable/pdf/190944.pdf?refreqid=excelsior%3Ad45e4cb9853b277f03d3f73d15b09934

"Obeying and Resisting Malevolent Orders". *American Psychological Association.* May 25, 2004, http://www.apa.org/research/action/order.aspx

Parsons, William. *Facing History and Ourselves: Holocaust and Human Behavior.* AbeBooks, 1978, https://www.facinghistory.org/holocaust-and-human-behavior/chapter-9/matter-obedience

Richardot, Sophie. "Testing the Limits of Human Obedience". *CNRS News.* Jan. 25, 2016, https://news.cnrs.fr/opinions/testing-the-limits-of-human-obedience

Romm, Cari. "Rethinking One of Psychology's Most Infamous Experiments". *The Atlantic.* Jan. 28, 2015, https://www.theatlantic.com/health/archive/2015/01/rethinking-one-of-psychologys-most-infamous-experiments/384913/

SparkNotes Editors. "SparkNote on Social Psychology." *SparkNotes LLC.* 27 Sept. 2018, http://www.sparknotes.com/psychology/psych101/socialpsychology/section7/

# UNIT SIX

# The Web Effect

## Readings, Responsibilities, & Objectives for Unit Six: The Web Effect

## Suggested Timeline: Two to three weeks

Experts in fields as diverse as economics, communications, anthropology, and other branches of human studies agree that we have entered a new era of human history in the 21st century. The Internet Era ranks in importance, say these experts, alongside the pre-historic Agricultural Revolution and the Industrial Revolution of the 18th and 19th centuries. It may be difficult to understand—or is it easy for young minds to understand?—that you are coming of age in an era that is separate and distinct from the one in which your parents or grandparents came of age.

Many facets of society have experienced profound transformation since the late 20th century. Economists tell us that the United States operates in a post-industrial economy. Communications experts describe the vast transformations that have taken place in the distribution of information and electronic data. Psychologists describe the intense effects of digitalization on the human experience.

Unit Six: The Web Effect gives us an opportunity to take stock of our new world, to weigh out some of the benefits, as well as some of the challenges and possible disadvantages, of this new age.

## Readings

Langdon Winner, "Mythinformation" (1986)

## Responsibilities

**Reader Response #7** identifies a topic for exploration in the **Unit Six Essay**.

# Objectives

✓ Students will annotate texts, engage in group discussions, and produce critical, creative connections in discussion and in formal compositions between the texts themselves and between the texts and the student's life experience.

✓ This unit aims to reinforce the development of sound critical and analytical thinking through the detailed evaluation of source materials.

✓ This unit challenges students to turn sound critical and analytical thinking on complex topics into clear prose.

✓ Students must produce writing with clear organization, appropriate logic, detailed text analysis, and solid support for their own views, with appropriately cited source information.

✓ Students will develop critical thinking, reading, and writing strategies in order to produce notes, drafts, and a final essay that exhibits synthetic connections between source materials.

✓ Students will demonstrate the ability to produce clear, accurate, and correct academic discourse that reflects an acceptable level of critical thinking while employing the conventions of standard written English.

# Resources

Brainstorming on "Mythinformation"
A Brief History of the Internet
Podcasting Your Abstract

Readings

What could someone know about the internet in 1986? Arguably, the "birthdate" of the internet is April 30, 1993. So what could someone know about the internet, and the profound effects that the internet would have on society, years before the internet was "born"? Langdon Winner reveals a great deal of foresight regarding the impact of computer networking in his 1986 article, an excerpt from his book entitled *The Whale and the Reactor*. As you read his article, take stock of Winner's predictions and measure his concerns with the hindsight of history. In other words, to what extent have his fears been realized in the 21st century? To what extent have the dreams of "computer utopians" who predicted great benefits for society come to pass?

Winner's prognostications seem especially accurate as he lists specific services that will arise from the "utopian promise of this new age: interactive television, electronic funds transfer, computer-aided instruction, customized news service, electronic magazines, electronic mail, computer teleconferencing, online stock market and weather reports, computerized Yellow Pages, shopping via home computer, and so forth." Other than rudimentary forms of email, none of these services existed (at least not in forms that we would recognize) when Winner published his article. In the 21st century, we enjoy all of these services and more.

So the question is this: If we enjoy all of the services that were promised to us in the age of computers, why aren't we living in utopia? Society still suffers from inequities of wealth and enfranchisement. Early internet pioneers predicted that we would make great strides on these fronts in the networking age, yet Winner predicts in this article that these concerns may only get worse in the wake of the "digital revolution." Where is the egalitarian paradise that networking advocates envisioned? What have computers and the internet actually done for the betterment of society?

These questions are at the heart of Winner's article. Clearly, he is pushing back against the utopianism of the "computer romantics" who sermonized on the rise of digital networking in the late 20th century. The assumption, Winner tells us, is that the advent of what we now call the Internet Era must spell good things for society. Winner wants us to question this assumption. How can we plan for the changes that will take place, he asks, if we only assume that good things will happen? In updating that question for the 21st century, we might ask what planning remains to be done in order to prepare for this century and beyond.

Students often have a difficult time with Winner's historical comparisons. Nineteenth-century European revolutionaries had specific social and political goals, but what exactly are the social and political goals of the so-called "computer revolution"?

Very likely, you have never thought much about the Computer Revolution, or the Digital Revolution, or the Networking Revolution, or any other iteration of this concept. You were born in a time and in a country when this "revolution" had already taken place. Yet the deep-seated issues surrounding the internet revolution are far from resolved. It is no exaggeration to say that your generation lives in a new era of human history. We have seen fundamental social, political, financial, and economic shifts that could not have taken place pre-internet. These historical changes warrant discussion.

To what extent do you share Winner's skepticism regarding the changes that have taken place in the Internet Era?

To what extent do you share the utopian vision of early internet pioneers who very clearly understood that computer and networking technology would fundamentally alter the world we inhabit?

As you read, identify specific themes that Winner touches upon. The "Questions to Consider" will help you to do so. Identify sections of the text where Winner discusses the possible social and political effects of what we have come to call the "internet." Specifically, how will computer technologies affect the following areas:

- labor and jobs
- the overall economy

- financial institutions
- education
- politics and democratic processes
- the rise of globalism

You will need to focus on one of these specific areas as you respond to the text in your next reader response.

## Questions to Consider

*Answer these questions as you read and annotate the text:*

- Look over the list of specific services which spell out the "utopian promise" of the new computer age. Remember, this list was compiled in 1986. Can you add to this list? Winner argues, "All of it is supposed to add up to a cultural renaissance." Obviously, he does not believe in 1986 that it all will add up to a cultural renaissance. Has it? In what ways do these computer services create a better society and a better world? In what ways do these services detract from the promise of a better society and a better world?
- Winner alludes to studies, including U.S. Bureau of Labor Statistics studies, that offer predictions regarding new jobs in the "information society." What do these studies predict? What other information can you find in regard to the issue of jobs in post-industrial America?
- Explain the following quotation (from a related section of Winner's book): "Current developments in the information age suggest an increase in power by those who already had a great deal of power, an enhanced centralization of control by those already prepared for control, an augmentation of wealth by the already wealthy." What does he mean when he wrote this in 1986? How has this idea played out in subsequent decades?
- Winner claims that a certain idea is "entirely faulty." Which idea does he mean?
- Winner draws an analogy regarding the impact of television in the 20th century on the level of political participation in our democracy. What is his analogy between television and the internet? What point is he trying to make? Do you find his point persuasive? In your view, what is happening to political participation in America in the Internet Era?
- Winner complains about superficial responses to social changes that result from computerization. What or who is to blame for these superficial, unreflective responses, in your opinion and in Winner's opinion?
- Near the end of his essay, Winner comments on the growing power of "transnational corporations." What are transnational corporations? How does the rise of computer power aid such corporations? What sorts of discussions regarding the power and influence of "transnational corporations" continue to affect our public discourse?

## Langdon WInner, Mythinformation

Mythinformation (n.): The almost religious conviction that a widespread adoption of computers and communications systems, along with broad access to electronic information, will automatically produce a better world for humanity.

The specter of computer revolution is haunting modern society. Books, magazine articles, and news-media specials declare that this upheaval is underway, that nothing will escape unchanged. Like political revolutionists, advocates of computerization believe that a glorious transformation is sweeping the world and that they are its vanguard.

Of course, modern society has long since gotten used to "revolutions" in laundry detergents, underarm deodorants, floor waxes, and other consumer products. Exhausted in advertising slogans, the revolution image has lost much of its punch. Those who employ it to talk about computers and society, however, appear to make much more serious claims.

According to visionaries like Edward A. Feigenbaum and Pamela McCorduck (The Fifth Generation) or Murray Turoff and Starr Roxanne Hiltz (The Network Nation) industrial society, which depends on material production for its livelihood, is being supplanted by a society in which information services will enable people to satisfy their economic and social needs. As computation and communication technologies become less expensive and more convenient, all the people of the world, not just the wealthy, will use the wonderful services that information machines make available. Gradually, existing differences between rich and poor will evaporate.

Long lists of services are meant to suggest the coming utopia: interactive television, electronic funds transfer computer-aided instruction, customized news service, electronic magazines, electronic mail, computer teleconferencing, on-line stock and weather reports, computerized yellow pages, shopping via home computer, and so forth. In the words of James Martin, writing in Telematic Society: "The electronic revolution will not do away with work, but it does hold out some promises: most boring jobs can be done by machines; lengthy commuting can be avoided; the opportunities for personal creativity will be unlimited."

In this interpretation, the prospects for participatory democracy have never been brighter, offering all the democratic benefits of the ancient Greek city-state, the Israeli kibbutz, and the New England town meeting. J. C. R. Licklider, a computer scientist at MIT, writes hopefully in a 1980 article called "Computers and Government": "The political process would essentially be a giant teleconference, and a campaign would be a months-long series of communications among candidates, propagandists, commentators, political action groups, and voters. The information revolution is bringing with it a key that may open the door to a new era of involvement and participation."

## Mythinformation in the High-tech Era

Taken as a whole, beliefs like these make up what I call mythinformation: the almost religious conviction that a widespread adoption of computers and communications systems, along with broad access to electronic information, will automatically produce a better world for humanity.

It is common for the advent of a new technology to provide occasion for flights of utopian fancy. During the last two centuries the factory system, railroads, the telephone, electricity, automobiles, airplanes, radio, television, and nuclear power have all figured prominently in the belief that a new and glorious age was about to begin. But even within the great tradition of optimistic technophilia, current dreams

---

An earlier version of this chapter appeared in Langdon Winner, "Mythinformation: Romantic Politics on the Computer Revolution," Research in Philosophy and Technology, JAI Press (1984), 287–304.

of a "computer age" stand out as exaggerated and unrealistic. Because they have such broad appeal, and because they overshadow other ways of looking at the matter, these notions deserve closer inspection.

As is generally true of myths, the dreams contain elements of truth. What were once industrial societies are being transformed into service economies, a trend that emerges as a greater share of material production shifts to the developing countries, where labor costs are low and business tax breaks are lucrative. However, this shift does not mean that future employment possibilities will flow largely from the microelectronics and information-services industries, even though some service industries do depend on highly sophisticated computer and communications systems.

A number of studies, including those of the US Bureau of Labor Statistics, suggest that the vast majority of new jobs will be menial service positions paying relatively low wages. As robots and computer software absorb an increasing share of factory and office tasks, the "information society" will offer plenty of work for janitors, hospital orderlies, and fast-food helpers.

The computer savants correctly notice that computerization alters relationships of social power and control; however, the most obvious beneficiaries of this change are large transnational business corporations. While their "global reach" does not arise solely from the application of information technologies, such organizations are uniquely situated to exploit the new electronic possibilities for greater efficiency, productivity, command, and control. Other notable beneficiaries will be public bureaucracies, intelligence agencies, and ever-expanding military organizations.

Ordinary people are, of course, strongly affected by these organizations and by the rapid spread of new electronic systems in banking, insurance, taxation, work, home entertainment, and the like. They are counted on to be eventual eager buyers of hardware, software, and communications services.

But where is any motion toward increased democratization and social equality, or the dawn of a cultural renaissance? Current empirical studies of computers and social change—such as those described in Computers and Politics by James Danzig—suggest an increase in power by those who already have a great deal of power, an enhanced centralization of control by those already in control, and an augmentation of wealth by the already wealthy. If there is to be a computer revolution, it will most likely have a distinctly conservative character.

Granted, such prominent trends could be altered. A society strongly rooted in computer and telecommunications systems could incorporate participatory democracy, decentralized control, and social equality. However, such progress would involve concerted efforts to remove the many difficult obstacles blocking those ends, and the writings of computer enthusiasts seldom propose such deliberate action. Instead, they suggest that the good society will be a natural spin-off from the proliferation of computing devices. They evidently assume no need to place limits upon concentrations of power in the information age.

There is nothing new in this assumption. Computer romanticism strongly resembles a common nineteenth- and twentieth-century faith that expects to generate freedom, democracy, and justice through simple material abundance. From that point of view, there is no need for serious inquiry into the appropriate design of new institutions for the distribution of rewards and burdens. In previous versions of this conviction, the abundant (and therefore democratic) world would be found in a limitless supply of houses and consumer goods. Now "access to information" has moved to the top of the list.

## Probing the Key Assumptions

The political arguments of computer romantics draw upon four key assumptions: 1) people are bereft of information; 2) information is knowledge; 3) knowledge is power; and 4) increased access to information enhances democracy and equalizes social power.

1. Is it true that people face serious shortages of information? To read the literature on the computer revolution, one would suppose this to be a problem on a par with the energy crisis of the 1970s. The persuasiveness of this notion borrows from our sense that literacy, education, knowledge, well-informed minds, and the widespread availability of tools of inquiry are of unquestionable social value.

Alas, the idea is entirely faulty. It mistakes sheer supply of information for an educated ability to gain knowledge and act effectively. Even highly developed societies contain chronic inequalities in the distribution of education and intellectual skills. The US Army must reject many of the young men and women it recruits because they cannot read military manuals.

If the solution to problems of illiteracy and poor education were a question of information supply alone, then the best policy might be to increase the number of well-stocked libraries, especially in places where libraries do not presently exist. Of course, that would do little good unless people were sufficiently well educated to use those libraries. Computer enthusiasts, however, are not known for their support of public libraries and schools; they call for electronic information carried by networks. To look to those instruments first while ignoring everything history has taught us about how to educate and stimulate a human mind is grave foolishness.

2. What is the "information" so cherished as knowledge? It is not understanding, enlightenment, critical thought, timeless wisdom, or the content of a well-educated mind. Looking closely at the writings of computer enthusiasts, "information" means enormous quantities of data manipulated by various kinds of electronic media, used to facilitate the transactions of large, complex organizations. In this context, the sheer quantity of information presents a formidable challenge. Modern organizations continually face "overload", a flood of data that threatens to become unintelligible. Computers provide one way to confront that problem; speed conquers quantity.

The information most crucial to modern organizations is highly time-specific. Data on stock market prices, airline traffic, weather conditions, international economic indicators, military intelligence, and public opinion polls are useful for very short periods of time. Systems that gather, organize, analyze, and use electronic data must be closely tuned to the latest developments. Information is a perishable commodity.

But is it sensible to transfer this ideology, as many evidently wish, to all parts of human life? A recent Business Week article on home computers concluded: "Running a household is actually like running a small business. You have to worry about inventory control-of household supplies-and budgeting for school tuition, housekeepers' salaries, and all the rest." One begins to wonder how running a home was possible before microelectronics.

3. "As everybody knows, knowledge is power," wrote Dr. Feigenbaum. This attractive idea is highly misleading. Knowledge employed in particular circumstances may well help one act effectively-a citrus farmer's knowledge of frost conditions enables him to fight the harmful effects of cold snaps. But there is no automatic, positive link between knowledge and power, especially power in a social or political sense. At times, knowledge brings merely an enlightened impotence or paralysis. What conditions might enable ordinary folks to translate their knowledge into renewed power? It is a question computer enthusiasts, ought to explore.

4. An equally serious misconception among computer enthusiasts is the belief that democracy is largely a matter of distributing information. This assertion plays on the valid beliefs that a democratic public should be open-minded and well-informed, and that totalitarian societies are evil because they dictate what people can know and impose secrecy to restrict freedom. But democracy is not founded primarily upon the availability of information. It is distinguished from other political forms by the recognition that the people as a whole are capable of; and have the right to, self-government.

There are many reasons why relatively low levels of citizen participation prevail in some modern democracies, including the United States. Perhaps opportunities to serve in a public office or influence policy are too limited; in that case, broaden the opportunities. Or perhaps choices placed before citizens are so pallid that boredom is a valid response; then improve the quality of those choices. But it is not reasonable to assume that a universal grid of sophisticated information machines, in itself, would stimulate a renewed sense of political involvement and participation.

The role of television in modern politics suggests why this is so. Public participation in voting has steadily declined as television replaces the face-to-face politics of precincts and neighborhoods. The passive monitoring of electronic news makes citizens feel involved while releasing them from the desire to take an active part, and from any genuine political knowledge based on first-hand experience. The vitality of democratic politics depends on people's willingness to act together - to appear before each other in person, speak their minds, deliberate, and decide what they will do. This is considerably different from the model upheld as a breakthrough for democracy: logging onto one's computer, receiving the latest information, and sending back a digitized response. No computer enthusiasm is more poignant than the faith that the personal computer, as it becomes more sophisticated, cheaper, and more simple to use, will become a potent equalizer in society. Presumably, ordinary citizens equipped with microcomputers will counter the influence of large, computer-based organizations. This notion echoes the eighteenth- and nineteenth-century revolutionary belief that placing firearms in the hands of the people would overthrow entrenched authority. But the military defeat of the Paris Commune in 1871 made clear that arming the people may not be enough. Using a personal computer makes one no more powerful vis-a-vis, say, the US National Security Agency than flying a hang glider establishes a person as a match for the US Air Force.

## The Long-term Consequences

If the long-term consequences of computerization are anything like the ones commonly predicted, they will require rethinking of many fundamental conditions and institutions in social and political life. Three areas of concern seem paramount. First, as people handle more of their daily activites electronically-mail, banking, shopping, entertainment, travel plans, and so on-it becomes technically feasible to inonitor these activities with unprecedented ease. An age rich in electronic information may achieve wonderful social conveniences at the cost of placing freedom-and the feeling of freedom-in a deep chill.

Second, a computerized world will renovate conditions of human sociability. Indeed, the point of many applications of microelectronics is to eliminate social layers that were previously needed. Computerized bank tellers have largely done away with local branch banks, which were places where people met and socialized. The so-called electronic cottage would operate well without the human interaction that characterizes office work.

These developments pare away the face-to-face contact that once provided buffers between individuals and organized power. Workers who might previously have recognized a common grievance and acted together to remedy it are now deprived of such contact, and thus increasingly influenced by employers, news media, advertisers, and national political leaders. Where will we find new institutions to balance and mediate such power?

Third, computers, satellites, and telecommunications may recast the basic structure of political order, as they fulfill the modern dream of conquering space and time. These systems make possible instantaneous action anywhere on the globe without limits imposed by the location of the initiator.

But humans and their societies have traditionally lived, acted, and found meaning within spatial and temporal limits. Microelectronics tends to dissolve these limits, thereby threatening the integrity of social and political forms that depend on them.

Transnational corporations of enormous size can now manage their activities efficiently across the whole surface of the planet. If it seems convenient, operations can be shifted from Sunnyvale to Singapore at the flick of a switch. In recent past, corporations have had to demonstrate at least some semblance of commitment to their geographical base; their public relations often stressed the fact that they were "good neighbors". But when organizations are located everywhere and nowhere this commitment easily evaporates. Towns, cities, regions, and whole nations must swallow their pride and negotiate for favors. Political authority is gradually redefined.

By calling the changes of computerization "revolutionary", people tacitly acknowledge that these changes require reflection; they may even require strong public action to ensure desirable outcome. Yet the occasions in our society for reflection, debate and public check are rare indeed. The important decisions are left in private hands inspired by narrowly focused economic motives. While it is widely recognized that these decisions have profound cumulative consequence for our common lives few seem prepared to own up to that fact. Some observers forecast that the computer revolution will be guided by new wonders in artificial intelligence. Its present course is influenced by something much more familiar: the absent mind.

## Questions for Comprehension

*Answer these questions as a comprehension reading quiz and/or for further clarification on the text:*

1. Fill in the blank from the final paragraph: *By calling the changes of computerization "revolutionary," people tacitly acknowledge that these changes require _____.*

2. True/False. Winner expresses optimism when it comes to the types of jobs that the new information society will produce.

3. Define the neologism "mythinformation." *Neologism*, literally, means "new word."

4. True/False. Winner disagrees with the "computer utopians" in their belief that the information age will distribute political and economic power to a wide range of people.

5. What is wrong with the following formula, according to Winner? *1) People lack information, 2) information is knowledge, 3) knowledge is power; therefore, 4) increasing access to information enhances democracy and equalizes social power.*

# Assignments

## Reader Response #7

Two pages in MLA format (about 500 words)

Focus on Langdon Winner's "Mythinformation."

**Writing prompt:** *1. Select a focus, 2. analyze Winner's concerns, and 3. respond/update.*

1. Select a general area of concern from the following list:
   - labor and jobs
   - the overall economy
   - financial institutions
   - education
   - politics and democratic processes
   - globalism
2. Briefly introduce Winner's text and identify his thesis or main point as it relates to your selected general area of concern. For example, if you select "labor and jobs," then convey Winner's claims regarding the effects of the computer age on labor and jobs. As always, be sure to quote and accurately paraphrase as you analyze the content of Winner's article.
3. Respond to Winner's concerns. Stay focused on the general area of concern that you have selected. Offer your personal insights on the subject matter. Incorporate relevant 21st century updates on the subject matter. You may have to do some study online in order to be able to define a relevant public discourse as it applies to today. The area of focus that you select from the list above will help you to determine how to define your public discourse.

Reader Response #7 prepares you for the Unit Six essay.

## Suggested Evaluation Criteria and Point Values

| | |
|---|---|
| Accurate representation of author's main point and concerns. Turned in on deadline. | 10 points |
| Ability to handle quotations and paraphrases: language selection, proper integration, and appropriate commentary or explanation | 10 points |

# Unit Six Essay Topics

Length: 1000 to 1200 words in MLA format *or another acceptable standard format as indicated by the instructor.* The topics below can be converted into research topics as well.

## OPTION #1.

Introducing one or more of Winner's main claims, offer a focused, coherent update on a relevant 21st-century technology that did not exist when the article was published in 1986. What is the relationship between this technology and Winner's claims? How does this technology tend to support or contradict the claims that Winner makes in his article?

## OPTION #2.

Introducing and incorporating Winner's main concerns, analyze the most significant societal shifts that have taken place as America has transitioned from an industrial to a post-industrial society. You may want to narrow your focus according to the general area of concern that you selected in Reader Response #7.

## OPTION #3.

Expand Reader Response #7 into a more comprehensive analysis of your chosen subject matter. Explore valid, authoritative source materials in order to update the relevant issues that exist in the 21st century when it comes to the Internet Era and your selected area of concern.

The best compositions will have a controlling voice and direction, that is, they will purposefully convey a main point or thesis in direct response to the source material. Your main point (or "thesis" or "claim" or "substantiated opinion") must be supported by evidence from the source text or from other valid, authoritative texts. Check with your instructor on assignment parameters. Suggested assignment parameters and suggested evaluation criteria appear below.

Follow best practices: As you introduce "Mythinformation" to your outside audience, be sure to address the "rhetorical situation" of the text. See "Rhetorical Situation" in Unit Five.

## Suggested Requirements:

As always, check with your instructor on final assignment parameters and requirements.

- ✓ You must present a thesis or major claim.
- ✓ You must clarify the thesis or major claim of the main source article.
  - If you incorporate minor sources, follow proper methods of attribution. See "Integrating Minor Sources" in Unit Five and "The Importance of Attribution" in Unit Three.
- ✓ As always, you must select and integrate an acceptable number of significant quotations from the source article. If you are unsure as to what constitutes an acceptable number, consult your instructor.
- ✓ It is helpful to identify a valid counter-argument or alternate viewpoint which tends to dispute your own thesis or some aspect of it. Note here that if you choose to counter or dispute a main claim of the source text, then you are probably already organically engaged in the process of identifying and offering a valid counter-argument. See "Offering a Contrary Viewpoint as a Rhetorical Strategy" in Unit Five.
- ✓ Your essay must present evidence from the source text or from other texts to support your major claim.
  - All source materials must be properly listed on a Works Cited page or other form of bibliography.

*Summary Notes:* Introduce and analyze the source text for the benefit of an outside audience. Communicate the thesis, concerns, evidence, and conclusions of the source text *as appropriate to your purpose.* That is, focus on your selected area of concern. Decide which points to paraphrase and which points to detail. Demonstrate reading comprehension through an accurate depiction of the author's views. You must also establish your own viewpoint. Support your points with evidence. Your essay must include significant quotation, sound paragraph development, and overall clear organization.

## Suggested Evaluation Criteria and Point Values

| | |
|---|---|
| **Holistic Assessment**<br>*The essay addresses the given topic in a thoughtful manner, and is: well-organized and purposeful in its presentation of ideas and supporting evidence; clear and accurate in its representations of source materials; meets length requirement; turned in on deadline.* | 20 points |
| **Controlling Idea**<br>*The student articulates a thesis statement/major claim/main point which is consistently pursued and supported.* | 20 points |
| **Accuracy**<br>*The essay accurately and concisely communicates the thesis, concerns, and/or conclusions of the source text and/or the author's relevant main points.* | 10 points |
| **Text Introduction**<br>*Effective introduction of source text presented to an outside audience.* | 10 points |
| **Quotations and Text References**<br>*Effective use of text references; effective quotation selection and integration with a minimum of (3) quotations or short quoted phrases from the source text and/or other valid authoritative sources.* | 20 points |
| **Controlling Voice**<br>*The student uses appropriate, effective grammar, usage, and syntax.* | 10 points |
| **Proper MLA Format (or another standard format as indicated by the instructor)**<br>*Includes proper header, Works Cited, in-text citation, and general formatting.* | 10 points |

# Resources

# Brainstorming on "Mythinformation"

Individually or in small groups, use the prompts below in order to brainstorm on your selected area of focus. This exercise prepares you for drafting Reader Response #7 and the final unit essay.

Understand that there are dozens, if not hundreds, of different sub-topics to pursue under each general category. Instead of feeling overwhelmed, try to find a specific sub-topic that interests you personally. Don't try to cover everything. Cover one thing in detail. Good writing is often the result of analyzing a narrow, specific sub-topic. Demonstrate how the specific sub-topic relates to the general claims of Winner and/or other experts. Obviously, you could easily turn this exercise into a research topic, but it is equally valuable to turn it into an important cognitive exercise in how to narrow down an overwhelming topic into a manageable piece of information. Arguably, this is one of the most important skills that young Americans need to develop in the 21st century.

With all of these topics, you may need to find reliable source materials online that can help you to participate in the discourse as it pertains to 21stcentury America.

Consider the following questions within each general area of focus. 1) Look for evidence as to what Winner claims in regard to these issues, and 2) update these issues with regard to what you know or what you can find out concerning these issues as they exist in the 21st century.

- Labor and Jobs
    - What does Winner claim will happen to American jobs as a result of the advent of the Internet Era? What has happened within American labor as a result of the rise of a post-industrial Internet Era economy? Look for reliable source materials online that can help you to participate in this discourse.
- Economy
    - It is difficult to separate "economy" from "jobs." Nonetheless, make a distinction to the best of your ability. How does Winner seem to deal separately with the issue of "economy" rather than "jobs" per se? What does current scholarship have to say regarding the overall effects that the internet has had on the American economy?
- Finance and Financial Institutions
    - What does Winner say regarding the effects of networking technologies on finance and financial institutions? How has the internet benefitted and/or disadvantaged consumers, banks, and financial institutions in 21st century America?
- Education
    - How has the internet impacted American education? Has anything fundamentally changed in education as a result of the internet? What are the benefits and/or disadvantages that that have arisen, or should arise, in American education as a result of internet technologies?
- Politics and the Democratic Process
    - What does Winner predict is likely to happen in this realm as a result of internet technologies? What do experts say has happened within the democratic political process as a result of internet technologies? It is noteworthy that both Presidents Obama and Trump made extensive use of social media in their election campaigns. What are the benefits and/or disadvantages that arise as a result of the internet when it comes to politics and the democratic process?
- Globalism
    - How does the internet contribute to "globalism"? Define this broad term. How or why does globalism become a more important concept in the Internet Era?

# A Brief History of the Internet

Scholars often give April 30, 1993 as the official "birthdate" of the Internet. Of course, there were many computer and networking pioneers who worked over a long period in order to develop the necessary hardware and software applications needed to create the global information network that we call the internet. The following list is not intended to be comprehensive or definitive, only brief.

Aug. 1962 – MIT professor and head of computer research program at DARPA (Defense Advanced Research Projects Agency), J.C.R. Licklider envisions a "Galactic Network" of interconnected computers.

1967 – After he and associates successfully connected two computers in Massachusetts and California via a telephone line in 1965, Lawrence G. Roberts publishes a plan for ARPANET, the Advanced Research Projects Agency Network, a pioneering network for sharing data between remote computers.

1972 – "Electronic mail" (email) is introduced as an application to run on ARPANET.

1972 – Bob Kahn proposes the concept of "open architecture" networking, allowing separate networks with different protocols to interact. There would be no universal or global controls. Early incarnations of routers would be designed to traffic the flow of information.

1973 – TCP/IP, or Transmission Control Protocol/Internet Protocol, is developed by Bob Kahn and Vint Cerf.

1973 – Ethernet technology is developed by Bob Metcalfe at Xerox PARC (Palo Alto Research Center).

1980s – The development of LANs (Local Area Networks), along with the advent and spread of PCs (Personal Computers), intimate the beginnings of the internet. A limited number of "host" computers provide networking services, while an increasing number of LANs makes it clear that early networking concepts involving single "hosts" must be modified. Paul Mockapetris of USC Information Sciences Institute invents the Domain Name System (DNS). Early "nodes" or routers have difficulty handling an increasing amount of diverse traffic.

1985 – The U.S. National Science Foundation Network (NSFNET) announces its intention to serve the entire higher education community. TCP/IP is selected to support the NSFNET program. From 1986 to 1995, the NSFNET program provides $200 million in funding to connect supercomputer centers, research facilities, and education networks. The NSFNET program provides a "demonstration" of the global internet concept, a large-scale, complex network that provides a "backbone" to connect numerous independently operated networks. After 1995, networking support largely transitions from public (government) to private (corporate) interests.

1989 – Tim Berners-Lee invents the "world wide web," a data system that linked hypertext documents that were accessible from any point on the network. Berners-Lee develops the first "web server" and the first "web browser" in 1990. In 1994, Berners-Lee defines a URL, or Uniform Resource Locator. The format modifies the existing DNS domain name system. Berners-Lee and his team at CERN (European Particle Physics Laboratory in Geneva, Switzerland) develop the first HTTP, or hypertext transfer protocol, a standard format for transmitting hypertext documents on the world wide web.

1989 – The World, the first commercial dialup ISP (Internet Service Provider), begins operations in the United States.

1992 – Congress passes legislation allowing NSFNET to interconnect with commercial networks.

Apr. 30, 1993 – CERN (European Particle Physics Laboratory) issues a document in which it formally gives up the right to charge royalties for world wide web technologies developed by Tim Berners-Lee and his team. According to Berners-Lee and other scholars, without the release of this intellectual property for public use, there would be no internet as we know it today. Some observers say that another technology may have eventually filled the space occupied by www technologies; however, there is little dispute that the rapid global growth of the internet is fueled primarily by the spread of these www protocols being released into the international public domain.

Oct. 24, 1995 – The FNC (Federal Networking Council) formally adopts the term "internet."

## Podcasting Your Abstract

As you probably know, an *abstract* is a brief encapsulation of an article. An abstract prefaces the actual article. It outlines the main argument, methodologies, and main points of evidence used in the article. While "abstract" tends to be an academic term, the idea of an abstract is much the same as an "executive summary" or "outline."

What resources are available to you to develop a brief podcast or web recording for broadcast to your classmates?

Find the means to record and podcast a brief abstract in order to forecast your Unit Six essay on web technology. Check with your instructor prior to undertaking any suggested assignment.

- Outline your thesis or main point.
- Summarize your argument and evidence.
- Identify your conclusions.

Podcast parameters:

- 150 words maximum
- Your recording must be under one minute, preferably closer to 30 seconds

Discover what resources your institution has to support you in this project.

## Further Inquiry & Research

Darnton, Robert. "The Research Library in the Digital Age." Harvard University Library, 2008, http://hul.harvard.edu/publications/Darnton_ResearchLibraryDigitalAge.pdf.

Leiner et al. "Brief History of the Internet." *Internet Society,* 1997, *https://www.internetsociety.org/internet/history-internet/brief-history-internet/*

Turkle, Sherry. "Connected, But Alone?" TED Talk, Feb. 2012, https://www.ted.com/talks/sherry_turkle_alone_together.

Winner, Langdon. "Who Will Be in Cyberspace?" *Information Society*, Vol. 12, No. 1, 1996, pp. 63–72, *https://www.tandfonline.com/doi/abs/10.1080/019722496129701*, published online July 29, 2006.

## Additional Source Materials by Topic

### Utopia/Dystopia

Castells, Manuel. *The Internet Galaxy: Reflections on the Internet, Business, and Society.* Oxford University Press, 2002, *books.google.com*

Davis, Randall. "Utopia or Chaos?: The Impact of Technology on Language Teaching". Central European Journal, 2006

Dworak, B., Lovett, J., & Baumgartner, F. "The Diversity of Internet Media: Utopia or Dystopia". *Midwest Political Science Association, Vol. 1, Issue 6, pp. 42–65.* April 3, 2014, http://www.unc.edu/~fbaum/papers/MPSA2014-InternetDystopia.pdf

Filchy, Patrice. *The Internet Imaginare.* MIT Press, 2007, *books.google.com*

Morais, Ricardo. "New Technologies and Deliberation: Internet as a Virtual Public Sphere or a Democratic Utopia?". *The Virtual Sphere.* Sage Publications, *2002,* pp. 223–226. http://agendadocidadao.ubi.pt/PSR/book/psr-ebook.pdf#page=223

## Internet and Politics

Browning, Graeme. *Electronic Democracy.* Information Today, Inc., 2002, books.google.com

Chadwick, Andrew and Philip Howard, editors. *Routledge Handbook of Internet Politics.* Taylor & Francis, 2010, books.google.com

Gibson, R.K., G. Nixon, and S.J. Ward editors. *Political Parties and the Internet: Net Gain?.* Routledge, Aug. 29, 2003, *books.google.com*

Graber, D. & Dunaway, J. *Mass Media and American Politics.* CQ Press, Jul. 20, 2017, *books.google.com*

Oats, S., D. Owen, and R. Gibson, editors. *The Internet and Politics.* Routledge, 2006, *books.google.com*

Selnow, Gary. *Electric Whistle Stops: The Impact of the Internet on American Politics.* Greenwood Publishing Group, 1998, *books.google.com*

## Cognition

Brand, Matthias et al. "Integrating psychological and neurobiological considerations regarding the development and maintenance of specific Internet-use disorders". *Science Direct, Neuroscience & Biobehavioral Reviews, Vol. 71, Dec. 2016, pp. 252–266,* https://www.sciencedirect.com/science/article/pii/S0149763416302627

Riva, G. & Galimberti, C. *Towards Cyberpsychology: Mind, Cognition, and Society in the Internet Age.* IOS Press, 2001, *books.google.com*

# Unit One Notes

## Questions for Comprehension – Asimov essay

1. False
2. True
3. The measurement of intelligence is always relative and subjective in nature. There are various sorts of intelligence. Society seems to value certain kinds of intelligence over other kinds of intelligence. Academics have become the "arbiters" of what it means to be intelligent.

## Questions for Comprehension – Baker essay

1. True
2. The concept of "dumb or smart" involves expectations: "If the teacher puts intelligent demands upon the child, the child learns he is smart. If the teacher expects little of the child, the child learns he is dumb."
3. Obviously, this question is subjective in nature and simply requires a thoughtful response. One might draw a valid analogy between the concerns that TV would "rot" kids' minds and negatively influence their values and the current concerns over the influence of social media, marketing, and even "fake news" propagated over the internet. The most alarmist of these concerns did not seem to come to pass regarding the influence of TV, but that doesn't mean that all concerns over the negative influences of TV media weren't valid. Perhaps the most reasonable conclusion is that with both TV and the internet some of the concerns are valid, while "slippery slope" or "end of the world" arguments ought to be toned down a bit.
4. The "smart" children who have been "happily telling testers what they want to hear for twelve years" appear to be the best candidates for college in a world that values "school" over real education. Meanwhile, children who have suffered from low expectations, i.e. the "dumb" kids, are admitted to "less joyous" colleges that may teach them to read. The worldview expressed here seems not only dour, but outright cynical. Of course, it's possible to read humor here as well.
5. Developing "a curious mind" is the beginning of true education. What has come before—testing, grades, busy work—is only "school."

## Questions for Comprehension – Rose essay

1. C – vocational
2. Essentially, Rose argues that some students find school so confusing and disorienting that they develop an "I don't care" attitude about school and education in order to protect themselves from feeling vulnerable. Unfortunately, writes Rose, "you have to twist the knife in your own gray matter to make this defense work."
3. There are numerous things that a student might note. For example, classmates seemed to gather, either formally or informally, in Mr. MacFarland's home. They read and discussed some of the canonical classics of Western culture. The assignments were difficult. Mr. MacFarland, a sort of beatnik who chain smoked and dressed sloppily, set a high bar for his students. He did not have low expectations that would allow his students to slide by.
4. False. He mentions the boundaries of Vermont Street at the very end of his text.
5. Rose's newfound learning allows him to connect to his teacher, to his classmates, and to the world. Although he drops the persona of the disaffected hipster within a couple of years, the concept of establishing a worldview based on the gaining of knowledge sticks with Rose for a lifetime.

# Notes for Composition Unit One

## Sentence Exercise #1

1. Note that normally a comma would appear after the essay title and before the end quotation mark. Since a question mark appears in that place as part of the title, we leave out the comma so that we do not double punctuate the introductory dependent phrase.
2. Note that there are two distinct sentences here.
3. Some instructors do not like the use of "we" or "us" in formal composition. Check with your instructor on his or her opinion.
4. Can you identify the faulty syntax in this sentence? How could you fix the sentence?
5. This is an example of weak syntax or sentence structure. Note that the author's name does not appear. The sentence could read "it is argued by Isaac Asimov that _____ ." Then you would have the author's name in there, but the sentence itself is still structured in the weak passive voice. We know the sentence features passive syntax due to the word "it" and the implication of "by Isaac Asimov." In order to make the sentence function with active voice syntax, we can attribute the action to the sentence subject, which in this case is the author Isaac Asimov: *Isaac Asimov argues in his essay "What Is Intelligence, Anyway?" that* _____ .

## Sentence Exercise #2

1. Note the necessary comma that follows the introductory dependent phrase. In American publishing, we place this comma inside the article title's second quotation mark. In other countries you might see this comma appear outside of the second quotation mark. As I like to point out to my students, we happen to reside in America so let's punctuate according to the rules of American publishing.
2. Note that we are *analyzing* content rather than *summarizing* content. You can look up the definitions of the verbs "analyze" and "summarize" instantly on *dictionary.com* or another web resource.
3. Some instructors do not like the use of "we" or "us" in formal composition. Check with your instructor on his or her opinion.
4. Identify and correct the faulty syntax.
5. This is an example of weak, passive syntax, also called *passive voice* sentence structure. There is nothing grammatically incorrect with this sentence structure. So what's the problem? In some cases, there may be no problem. Ask your instructor his or her opinion on the use of passive voice sentence structure. In order to make the sentence function with *active voice*, we identify the subject and provide an action verb for that subject: *Russell Baker argues in his essay "School vs. Education" that* _____ .

## Three Effective Ways to Integrate Quotations

1. "Atwood claims" is the signal phrase that must be set off with a comma. Note that we have replaced "It's also" in the original text with the bracketed phrase "Pornography is." The beginning of this quotation (which is a full sentence) requires a capital letter "P" on "Pornography." Avoid quoting faulty fragment sentences with the signal phrase method. With the signal phrase method, you want to quote or create a full sentence quotation.

2. Note that we have set up the original quotation with a complete sentence that is capable of standing on its own. A colon follows this complete sentence in order to set up the quotation. We use the colon to display the relationship between the set up and the quotation.

3. Note that there is no comma after "is." Punctuate this sentence as you would a normal sentence of your own.

# Unit Two Notes

## Questions for Comprehension – Brady essay

1. False
2. Take the kids to the doctor and dentist, take care of all traditional domestic duties, take care of the husband's physical needs, etc.—essentially, to take a backseat to the husband's desires and goals.
3. Brady writes that a husband can divorce his wife at will. After the divorce, the assumption is that the wife will take the children. Legally, divorce has become more easy to accomplish in most states since the early 1970s. At the same time, arguably, attitudes have significantly changed regarding which parent will take custody of the children. In many states, the current presumption of the law is "joint custody."

## Questions for Comprehension – Atwood essay

1. Students might speculate that the internet has enabled more viewers of all sorts, male and female.
2. The matter of sexual harassment in the workplace appears pervasive in light of these social movements. Feminists have long commented on the "glass ceiling" and oppression of women in the workplace. Just as pornography allows for the objectification of women, harassment in the workplace tends to treat women as objects who are subject to male power rather than as equal business partners.
3. Atwood writes that "hard core" porn use may function "as alcohol does for the alcoholic: tolerance develops, and a little is no longer enough." In this case, Atwood speculates, "the quality of explicitness must escalate, which may account for the growing violence."

## Questions for Comprehension – Steinem essay

1. Erotica
2. Much like Atwood, Steinem describes pornography as a matter of violence and male dominance. Steinem writes that pornography "is about power and sex-as-weapon." Their viewpoints are so similar that some students, if they are not careful, may even confuse these two authors.
3. "We" is clearly women. This can be an opportunity to consider "audience" as a component of sound composition. A composition instructor might note the awkward nominalization of "expertise erotic," but let's not nitpick! What Steinem means by the idea of developing "those qualities" may not be entirely clear, but taking control of one's own sexuality appears to be an important idea. Steinem's main concept is clarified at the end of the paragraph: "As some men replace the need for submission from childlike women with the pleasure of cooperation from equals, they may find a partner's competence to be erotic, too." She expresses feminist concerns for equality in matters beyond the political realm. Steinem treats sexuality not as a fixed entity but as a fluid entity capable of changing.

## Questions for Comprehension – McElroy essay

1. False. She criticizes academic feminists for maintaining this belief. Looking forward: John Taylor and others likewise criticize advocates of "political correctness" for claiming that anyone who disagrees with them is a victim of "false consciousness" who has been duped by predominant cultural mores.
2. McElroy implies that academic feminists may favor censorship of pornography while "liberal feminists" are split on the subject but tend to be bullied into silence by the academic feminists. She writes, "Liberal feminists share the general liberal bias toward free speech, but they are in flux on pornography." Some feminists, according to McElroy, staunchly defend sexual freedom, while others

merely tolerate pornography as an unfortunate reality that exists in a society that values free speech. These feminists who tolerate the existence of pornography are not, however, "pro-pornography," she points out. In this essay, she attempts to stake out her own "pro-sex" and "pro-pornography" feminist position.

3. None of these "definitions" are set in stone, of course. We probably ought not to expect our students to understand these distinctions. However, a little bit of poking around on the internet will provide students with enough information for a good discussion. Second wave feminism stems from 1960s activism and the push for equality. From there, academic feminists, using the insights of language theorists, became concerned with the role of culture or "patriarchal" culture in proscriptive under-standings of gender. Second wave feminism spans circa 1960s to 1990s. Third wave feminism started up in the 1990s. Martha Rampton writes, "An aspect of third wave feminism that mystified the moth-ers of the earlier feminist movement was the readoption by young feminists of the very lip-stick, high-heels, and cleavage proudly exposed by low cut necklines that the first two phases of the move-ment identified with male oppression." A distinct aspect of third wave feminism involves the idea of sexuality as empowerment. Some "fourth wave" feminists, according to Rampton, have trouble with the very word "feminism" which seems to imply to them "for women only."

## Questions for Comprehension – Brownmiller essay

1. False. This quotation—really it's a partial quotation—shows how the meanings of texts can be dis-torted when taken out of context. In fact, she is expressing her opinion of society's view of women and femininity. Brownmiller questions why a woman must be considered weak, vulnerable, and girl-ish if she is to be considered "feminine."
2. Femininity, she argues, is a very active endeavor. Femininity is granted to women who comply with society's demands. In this sense, femininity is a matter of *nurture* rather than *nature*. Simple biology is not enough for women to be considered feminine.

## Questions for Comprehension – Paglia essay

1. True. "Society is not the enemy, as feminism ignorantly claims. Society is woman's protection against rape."
2. She finds this essence in football and rock music. She finds certain "fundamental, unchanging truth about sex" in "the jock and the noisy posturing of the heavy-metal guitarist." This question/answer begs for a moment of reflection. Long-haired 1980s metal guitarists with stupendous mullets are her idea of "extreme" masculinity? OK. Pull up a YouTube video of the rock band Cinderella and have some fun with that one. Seriously, though, Paglia clearly revels in her role as provocateur, but some of her claims will certainly prove odd, if not disturbing, to a majority of Millennial men and women when they pause a moment to consider her implications. One teaching point here—as students meld the concepts of *nature* or *nurture* as it applies to gender identity and sexual development—is that ideas about "masculinity" and maybe "femininity" too seem to have changed substantially since 1991. I can only speak as a heterosexual man, of course. I tell my students that as an intellectual I felt back then as I do now that the power of the mind—reading books and playing chess, for example—struck me as just as "manly" as rocking my ax, i.e. strumming my electric guitar.
3. "Stereotype" must convince the audience that Paglia indulges in stereotypes about young men, while "Reality" must convince the audience that she offers a realistic depiction of young men. Each side (or each writer) must cite and critique evidence from Paglia's text to support its point of view.

# Notes for Composition Unit Two

## Sentence Exercise #3

1. Note that "xx" stands for the page number citation that appears in MLA format. Note that you are likely to quote a full sentence given this particular quotation format.

# Unit Three Notes

## Questions for Comprehension – Nilsen essay

1. Nilsen claims that language provides evidence of "thoughts" in her final paragraph. To what extent does this premise cause problems in the age of political correctness? To what extent might understanding this concept solve problems in the age of political correctness? It might be useful to discuss the idea that many people use language somewhat thoughtlessly and even arbitrarily. Some students won't understand, therefore, that a person's language can reveal his or her thoughts. Here students can be introduced to the concept that language reveals "attitudes" or "unspoken thoughts." People don't always use offensive language with the intent to offend; nonetheless, the use of the language remains offensive in that it appears to reveal a certain attitude, possibly even a thoughtless stance or position that the person has taken up through the use of that language. It might have been difficult to explain many decades ago that the seemingly innocuous word "Oriental" was usually both inaccurate and offensive. The "Orient" may have originated as a geographical term, but its connotations soon made it inaccurate and offensive.

2. In a general sense, the answer is that there is sexism in the English language. More specifically, she writes that a careful look at English will reveal the attitudes—presumably, sexist attitudes—that our ancestors and the culture held. She divides these "obvious facts" into three main points in accordance with the subtitles in her article.

3. There is no "correct" answer here. This is a "chicken and egg" query that cuts to the heart of the social movement called political correctness. To a certain extent, language can instigate thought, and so PC advocates have a point in wanting to eliminate offensive language, which might have the benefit of eliminating offensive thoughts that are passed down from generation to generation. However, the idea that sexist language causes sexist thinking is simplistic at best. The origins of language and thought are intimately interwoven. Does offensive thinking cause offensive language? Is this the predominate paradigm? The idea here is not to get students to come to the "correct" conclusion; the idea here is to get them to understand the question on a deep level.

## Questions for Comprehension – Orwell essay

1. False. These passages demonstrate the two grave sins of modern speech and writing, in Orwell's view: "staleness of imagery" and "lack of precision."

2. "drinks"

3. The phrases "it is generally assumed" [note the passive voice construction] and "so the argument runs," set off by em-dashes, clue us into his rhetorical strategy that his opinion runs contrary to the general assumptions regarding this topic.

4. Concrete words and imagery are key elements to good writing, according to Orwell. Sometimes I provide students a silly litmus test: "concrete" means you can pour coffee [or "hot chocolate" or "beer"] on it, while "abstract" means you can't. You can't pour coffee on *love* but you can pour coffee on *the young woman waiting in line*. That wouldn't be very nice, though, and it would definitely be an ill-advised strategy to make friends with someone. Orwell's essay puts me in mind to examine how we use and respond to abstract terms like "freedom," "liberty," and "patriotism." Different people can mean very different things even if they are using the same words. This is why it's essential, in Orwell's view, to specify concrete meanings and ideas.

5. Well, we can let the imagination run wild here, and that's Orwell's point. A meaningful sentence doesn't allow the imagination to run wild to any possible conclusion. The basic idea here is to take a

passive voice sentence and transform it into an active voice, in accordance with his fourth rule. The passive voice hides the real actor of a sentence. *The people were relocated by whom?* Maybe this: *Government officials relocated the people using available roadways.* Why say "populace" when "people" is available? Or maybe a keen student comes up with: *Soldiers chased citizens out of the city on northbound highways.* If the discussion turns toward how government and media [and even lecturers and teachers] can cover up the truth and the way of things with sentence structure and usage, I would think that Orwell would approve.

## Questions for Comprehension – Chait essay

1. According to Chait, Mahmood wrote a satirical column in the school newspaper that mocked the campus culture of hyper-sensitivity and the propensity to take offense at imagined slights.
2. False. Chait mocks this mindset and writes that "Trigger warnings aren't much help in actually overcoming trauma."
3. True. He claims, on the other hand, "Political correctness makes debate irrelevant and frequently impossible."
4. False. Chait argues that "Under p.c. culture, the same idea can be expressed identically by two people but received differently depending on the race and the sex of the individuals doing the expressing." This subtle point is maybe one of the most important points that Chait makes. He is uncomfortable with the notion that words and ideas are validated or invalidated according to the gender, race, and/or sexual identity of the speaker.
5. Naturally, this concept may take more than a few words to explain. I would recommend allowing students access to the text as they answer this question. One core argument here is that PC culture prevents free speech and meaningful public discourse. Representative democracies such as ours, Chait seems to say, depend on free and open discourse. Chait seems especially concerned with leftist "thought police" who shut down any speech or ideology with which they disagree. Such a mindset challenges the traditional American veneration of free speech enshrined in the First Amendment to the U.S. Constitution. Other reasonable answers may suffice, of course, as we seek to stimulate deep thinking on the topic at hand.

# Unit Five Notes

## Questions for Comprehension – Milgram and Hollander essay

1. True.
2. Assuming someone else had done so, inability to form a whole picture from the fragment of information that was available, sheer disbelief that violence was actually occurring in a nice neighborhood, hesitance to perform a less than ideal response in the knowledge of the ideal response to go down and physically intervene, fear of intervention, the fact that a city resident cannot respond to every possible needy person, an indifference that is a necessary part of city life. There are other acceptable responses, obviously.

## Questions for Comprehension – Milgram essay

1. False.
2. the Teacher, the Learner, and the Experimenter
3. Teacher
4. She exerts her "free will" to stop the experiment. She remains calm. She appears to model the behavior that we all hope we would have in such circumstances.
5. True.

# Unit Six Notes

# Questions for Comprehension – Winner essay

1. "Reflection" is the correct response; other (incorrect) choices for multiple choice could be "thoughtlessness," "truth," and "disdain." You can also make this an "open book" question, requiring the student to study the text for the correct response.

2. False. He cites Bureau of Labor statistics that indicate that most of the new jobs will be in the service sector. Winner does not believe these are good jobs.

3. Mythinformation is the "almost religious conviction that a widespread adoption of computers and communications systems . . . will automatically produce a better world for human living."

4. True. He does not believe this. In a related section of Winner's book, he claims that "Current developments . . . suggest an increase in power by those who already had a great deal of power, an enhanced centralization of control . . ., an augmentation of wealth by the already wealthy." In this regard, you might update your students on public discourse surrounding the issue of the so-called "1%," the wealthiest members of our society. It's fascinating that this discourse emerged early in the 21st century, arguably seeming to validate Winner's reading of the situation. It might also be interesting to discuss with students the role of "social power" in the age of the internet. "Arab Spring" political movements were fueled by social media technologies. Is this a good point of defense in terms of the idea of spreading political power among the masses?

5. Winner claims that the concept mistakes the sheer supply of information with the ability to translate the information into useful knowledge. In other words, the idea that "information is knowledge" is faulty. If you don't know what to do with the information that you have, then you are no better off than you were before.

# COURSE THEORY AND DESIGN

## Afterword for Deans and Department Chairs

Whenever folks at a social gathering hear that I'm a college English teacher, an inevitable question follows: "Can college kids write these days?" Clearly, it is a rhetorical question to which I am supposed to respond, "No, they're awful! They don't even know how to use semicolons." Never mind that I'm likely speaking to a successful career professional who doesn't understand semicolons.

I surprise people by saying, "Of course they can write . . . *if* they have something to write about. When they care about what they're writing, they write well." These folks make the same conceptual mistake that some of my academic colleagues make. They conceive of English 101 or first semester college composition as a how-to mechanical process instead of what it must be in 21st century American higher education: a keystone course that fosters the development of critical thinking.

The mechanical aspects of good composition are the byproducts of good critical reasoning. You can't develop solid thinking skills with multiple-choice tests. After twenty years of college teaching, it's still wondrous to me that sometimes grammar and syntactical problems seem disappear once a student actually engages with a given public discourse. In other words, once the student *cares* about what he or she is writing, that care translates into better, more clear prose. Our students, for the most part, come out of high school with the bare mechanical essentials of prose in place. My claim here doesn't stem from naivety. I've spent more of my career working with first generation college students than with the academic elite. And, not incidentally, let me add here how little difference there is in terms of cognitive development between a first generation student and a student prepped for the Ivy League. There is often a great deal of difference when it comes to familial environment, mechanical skills, and the ability to process text. On the core objectives regarding the development of critical thinking, however, I find that these students are starting from the same place.

It doesn't help when we throw topics at our students that promote a binary yes/no response. We ask a first semester college student to write a research paper on global warming or abortion then bemoan our fates as graders of awful prose. Worse, we ask first semester students to engage in our own pet projects, along these lines: Using multiple sources, write an analysis of social mores and gender politics in 18th century England. Say what? I love Jane Austin, but I'm with the students on this one. Can we find public discourse in which all of our budding scientists, engineers, health care professionals, *and* literary critics can engage? Instead of focusing on what *I* as teacher know about, maybe we ought to focus on what the students know about.

The experts tell us that two-thirds of our college-age kids in the 21st century will never get a four year degree. At the same time, obtaining a college education has never been more critical for the personal or public good. When I tell my students that a college education is a matter of life and death, I inform them that I mean it literally. In the early 2000s, an unprecedented statistic emerged. Americans in my basic demographic (white, male, middle aged) are, statistically speaking, leading shorter lives. There's one exception, though. Those who are college educated are not experiencing the same shortening of life expectancy. English 101 (i.e., first year college composition) is critical for the health of the person and the nation. For an increasing number of students, including many certificate and associate's degree holders, English 101 is a student's single interaction with the sort of literary analysis, source analysis, cognitive development, and independent thinking that seems so sorely wanting in the public life of our nation. If, upon reading that last sentence, your mind immediately goes to the dangerous partisan quarantine of *liberal versus conservative*, then you yourself are living proof of the great need for this course and textbook. As I put it, our job is to inform students *how* to think, not *what* to think.

This critical mission often has to be carried out by part-time instructors, adjunct faculty, and graduate students. The challenge I gave myself was to develop a straightforward tool that could be used with little prep time to accomplish the critical objectives and learning outcomes mentioned above. The entire curriculum also had to honor the values of academic freedom set forth in 1940 by the American Association of University Professors in its Statement of Principles on Academic Freedom and Tenure. And the tool could be used to measure and assess an institution's general education and course learning outcomes. This *Engaging Discourse* textbook checks all of the boxes.

Maybe I'm simply aggrandizing my own profession, but I believe that this course is vital for the future of our country and for the individual futures of my students.

Accessibility and ease of use have become common expectations for the 21st century American college student. You don't have to be a crotchety antiquarian to note that the Internet Era—representing one of the great fundamental shifts in human history—has changed the learning experience. "Changed" does not mean for the better or for the worse. In fact, it's both for the better and for the worse simultaneously. It is irresponsible of us as educators not to adjust to the realities of the world in which we live. So I offer my contribution. It's not really a "flipped classroom," whatever that term is supposed to mean. *Engaging Discourse* is not a vast anthology without personal guidance, nor is it a how-to manual devoid of content. This textbook is a sensible balance for students and instructors who are increasingly both time and money stressed. Maybe I am charging at windmills; however, two decades of college teaching experience informs me otherwise. And please do note the clever and grammatically correct use of a semicolon in that last sentence!

In its "Framework for Success in Postsecondary Writing," the Council of Writing Program Administrators (CWPA), National Council of Teachers of English (NCTE), and the National Writing Project (NWP) enumerate the habits of mind that are critical to student success in college writing: curiosity, openness, engagement, creativity, persistence, responsibility, flexibility, and metacognition. My firm belief is that this course encourages these habits of mind. Furthermore, *Engaging Discourse* develops rhetorical knowledge, critical thinking, knowledge of conventions, and the ability to compose in multiple environments in accordance with the joint CWPA, NCTE, and NWP guidelines.

Delve into these pages with us. We'll have fun along the way, and we are all in danger of learning something, even you deans and department chairs. Will I teach you something? Highly unlikely. The students will teach us. All we need to do is to provide interesting subject matter and an opportunity to reason critically and write correctly.

Here's the bottom line: experienced teachers will appreciate this curriculum's flexibility and, in an emergency, you can hand this textbook to a graduate student or part-time instructor a few days before the semester begins and rest assured that your students can experience a high quality course with high quality instruction metrics. Moreover, if need be, you can pull meaningful assessment data from the evaluation rubrics.

###

# Outcomes & Objectives for First Year College Composition

*Engaging Discourse* is a writing-intensive course designed to strengthen college-level writing, with particular attention to persuasion, analysis, synthesis, and an introduction to research methodologies. Generally, an in-depth research paper represents the culminating assignment, typically produced toward the end of the second semester or first academic year. The general goal of *Engaging Discourse* is to improve the reading, thinking, and writing processes associated with academic study. Students must write and edit for clarity and standard usage. The course requires the proper treatment and documentation of source materials.

## Course Objectives

✓ The course aims to develop and to reinforce literacy skills and communication skills, with special emphasis on the student's ability to communicate in clear, standard English language prose.
✓ The course aims to model and strengthen sound critical and analytical thinking.
✓ The course aims to explain, develop, and clarify methods for the evaluation of source materials.
✓ The course aims to offer insights on 21st century research methodologies.

## Student Learning Outcomes

✓ Student will employ the conventions of standard written English, as evidenced by competency in format, grammar, mechanics, punctuation, and sentence structure.
✓ Using college level academic discourse, students will write a variety of essays that demonstrate critical thinking.
✓ Students will incorporate critical reading and writing strategies that include the use of secondary sources in the production of drafts and final essay assignments that exhibit synthetic connections between varied source materials.

To these ends, students will produce 20–25 pages of revised prose per semester with multiple drafts leading to final essays formatted in Modern Language Association (MLA) style or another style as specified by the instructor. Beyond these minimum requirements, instructors and/or departments may require additional pages and/or assignments, including the production of an in-depth research paper in the first and/or second semester.

# Suggested Course Structure, Hierarchy of Assignments, Timelines, & Point Values

## Course Structure & Hierarchy of Assignments

*Engaging Discourse* is a complete course and curriculum for first year college composition. Each unit includes a build-up of exercises and assignments, from pre-reading activities to final composition assignments. In addition, each unit provides opportunities for research. There is also a unit that introduces students to 21st century research methodology and that allows the instructor to incorporate a novel into the course (with three suggestions provided). Each subject matter specific unit offers:

- ✓ pre-reading guidance
- ✓ readings designed to engage student critical thinking
- ✓ discussion guides
- ✓ exercises to develop cognitive and prose skills
- ✓ formal reader response assignments to produce essay draft material
- ✓ essay assignments with specific required parameters and thoughtful prompts
- ✓ evaluation rubrics with specific criteria and suggested point values

Suggested point values rise from sentence and paragraph exercises (10 points) to reader response assignments (20 points) to essay assignments (100 points). An instructor may want to complete the annotated bibliography assignment (100 points) or assign a research or other composition assignment. The evaluation rubrics may be adjusted to reflect an instructor's preferences and/or adapted for course or classroom assessment activities.

## Course Outline with Suggested Timelines & Point Values

*Suggested timelines are based on a 15-week college semester with two classes per week, plus a finals week. Sentence exercises and reader response assignments would be due within the suggested time periods, while culminating unit assignments (i.e., essays) would be due in the week following the suggested time periods. The suggested timelines total 14 weeks, so there is one regular semester week plus the finals in order to accommodate flexibility in the schedule.*

*Each unit contains pre- and post-reading discussion questions which may be assigned point values. In addition, each unit features "Further Inquiry & Research" and "Additional Source Materials by Topic" which may be used for associated research or alternate composition assignments.*

*Instructors may select a novel or nonfiction book to read for Unit Four and/or assign an annotated bibliography. Novel suggestions (with related assignments included) are:* The Curious Incident of the Dog in the Night-Time *(2003) by Mark Haddon,* The Color Purple *(1982) by Alice Walker, or* 1984 *(1949) by George Orwell.*

Unit One: Education

*Two weeks or four class periods, 160 points*

*Sentence exercises, 20 points*
*Reader responses, 40 points*
*Unit essay, 100 points*

Unit Two: Feminism

*Three weeks or six class periods, 160 points*

*Sentence exercise, 10 points*
*Paragraph exercise, 10 points*
*Reader responses, 40 points*
*Unit essay, 100 points*

Unit Three: Political Correctness     *Two weeks or four class periods, 110 points*

*Paragraph exercise, 10 points*
*Unit essay, 100 points*

Unit Four: An Introduction to     *Two or three weeks or four to six class*
21st Century Research     *periods, 120–280 points*

*Library and related assignments, 80 points*
*Unit essay, 100 points*
*Annotated bibliography, 100 points*

Unit Five: Social Psychology     *Three weeks or six class periods, 140 points*

*Reader responses, 40 points*
*Unit essay, 100 points*

Unit Six: The Web Effect     *Two weeks or four class periods, 120 points*
*Reader response, 20 points*
*Unit essay, 100 points*

## Suggested Timelines

The suggested timelines for this course (one to four weeks per unit) are based on the assumption of a traditional 16-week semester, with 15 weeks of two classes per week (approximately one and a quarter hour per class) plus a finals week. Obviously, instructors may need to make adjustments based on the academic calendar in which they are working.

## Suggested Point Values

| Category: | Description: | Points: |
|---|---|---|
| Essays | 5–6 x 100 points | 500–600 |
| Annotated Bibliography | | 100 |
| Reader Responses | 7 x 20 points | 140 |
| Sentence and Paragraph Exercises | 10 x 10 | 100 |
| Library Assignments | 2 x 20 / 1 x 40 | 20–80 |
| Discussions and Participation | | *To be determined by instructor* |
| Reading Comprehension Quizzes | | *To be determined by instructor* |
| Required Tutoring | | *To be determined by instructor* |
| ***Course Total* to be determined by instructor** | | |

## Customization

Instructors may modify the curriculum, modify reading requirements, modify existing assignments, and/or develop entirely original assignments by making use of the extensive "Further Inquiry & Research" and "Additional Source Materials by Topic" resources listed at the end of each unit.

# Reading, Literacy, & Composition Standards

Let's establish not only *what* we will do but *why* we will do it. Luckily, as literary and composition professionals, we can rely on the work of professional organizations in addition to our own experience and good sense. In 1996, the International Reading Association (IRA) and the National Council of Teachers of English (NCTE) set out a common purpose which can also stand in for our global objectives in a first semester college composition course: "Our shared purpose is to ensure that all students are knowledgeable and proficient users of language so that they may succeed in school, participate in our democracy as informed citizens, find challenging and rewarding work, appreciate and contribute to our culture, and pursue their own goals and interests as independent learners throughout their lives." Students, in order to fulfill their job and career potentials and in order to become contributing citizens, must learn how to analyze the multi-various digital and print texts that are set before them in the 21st century. They must learn how to engage with these texts and with the language (formal and informal, oral and written, explicit and implicit) that is used to present these texts. That means they must be able to discuss and to write about these texts. They must learn how to engage in public discourse. They must learn how to engage in critical, independent thinking about the world in which they live.

More recently, NCTE has defined (2008) and updated (2013) its definitions of 21st century literacies. NCTE points out, "Literacy has always been a collection of cultural and communicative practices shared among members of particular groups. As society and technology change, so does literacy." The Committee on College Composition (CCCC) has also established (1989) and revised (2013, 2015) an insightful and useful set of guidelines in its "Principles for the Postsecondary Teaching of Writing." As college composition instructors, we must acknowledge the reality of the post-industrial internet society into which our students were born. That does not mean abandoning print texts. Study after study indicates the difficulties involved with the reading and processing of electronic texts. We cannot pretend, however, that 21st century students and citizens will procure most of their information from printed texts. Barring a societal shift of apocalyptic proportions, the internet is here to stay. People, for the most part, will visit a search engine before they visit a library or even a library database. To me, this reality does not imply the inevitable death of the library, the database, or the printed book. As I like to point out to my students, simple supply and demand economics tells us that if books become more rare then they become more valuable, at least for as long as some of us want and value them over other forms. (I read on screen for work, a computer and a server being at the core of my composition courses, but for pleasure and personal study I'll take a book every time.) *Engaging Discourse* has been designed to encourage the development of timeless literacy skills within the context of our 21st century world.

# The Role of Two-Year Colleges in American Higher Education

For many 21st century students, first year college compostion represents the single intersection of a student's education and career path with the sorts of explicit literacy skills which English department professors, and much objective evidence, claim to be so essential to the development of a meaningful, economically sound, and civicly engaged life. This dynamic is particularly true in the context of the two year college. All evidence suggests that two year colleges have a role of increasing importance in American higher education.

*Engaging Discourse* works as a first semester composition course in a university, two year college, or advanced high school context. This course has been designed with an acknowledgement of the needs of a growing majority of 21st century American learners. It is important to maintain—or, in fact, to elevate—traditional expectations and standards as we prepare our students to reach their potentials.

- A growing demand for so called "middle-skill" jobs that require specialized training, such as technicians, police, electricians, firefighters, plumbers, welders, dental hygienists, respiratory therapists, radiologic technicians, and others, are "essential for the U.S. infrastructure development and overall economic growth." In addition, "There is a growing demand for such jobs among millennials that have suffered from unemployment issues despite their graduation degrees. As these jobs cannot be outsourced, it is essential that there is great demand for specialized skills required for these jobs." (Rhea, Kelly. "Top 3 Trends to Impact Community Colleges by 2021." *CampusTechnology.com*, July 3, 2017.) (https://campustechnology.com/articles/2017/07/03/top-3-trends-to-impact-community-colleges-by-2021.aspx)
- Currently, the median salary for someone with only a high school diploma is $36,000. For those with a community college degree, it's $42,600. This gap is projected to grow as automation transforms the U.S. workforce. Forty-eight percent of small businesses reported recently that they couldn't find qualified job applicants to fill open positions, according to the National Federation of Independent Business (Sanburn, Josh. "The Case for Community College." *Time.com*, June 1, 2017.) (http://time.com/4800811/the-case-for-community-college/)
- According to a recent report from the National Student Clearinghouse (NSC), nearly half (46 percent) of all students who completed a degree at a four-year institution in 2013–14 had enrolled at a two-year institution at some point in the previous 10 years. These enrollment patterns are not just picking up the occasional community college course taken by students; of those students who had attended a two year institution, 47 percent had enrolled in that sector for five or more terms. (Ma, Jennifer and Sandy Baum. "Trends in Community Colleges." College Board Research, Research Brief, April 2016.) (https://trends.collegeboard.org/sites/default/files/trends-in-community-colleges-research-brief.pdf)
- It is well documented that community colleges serve a large proportion of minority, first-generation, low income, and adult students. In 2011–12, 36 percent of dependent students in the public two-year sector were first generation college students, compared to 24 percent of those in the public four-year sector and 19 percent in the private nonprofit four-year sector. Almost half of all undergraduate students in the for-profit sector were first generation college students. (Ibid.) (https://trends.collegeboard.org/sites/default/files/trends-in-community-colleges-research-brief.pdf)

- Increasingly, community colleges provide career training through vocationally oriented courses that lead to a certificate. This type of career training previously was offered mainly by proprietary schools and vocational institutions, but community colleges now have similar programs to better serve the needs of local businesses and communities. This service has increased the importance of community colleges, especially in rural areas where career training is difficult to obtain. Due to this dynamic, community colleges have seen an enrollment surge that outpaces the enrollment growth of educational institutions offering bachelor's degrees. Enrollment at public four year colleges and universities roughly doubled from 1965 to 1999, while enrollment at public community colleges increased about fivefold. (Kasper, Henry T. "The Changing Role of Community College." *Occupational Outlook Quarterly*, Winter 2002–03.) (https://www.bls.gov/careeroutlook/2002/winter/art02.pdf)
- Short-term certificate programs allow students to train quickly to enter the workforce, requiring less than one year to complete. From academic year 1989–90 to academic year 1999–2000, the number of short-term certificates awarded by community colleges rose from 46,447 to 85,941, an increase of 85 percent. (Ibid.) (https://www.bls.gov/careeroutlook/2002/winter/art02.pdf)

Special thanks to the Institutional Research Office, Truckee Meadows Community College, Reno, Nevada, October 31, 2017.

## Acknowledgments

I would like to thank my English 101 students MaryBeth Greig, Anthony Williams, and Tyler Wozynski for allowing me to use their compositions in this textbook.

I would like to thank Truckee Meadows Community College in Reno, Nevada, for generously providing me a sabbatical period in the fall semester of 2018 so that I could complete a portion of *Engaging Discourse,* Volumes 1 and 2.

I would like to give a big shout out to Truckee Meadows Community College librarian Neil Siegel for helping me track down many valuable "Additional Source Materials by Topic" which appear at the end of each unit. The sources listed here are largely culled from Open Educational Resources (OER) databases. As a teacher, I value the possibilities and potentials of OER. As a writer and artist, I value copyright. As an intellectual, I am intrigued by our often ridiculous legal conceptions regarding copyright. I believe that 21st century "Open" movements are bound to modify some of our most antiquated 20th century legal notions regarding copyright and IP (intellectual property). I hope that high school and college students of the 21st century will continue to study, value, and acknowledge both copyright protection and the public domain.

# INDEX